Christmas 1994

To : Marie

From : Don, Betty + Robin

Xr

THE PERSONALITY OF THE CAT

THE PERSONALITY OF THE CAT

EDITED BY BRANDT AYMAR

WINGS BOOKS
NEW YORK • AVENEL, NEW JERSEY

This edition is published by Wings Books,
distributed by Outlet Book Company, Inc.,
a Random House Company, 40 Engelhard Avenue,
Avenel, New Jersey 07001.

Random House
New York • Toronto • London • Sydney • Auckland

Printed and bound in the United States of America

Library of Congress Cataloging-in-Publication Data
Main entry under title:

The Personality of the cat.

Reprint. Originally published: New York: Crown
Publishers, 1958.
1. Cats—Literary collections. 2. Literature,
Modern. I. Aymar, Brandt.
PN6071.C3P47 1983   808.8'036   82-23658
ISBN 0-517-00016-4
22 21 20 19 18 17 16 15

Acknowledgments

I DEEPLY appreciate the cooperation of the following authors and
publishers for their kind permission to include these selections in
this book:

MAZO DE LA ROCHE for "The Ninth Life" and "Cat's Cruise."

ALFRED A. KNOPF, INC. for "Jennie's Lessons to Peter on How to
    Behave Like a Cat" reprinted from *The Abandoned* by Paul
    Gallico, copyright 1950, and for "The Piebald Devil" reprinted
    from *Kittens: A Family Chronicle* by Svend Fleuron, copyright
    1920 by Svend Fleuron, 1922 by Alfred A. Knopf, Inc.

THE WORLD PUBLISHING CO. for the selection from *Little White
    King* by Marguerite Steen, copyright 1956.

FARRAR, STRAUS AND CUDAHY, INC. for "Sentimentalities" and "The
    Long-Cat" from *Creatures Great and Small* by Colette, copyright
    1904 by Colette Willy and translated by Enid McLeod.

R. Piper and Co. Verlag for "Hurrli, Bold, Proud, and Amiable Master of Elk House" from *My Cats and I* by Paul Eipper, translation by Anne Bostock courtesy of Hutchinson and Co., Ltd.

Intercultural Publications Inc. and Adriaan Morrien for his story "The Cats," which appeared in *The Atlantic Monthly*, April 1954, from *Perspective of Holland and Belgium*, copyright 1954 by Intercultural Publications Inc.

Houghton Mifflin Company for "Agrippina" by Agnes Repplier, for "How a Cat Was Annoyed and a Poet Booted" from *Grimm Tales Made Gay* by Guy Wetmore Carryl, for "Lives of Two Cats" by Pierre Loti, and for "Calvin" from *My Summer in a Garden* by Charles Dudley Warner.

Little Brown and Company for "Hodge, the Cat" by Susan Coolidge.

G. P. Putnam's Sons for "The Mysterious Ra" from *The Soul of a Cat and Other Stories* by Margaret Benson.

Marvin R. Clark for "Nellie and Tom" from his book *Pussy and Her Language*.

Geo. H. Richmond and Son for "The Paradise of Cats" from *Stories for Ninon* by Emile Zola, translated by Edward Vizetelly.

William Blackwood and Sons for "Songs of the Tom-Cat Hiddigeigei" from *The Trumpeter* by Joseph Victor von Scheffel, translated by Jessie Beck and Louise Lorimer.

D. C. Heath and Co. for "Puss in Boots" from *The Tales of Mother Goose* by Charles Perrault translated by Charles Welsh.

Mildred R. Howland for her poem "Muff of Fur," which appeared in *The Atlantic Monthly*, July 1954.

Vincent Starrett for his poem "My Lord's Motoring."

Frances Frost for her poem "Park Avenue Cat."

CONTENTS

Th<small>IS</small> book is for people who love cats and for cats who love people.

Ever since this feline friend or beast, depending upon which side of the fence your cat's feelings fall, appeared on man's hearthstone some several thousand years ago, he has been a controversial figure in literature and in art. Worshipped in Egyptian times as the great god Bast, he fell headlong into disrepute in the witch-baiting days of the Middle Ages, and it took many years before the cat recovered his present-day composure.

No wonder, then, that much has been written about cats, enough to fill a many-volumed encyclopedia. The problem of what should be included and what omitted thus arises for the compiler of a collection such as this. I decided to solve the problem by selecting pieces that would reflect the personality of the cat; to carry out this purpose it was necessary that the cat, not man, should be the main character of each piece.

As any cat lover knows, the personality of the cat is as variable as the shimmering shadows of a sunbeam and just as elusive, and it is to the credit of so many good writers that they have understood and interpreted for us this personality so well. They have given us good cats and bad cats, loyal cats and murderous cats, demure cats and devil-raising cats. Pick almost any adjective to describe personality and you'll find a cat lurking underneath it.

In setting these limits for my selections, I narrowed considerably the wide range of cat literature from which to choose. For instance, Edgar Allan Poe's masterpiece of horror "The Black Cat" automatically had to be excluded because here the cat itself was only incidental, the main emphasis being on the story teller's own foul deed. In the same manner, much of what has been written about the cat in ancient times, its medieval role in sorcery, and in many modern stories and essays, has no place in this book because the cat is not the main personality involved. If this were to be a book for cat lovers, then cats—not humans—must be its heroes.

Four categories in general make up the format of these selections. There are short stories, excerpts from longer works which in themselves are complete units, personal tales or essays of a writer's own cat or cats, and poetry.

The first and last stories in this book are by Mazo de la Roche. Of all the short stories written about the cat my two favorites are these. In *The Ninth Life* Harriet, left behind on a summer island, finds her way home to the Boyds after overcoming virtually impossible obstacles. Her courage is superhuman, but perhaps just normal cat. In *Cat's Cruise* we find the best example in literature of the cat's completely independent spirit. Oblivious to the many favors bestowed on Cat on her various cruises aboard freighters or luxury liners, in the end she ships out on a cattle-ship, "and all her past was as nothing to her."

Since there have been numerous anthologies of cat literature published in this Twentieth Century, it is inevitable that many of the same selections show up in each. If, in the opinion of the compiler these are the best, this is how it should be. But it is also his duty to include excellent selections which are new to the anthology set. One such story I came across is Arthur Stanley Riggs' *The Cat That Was Fey*. This curious tale of Peter the cat was told to Commander Riggs in Ancon, Panama, as a factual story. The question, however, of whether fact or fiction, we leave to the reader. Suffice it to say Peter's cat-like intuition saved the good ship *Calyx* from foundering on the rocks with all hands consigned to a watery grave. Some cats can navigate better than skippers.

Two stories that bring a catch to the reader's throat at their ends, but in quite different ways, are Sylvia Townsend Warner's *The Best Bed* and Q. Patrick's *The Fat Cat*. The first is a touching tale of a lonely, cold and bedraggled cat who on Christmas Eve finds shelter and warmth in a model manger inside a church. The second is that of one of the bravest cats known, to whom a marine named Randy, fighting in the South Pacific jungle, owes his life.

Two more of the stories included are perhaps well-known to most readers, but nonetheless can be read and reread over and over again.

Rudyard Kipling's *The Cat That Walked by Himself* is an example of one of his many children's stories which have been appropriated by adults. Saki's *Tobermory*, the devastatingly outspoken cat, could not, under any circumstances, have been omitted.

What the deep, unfathomable love of a cat for a man will accomplish is the theme of Mary E. Wilkins' story *The Cat*. "It was a face with the grimy grizzle of age upon it, with fever hollows in the cheeks, and the memories of wrong in the dim eyes, but the cat accepted the man unquestioningly and loved him."

With tongue in cheek, Emile Zola tells "what my cat related to me, one winter night, before the warm embers." Discontented with "the paradise of cats" in which he luxuriated, this Angora longed for the adventures of the world outside. But bitter experience soon turns his hopeful dreams into nightmares, and he is well contented to return to being "shut up and beaten in a room in which there is meat."

Strictly speaking Adriaan Morrien's story of the absent cats in *The Cats* is not one of an individual cat personality and therefore might not seem to fit into this collection. But the effect of the complete absence of any cat personalities upon a Dutch village during the last war is so startling and effective that I have included it on the theory that all cat personalities rolled into one might be considered individual. Charles Perrault's *Puss in Boots* is here because it is a classic that never tires.

I am very fond of cats in literature that appear wholly human. Our two Siamese "devils," Sua and Suda, are like members of the family, and we talk to them constantly just as we would to any of our friends or relatives. They in turn talk right back to us. Perhaps that is why my favorite selection in the second category of excerpts from longer works is from Paul Gallico's *The Abandoned*, a delightfully touching novel about an eight-year-old boy who becomes a large white cat, and his adventures with Jennie, a mangy tabby. In the scenes where Jennie instructs Peter in the ways of a cat, Paul Gallico, better than any writer, senses and conveys to the reader the true characteristics, mannerisms and psychology of the cat. The title of this selection, *Jennie's Lessons to Peter on How to Behave Like a Cat*, is my own. Three separated excerpts are joined together, all related to Jennie's excellent teachings, the by-now-classic one being "When in doubt, wash."

Poor Minette, like many an unfortunate damsel today, listened to the smooth tongue of a Don Juan cat instead of to her conscience and came upon evil days. In a series of letters to and from her sister Bébé, she pours out her woes. But all ends happily for the disillusioned Minette in *Love Adventures of a French Cat* by P-J. Stahl, even though she determinedly resolves "I shall end my days in widowhood."

Frances and Richard Lockridge have long been known for their astute understanding of all aspects of the cat. In *The Cat's Behavior in Two Worlds* they explore how the cat lives emotionally in both the human world and his own. Their own cats—Gin, Sherry, Martini, and all the others—form their laboratory of cat observation, and it is instructive as well as a great pleasure to read the conclusions of their research.

All cats, by human standards, are not good cats. One of the most dastardly in literature is Svend Fleuron's *Piebald Devil*, "a giant cat with the demon of passion seething in his blood and hate flaming from his eyes." No other rival for Grey Puss' affection could match him. Nor could Grey Puss herself trust him for an instant with their own kittens. This is the best characterization of the murderous instincts of a cat I have found.

Not all cats are successful in their *amours*. In *James Goes Serenading* James finds himself not alone in his attentions to Muffet. His sonorous caterwauling brought down on him something less inviting than applause. Jennie Laird's humorous adventure story is full of the charm and wisdom found in cats.

No man can be lonely if he has a cat. But not all men love cats, so more's the misfortune for never knowing of their loss. George found this out the hard way in *Birl Forms A Friendship* by Alexander M. Frey. When his mother dies he inherits her house and her cat, but it is some time before a lonely man and a bereaved cat find shelter in one another.

Cats are very sensitive to sounds. One strange noise and they're off like a shot to the protective shelter underneath the bed. Some sounds they love. Our cats can listen to music on the radio from morning to night. They seem to like all music, as long as it is not so loud as to destroy their placid mood. But one cat John Hickey and Priscilla Beach have come across is very critical of just which composer he likes. *Tut As a Music Critic* will come running whenever his mistress plays *Clair de Lune*. Let her start on a Bach fugue, however, and Tut is off like a shot. (I can hardly say I blame him.) When Tut was around she found herself being far more meticulous about the way she played.

One little tidbit I have included was written in 1811, by whom no one knows. *Felissa, a Kitten of Sentiment* is a very persecuted pussy, indeed. The trials she endures and survives would turn a modern soap-opera writer greenish with envy. She tells of them in her own words, and I'll let her speak for herself. Another selection that speaks for itself, of course, is Lewis Carroll's *Alice and the Cheshire Cat*.

The third category of this anthology consists of personal narratives about authors' own cats. In these, more than in the other writings, the reader can associate his or her own cats with the varied personalities of those who are the heroes of these pieces. To Michael Joseph, among all his cats *Minna Minna Mowbray* was the outstanding personality. She had no voice, her vocal cords being partially paralysed. She was an extremely gentle cat and an exemplary mother. She thoroughly disliked travelling. And she would brook no interference in her private affairs. I'm sure everyone will enjoy meeting her.

Another cat with an impediment is sure to beguile you. Although he was deaf, Marguerite Steen's *Little White King* had all the attributes to endear him to her. He was imperious and very autocratic in his requirements. Toward birds and field mice his attitude was benign. He had a mania for social life. To her there never was a cat with such sweetness, intelligence and affection.

Surely there must be some affinity between good newspaper sports writers and good writers about cats. Two of the authors between these covers are shining examples of both. Paul Gallico is joined by Murray Robinson, who as a longstanding pushover for cats warns you of what to expect from them in *Danger—Crazy Cats*. Of the 21,000,000 cats in the United States he claims his Willie is the wackiest of the lot and goes on to prove it. Second was Chauncey, in a heck of a fix because he was allergic to cat hair. Writing in staccato, journalistic style Murray Robinson soon has the reader in stitches at the antics of his feline furies.

Who will ever forget Pierre Loti's Moumoutte Blanche and Moumoutte Chinoise, the two cats associated in memory with the happiest years of his life. *Lives of Two Cats* is included here in its entirety. What of it, indeed, could be excluded? It stands as the perfect baring of the animal soul seeking the author's own with tenderness, supplication or terror. Pierre Loti looks deep into the eyes of his beloved cats and unfolds their lives with infinite pity and understanding.

"I have long known" writes Agnes Repplier "that cats are the most contemptuous of creatures, and that *Agrippina* is the most contemptuous of cats." With that she launches into a fine essay on cats in literature. To be sure Agrippina comes and goes, with catlike irregularity, in this informal literary discussion of cats of past and present, yet she always emerges in all her dignified, capricious personality.

Cats are nothing if not prolific in their breeding habits. In *The Immortal Cat* Karel Capek tells of his four generations (with more to come) of Pudlenkas and their offspring. After the twenty-first kitten he found he really had no market to give them away to, with the consequence that kittens were literally coming out of his sleeves.

There is little I can say about Charles Dudley Warner's *Calvin*. It is, and will always remain, the perfect tribute to a perfect cat. Innumerable are the times it has appeared in anthologies of cat literature, but it would be as unthinkable to leave it out as to write a history of our country omitting the Gettysburg Address. Were all cats to have tombstones—were these tombstones large enough—this magnificent epitaph to Calvin should surely be engraved upon them.

Infidelity is a figment of man's dubious imagination. It never bothered a cat. That is it never bothered Tom who belonged to Marvin R. Clark. Nellie to whom he brought home Tom as a mate thought differently after his flights into debauchery began. For a time she could forgive as he returned contrite and somewhat worse for wear. But there was a limit!

Cats can smell the ones they love. Neither distance nor strange surroundings can deter them from returning to their loved ones. Paul Eipper has had many cats, but Hurrli enjoyed to the fullest the freedom of his wild nature and the love of human beings. How he left and found his way back to their new home is an inspiring story of a cat's dauntless fidelity.

The story of Margaret Benson's *Mysterious Ra* is typical of a self-supporting cat. Much as cats love us they can exist without us. Whether they'd rather or not is not a question I'm prepared to answer. Ra was addicted to foraging. He was fond of not only mice and small game, but inordinately of rabbits. The last straw was the gardener's hundred crocus bulbs which he had so carefully planted and which Ra so dexterously unearthed, not once but twice.

Into what category should I put Colette's *Sentimentalities,* Colette who defies being categorized? The dialogues between Kiki-the-Demure, an Angora tabby, and Toby-Dog, a brindled French bulldog, are sheer delight of satirical and poetical insight into the three vastly different worlds of cat, dog, and Two-Footed Ones. It is no surprise that the cat comes off best. As the dialogue ends, Kiki wakes "quivering with youth again, sitting facing the sun, pearled by the dew with a silver halo which makes me appear to be indeed the God that once I was."

Colette's other selection is about *The Long-Cat,* her short-haired blackie, whose favorite pastime was poaching strawberries from the next-door neighbor. Impelled by a vegetarian craving, he would return home with the vestiges of not only berries, but melons and asparagus in the grooves of his claws. Another strangely different personality trait was Long-Cat's ability to glide through the water like a serpent. This trait, as you will see, he uses only to save himself or effect a rescue.

Too often in poetry the cat is treated with widely generalized eulogies. The poetic selections in this.volume are more specific. If they are not all named cats with distinctive (not always distinguished) personalities, then they are at least individual cats caught up in a web of circumstances rather than in a languorous mood.

"Macavity's not there!" Whatever feline crime has been committed in the community you can be sure of the culprit's identity, but even Scotland Yard's master sleuths are stumped. When they reach the scene of the crime, why naturally—*"Macavity's not there!"* There is no other poem that can match T. S. Eliot's *Macavity: The Mystery Cat* for characterization in verse. You'll shudder when you meet this "Napoleon of crime!"

"well, boss, wotthehell if mehitabel is a trifle *too* gay. after all, her spirit *did* once inhabit the body of cleopatra and that gives her the divine right to a fling now and then. there s life in the old

dame yet; toujours gay she ll always say." No one will ever forget
Don Marquis' *mehitabel* once they've listened to her song.

It is an unopposed truism that all cats were once kittens. Of all
the verses written about kittens, I like Joanna Baillie's one about
the romping, playful puss the best. "Whence hast thou, then, thou
witless Puss, The magic power to charm us thus?" she asks and
admirably answers her own question in *The Kitten*.

Was there ever a more unfortunate cat than the one Thomas
Gray drowned in a tub of gold fishes? From which cat catastrophe
we learn that all that glitters is not gold. Indeed, it is often apt to be
something fishy.

Pressed beyond endurance at the stupidity of the human race the
Hero-Cat, Hiddigeigei, "sings in wildest measure, his old feline
battle-song." In *Songs of the Tom-Cat Hiddigeigei* Joseph Victor
von Scheffel's worldly-wise cat castigates the people of his day (and
of our day for that matter) for their languorous living, lack of bold
initiative, and the useless wounds and pains they suffer from senseless fighting. At the end of the song, long after the Hero-Cat has
been laid to rest, the poet warns the world:

> *"Flee, ye fools, from worse than ruin!"*
> *Hark to Hiddigeigei's cry;*
> *Hark, his wrathful ghostly mewing:*
> *"Flee from mediocrity!"*

Circumstances can be cruel to a cat, she who loves her comfort
and repose. What feline favorite would ever suspect that, having
snugly settled down for a nap on the soft linen in an open bureau
drawer, some thoughtless chambermaid would shut it fast and im-
prison poor pussy within. "Was ever cat attended thus!" wails the
doubtful heroine of William Cowper's *The Retired Cat*.

Everyone knows how fond Dr. Samuel Johnson's cat Hodge was
of oysters. Boswell, because he loathed cats, has referred to it somewhat disdainfully in his biography. But the stern and menacing
doctor's one indulgence in sentimentality is admirably described in
Susan Coolidge's *Hodge, the Cat*.

Puns, I will defend, since as long as my friends can remember
I have affronted them with this form of wit. For this reason I have

included Guy Wetmore Carryl's *How a Cat Was Annoyed and a Poet Was Booted*. Skip it if you must, but I believe, like the Poet, you'll get a kick out of it. Antoinette Deshoulières has penned a little tidbit, too, in *Grisette Dines*.

Contemporary poetry is well served by Mildred R. Howland's *This Muff of Fur*. However black the soul of Smudge her cat, she worships him. Another sinning cat is Frances Frost's *Park Avenue Cat* who contemplatingly looks forward to Saturday night's rakish exploits, and in Vincent Starrett's *My Lord's Motoring* you meet a wisely arrogant cat.

Compiling this anthology has been sheer pleasure. A fatal fondness for cats and a love of literature have combined to achieve the result that follows. I only hope all other cat lovers will enjoy it as much.

BRANDT AYMAR

THE NINTH LIFE

BY *Mazo de la Roche*

"HARRIET! HARRIET! HARRIET!" Her name echoed through the pipe woods. It echoed across the water to the next island, was flung back from its precipitous shore in a mournful echo. Still she did not come.

The launch stood waiting at the wharf, laden with the luggage attendant on the breaking up of the holiday season. Summer was past, October almost gone, wild geese were mirrored in the lake in their flight southward. Now, for eight months the Indians and the wild deer would have the islands to themselves.

The Boyds were the last of the summer people to go. They enjoyed the month of freedom at the end of the season, when tourists were gone. They were country people themselves, bred in the district. When they were not living on their island they lived in a small town at the foot of the lake, thirty miles away. The year was marked for them by their migration to the island in the middle of June and their return to winter habitation in October.

They were well-to-do. They owned their launch which now stood waiting at the wharf, with the Indian, John Nanabush, at the wheel. He stood, dark and imperturbable, while Mrs. Boyd, her daughter and her cook raised their voices for Harriet. Mr. Boyd prowled about at the back of the cottage, peering into the workshop, the icehouse, behind the woodpile, where freshly cut birch logs lay waiting for next year's fires. Now and again he gave a stentorian shout for Harriet.

They had delayed their departure for hours because of her. Now they must go without her. Mrs. Boyd came to the wide veranda where the canoe lay covered by canvas. She lifted the edge of the canvas and peered under it.

"Why, mother, what a place to look!" said her husband. "The cat wouldn't be in there."

"I know," said Mrs. Boyd. "But I just feel so desperate!"

"Well, we've got to go without her."

"And it's getting so cold!"

On the wharf the girls wailed, "Oh, father, we can't leave Harriet on the island!"

"Find her, Pat! Find Harriet!" said Mr. Boyd to the Irish terrier.

Pat leaped from the launch, where he was investigating the hamper of eatables, and raced up the rocky shore. In his own fashion he shouted for the cat. A chipmunk darted from the trunk of a jack pine, sped across a large flat rock, ran halfway up a flaming red maple and paused, upside down, to stare at the group on the wharf.

John Nanabush raised his soft, thick, Indian voice. "You folks go along home. I'll find Harriett. I'll keep her for you."

"That's a good idea," said Mr. Boyd.

"Harriet would never stay with John," said Mrs. Boyd. "She's devoted to us."

"Guess she'd rather stay with me than freeze," said the Indian.

"Will you promise to come back to the island tomorrow and search till you find her?"

"Oh, I'll find her," said Nanabush, in his comforting, sly voice. "We ought to be gettin' on now, if you folks want to be home before dark."

"Pat! Pat! Oh, where is Pat gone?" cried the young girls.

Pat came bounding out of the woods, rushed at the launch, scrambled on board, and sat there grinning.

"He's got some sense, anyhow," said the Indian.

"Sound the whistle, John," said Mrs. Boyd. "That might fetch her."

"What if she's dead!" cried the younger girl.

"You can't kill a cat," said Nanabush. He stretched out his dark hand and blew the whistle.

All eyes were turned to the woods.

The cook said, "I left a bowl of bread and milk for her, by the back door."

"Come, mother," said Mr. Boyd, "it's no use. We can't wait any longer."

The launch looked like a toy boat as it moved among the islands. The reflection of the islands lay on the dark blue lake, more perfect than the reality. They were deserted.

WINTER. Theophile Steinlen. *Color lithograph. The Museum of Modern Art, New York, acquired through the Lillie P. Bliss Bequest*

It was only an hour later when Harriet came bac... She was tired and hungry, for she had been on a more strenuous hunt than usual. She had cut one of her feet and the hunt had been unsuccessful. She had curled up in the hollow of a tree and slept long, on the far side of the island. She had heard faint shouts for her, but feline perversity had made her curl herself closer.

Now she circled the cottage, meowed outside the doors, leaped to the window sills and peered into the rooms. There was a desolate air about it. She went to the wharf and saw that the launch was not there. The family would return in the launch.

She glided back to the cottage and found the bowl of bread and milk. She attacked it greedily, but after a few mouthfuls her appetite left her. She began to wash her face, then to lick her coat to cleanliness and luster. Her coat was a pleasing combination of tawny yellow and brown. She had a hard, shrewd face, but there was affection in her.

The October sun sank in spectacular grandeur among the islands.

There was no twilight. A blue, cold evening took possession. A few glittering stars were reflected in the lake. The air became bitterly cold, and a white furry frost rimed the grass. Harriet crept into the canoe where Mrs. Boyd had lifted the canvas. There was a cushion in it. She curled herself up and slept.

At sunrise she leaped from the canoe and ran to the kitchen window. From its ledge she peered into the room. There was no fire. There was no cook. Harriet gave a faint meow of disappointment. She bent her acute sense of hearing to catch a sound of life in the cottage. All she heard was the whisper of little waves against the shore. Pointed leaves from the silver birches drifted in the golden air. It was very cold.

Harriet went to the bowl of bread and milk and began to eat it. She discovered that she was ravenous. But there was so much of it that she had to take breath before she could finish it. Even in her repletion she muttered a meow of longing. She was four years old, and she had never been separated from the Boyds before. Her mother and her grandmother had belonged to the Boyds. She knew their movements and their life as she knew the pads of her own paw.

The bowl was emptied. As empty and hollow as the world in which she now found herself. Mechanically she began to wash her face, groom the fine hair behind her ears till it was erect as the pile of fine velvet. She stretched out her hind leg and swiftly licked the fur on the rim of her thigh. In this attitude it could be seen that she was with young. Her little teats showed rosy and fresh.

She heard a rustle in the fallen leaves and turned her green eyes defensively, fearfully, in that direction. A pair of porcupines stood staring at her, side by side, their quills upright, their yellow teeth showing in their trepidation. They had come to investigate the empty cottage.

Harriet gave a hissing scream at them, making her face as horrifying as she could. She stared with her back to the kitchen door, screaming and making faces. The porcupines turned and ambled away, pushing into a dense growth of junipers.

An acorn clattered across the roof of the cottage and fell close to Harriet. She stood up, wondering what was coming next. The chipmunk that had watched the departure yesterday now looked over the eave at her. He knew she could not get at him where he was, but he longed to retrieve his acorn. His neat striped head darted from side to side, his eyes questioned her. Her tail lashed its implacable answer. He put his little paw against the side of his face and settled down to watch her.

With a sudden leap she sprang toward the acorn, curved her paw about it, toyed with it. Beneath her fur her muscles flowed as she bent low over the acorn as though loving it, leaped back from it in disdain.

Paw to cheek, the chipmunk watched her.

Then, from all the empty world about her, her misery came to taunt her. She was alone, except for the helpless kittens that stirred inside her. She sank to her belly and gave a plaintive meow.

For a long while she lay with closed eyes. The chipmunk longed for his acorn. No other acorn could take its place. He kept elongating his neck to see into Harriet's face. She seemed oblivious of everything, but he was not deceived. Still he could not resist. He darted down the wall of the cottage, made a dash for the acorn, snatched it.

He almost succeeded. But his nearness electrified her. In a flowing curve she sprang at him. He dropped the acorn and turned himself into wind and blew back against the wall of the cottage. From the eaves he chattered at her. She stared out across the lake, ignoring him.

As the sun neared the tops of the pines she heard the delicate approach of a canoe. She ran to a point of rock and crouched there, among the junipers, watching.

It was John Nanabush come to look for her. The lake was very still and the reflection of canoe and Indian lay on the glassy water, in silent companionship. He dipped and raised his paddle, as though caressing the lake. He gave glittering diamonds to it from the tip of his paddle. He called, in his indifferent Indian voice: "Horriet! Horriet! You there?"

She crouched, staring at him. She watched him with acute but contemptuous interest.

"Horriet! Horriet!" The canoe moved on, out of sight, behind a tumble of rocks, but the Indian's voice still echoed dreamily.

She would not go with him! She would not go. Surely there was a mistake! If she ran very fast to the house, she would find the family there. Harriet ran, in swift undulations, up the rocky, shaggy steep to the cottage.

The chipmunk watched her approach from the eave, his little paws pressed together as though in prayer. But he reviled her shrilly.

She ran along the veranda and sprang to the sill of the kitchen window. Inside it was almost dark. There was no cook. The frying pan hung against the wall. She heard the chipmunk scampering across the roof, in haste to get a good view of her. She sat down on the sill and opened her mouth, but no sound came.

The chipmunk peered down at her, turning his striped head this way and that, quivering in his excitement. She lashed her tail, but she would not look up at him. She began to lick her sore paw.

The red of the sky turned to a clear lemon color. There was an exquisite stillness, as the trees awaited the first hard frost. An icy fear, a terrible loneliness, descended on Harriet. She would not spend another night on the island.

As she ran to the water's edge she meowed without ceasing, as in protest against what she must do. A wedge-shaped flock of wild geese flew strong and sure against the yellow sky.

Before her the lake stretched dark blue, crisping in its coldness, lapping icily at her paws. She cried loudly in her protest as she walked into it. A few steps and she was out of her depth.

She had never swum before, but she could do it. She moved her paws knowingly, treading the icy water in fear and hate. A loon skimming the lake was startled by her stark cat's head rising out of the water, and swung away, uttering his loud, wild laugh.

The next island was half a mile away. The last sunlight was held in the topmost branches of its pines. It seemed almost unattainable to Harriet, swimming in bitter stubbornness toward it. Sometimes she felt that she was sinking. The chill all but reached her heart, still she struggled toward the blackness of the rocks.

At last the island loomed above her. She smelled the scents of the land. All her hate of the water and her longing for home tautened her muscles. She swam fiercely and, before she was quite exhausted, clambered up on the rocks.

Once there, she was done. She lay flattened, a bit of wet draggled fur. But her heaving sides and gasping mouth showed that life was in her. The wet hairs of her fur began to crisp whitely in the frost.

Her tail began to look stiff and brittle. She felt the spirit going out of her and the bitter cold coming in. The red afterglow on the black horizon was fading. It would soon be dark.

Harriet had a curious feeling of life somewhere near. Not stirring, just sending its prickly essence, in a thin current, toward her. Her eyes flew open in horror of being attacked in her weak state. She looked straight into the eyes of a wild goose, spread on the rock near her.

One of his wings had been injured and he had been left behind, by the flock, to die. He was large and strong, but young. This had been his first flight southward. His injured wing lay spread on the rock like a fan. He rested his glossy head on it.

They stared at each other, fascinated, while the current of his fear pricked her to life. She tightened the muscles of her belly and pressed her claws against the rock. Their eyes communed, each to each, like instruments in tune. She drew her chin against her frosty breast, while her eyes became balls of fire, glaring into his.

He raised himself above his broken wing and reared his strong other wing, as though to fly. But she held him with her eyes. He opened his long beak, but the cry died in his throat. He got onto his webbed feet and stood, with trailing wing, facing her. He moved a step nearer.

So, they stared and stared, till he wanted her to take him. He had no will but hers. Now her blood was moving quickly. She felt strong and fierce. His long neck, his big downy breast, were defenseless. She sprang, sunk her teeth in his neck, tore his breast with her hind claws, clung to him. His strong wing beat the air, even after he knew himself dying.

It was dark when she had finished her meal. She sat on the rock, washing her face, attending to her sore paw. The air had grown even colder, and snowflakes drifted on the darkness. The water in pools and shallows began to freeze. Harriet crept close to the body of the goose, snuggling warmly in its down. She pressed under its wing, which spread above her, as though in protection.

She meowed plaintively as she prowled about the island next morning. The people who owned it had gone to their home, in a distant American city, many weeks ago. The windows of the cottage were boarded up. The flagstaff, where the big American flag had floated, was bare. Harriet prowled about the island, looking longingly at the mainland, filled with loathing of the icy water.

As she crept to its frozen rim she lifted her lip in loathing. A bit of down from the goose clung to her cheek. She crept onto the thin ice and, as it crackled beneath her, she meowed as in pain. At last, with a despairing lash of her tail, she went into the lake and set her face toward the mainland. It was three quarters of a mile away.

This ordeal was worse than last night's. The lake was more cruelly cold. But it was smooth, stretched like cold steel beneath the drifting snowflakes. Harriet's four paws went up and down, as though the lake were a great barrier of ice she was mounting. Her head looked small and sleek as a rat's. Her green eyes were unwinking. Like a lodestone, the house at the foot of the lake drew her. Her spirit drew courage from the fire of its hearth.

A snake also was swimming to the mainland. Its cold blood felt no chill. Its ebony head arched above the steel of the lake. A delicate flourish on the steely surface followed it. The two swimmers were acutely conscious of each other, but their cold eyes ignored.

Harriet scrambled onto the crackling ice at the shore and lay prone. The life was all but gone from her. She remembered neither food nor fire nor shelter. The snake glided over the stones near her, slippery and secure. She tried to rise but could not.

The flurry of snow passed. A wind from the southwest made a scatteration among the clouds. They moved north and east, settling in gray and purple on the horizon. The sun shone out strongly, turning the October foliage to a blaze of scarlet and gold. The sunlight lay warm on Harriet's sagging sides.

She felt new life creeping into her. She raised her head and began to lick her sore paw. Then she ran her tongue, in long eager strokes, across her flanks. Her fur stood upright. Her flesh grew warm and supple.

She crept out on a rock, from whose crevices hardy ferns and huckleberry bushes grew. A few huckleberries glimmered frostily blue among the russet leaves. Harriet peered into the pool below the rock. She saw some small bass resting there in the watered sunshine.

She crouched, watching them intently. Her colors mingled with the frost-browned fern and bronzed leaves. She settled herself on her breast, as though to rest, then her paws shot into the pool, her claws like fishhooks drove into the bright scales. The bass lay on the rock, its golden eye staring up at her.

Now she felt refreshed and strong. She found the sandy track through the woods and trotted along it toward the foot of the lake. All day she pressed forward, meeting no one. She stopped only to catch a little mouse and eat it and rest after the meal.

At sundown a deer stepped out of a thicket and stood before her, his antlers arching like the branches of a tree, his great eyes glowing. He looked at her, then bent his antlers, listening. He raised a shapely hoof and stood poised. Harriet saw something shining among the leaves. There was a sharp noise. The shock of it lifted Harriet from her feet, made every hair of her tail vibrant.

The tall deer sank to his knees. He laid the side of his head on the ground and his great eyes were raised imploringly to the face of the hunter who came out of the wood. The hunter knelt by him, as though in compassion. Then a stream of red gushed from the deer's throat. A dog came and sniffed his flank. Harriet peered down from a tree where she had hid. It was long before she dared to go on.

She had gone only a short way when she saw a doe and a fawn, standing as though waiting. The doe lowered her head at Harriet, but the fawn looked proudly aloof, holding its head, with the face innocent as a little child's, high on its strong neck. Harriet glided away, her paws brushing the snow from the dead leaves. She curled herself in a hollow in a tree and lay licking her sore paw. She thought of the dead deer's great body and the large pieces of flesh she had seen cut from it.

In the morning she was very hungry, but there was nothing to eat. The sky was dark, the snow had turned to a rain that dripped from the trees and soaked her fur till it clung to her. But she ran steadily along the track, always drawn by the lodestone of the house at the foot of the lake. Passing toward it, she sometimes gave a meow as faint and thin as the fall of a pine needle. She ate a few blueberries from the dried bushes. She came to a space carpeted by glossy wintergreen leaves. She even ate some of the scarlet berries, eating them with distaste and curling lip, but she was so hungry because of the kittens she carried. There seemed nothing living abroad except her.

The path crossed a swamp dense with a growth of cranberries.

Beyond this she came to a settler's cottage, clean and neat, with poultry in a wire run. There was a hen turkey in the yard, followed by three daintily moving poults. A girl was milking a cow in an open shed. Harriet stood staring, lonely, hungry. She felt weighted down, almost too tired to go on.

A man came out of the house with a bucket. He saw her, and a piercing whistle brought two hounds. He picked up a stone and threw it. It struck her side.

Harriet turned into a fury, an elongated, arched, fiery-eyed, sneering fury. The hounds hesitated before her claws that reached for their eyes. She whirled and flew down the path. They came after her, baying, sending up the volume of their voices in the rain. They urged each other on with loud cries. With her last strength she clambered into a tree and sat sneering down at them, her sides palpitating.

The hounds stood with their paws against the trunk of the tree, baying up at her. They changed places, as though that would help them. They flung themselves down, panting beneath the tree, then sprang up again, baying. But when the shrill whistle sounded again they ran without hesitating back to their master.

On and on Harriet limped over the rock track. Sometimes she had a glimpse of the lake between trees, but she scarcely looked to right or left. The homeward cord drew her ever more strongly. One would scarcely have recognized the sleek pet in this draggled tramp, this limping, heavy-eyed, slinking cat.

She could see the twinkling lights of the town across the bay, when her pain came on. It was so piercing, so sudden, that she turned, with a savage cry, to face what seemed to be attacking her in the rear. But then she knew that the pain was inside her.

She lay writhing on the ground and before long gave birth to a kitten. She began to lick it, then realized that it was dead. She ran on toward the town as fast as she could.

She was still two miles from it when she had two more kittens. She lay beside them for a while, feeling weak and peaceful. Now the lights of the town were out. Harriet picked up one of the kittens and limped on. With it in her mouth she went along the paved street. She gave a meow of delight as she reached the back door of her own home.

She laid the kitten on the doorstep and herself began limping back and forth, the length of the step, rubbing her sides against the door. For the first time since she had been left on the island she purred. The purr bubbled in her throat, vibrating through her nerves in an ecstasy of home-coming. She caressed the back door with every bit of her. She stood on her hind legs and caressed the door handle with a loving paw. Only the weak cry of her kitten made her desist.

She carried it to the tool shed and laid it on the mat where the terrier slept in warm weather. She laid herself down beside it, trilling to it in love. It buried its sightless face against her lank belly. She lay flat on her side, weary to the bone.

But the shape of the kitten she had abandoned on the road now crept into her mind. It crept on silken paws, with its tail pointed like a rat's and its eyelids glued together. Round and round it crept in its agony of abandonment, tearing her mind as its birth had torn her body. She flung herself on her other side, trying to forget it, but she could not.

With a piteous meow of protest against the instinct that hounded her, she left the kitten's side and went out into the dawn. The rain had stopped and there was a sharp clear wind that drove the dead leaves scurrying across the frozen ruts.

The pain of her sore paw on the ice ruts was like fire, but she hurried on, draggled, hard-faced, with the thought of the bereft kitten prodding her.

The dreadful road unrolled itself before her in an endless scroll of horrible hieroglyphics. She meowed in hate of it, at every yard. She covered it, mile after mile, till she reached the spot where she had littered. There in the coarse wet grass, she found the kitten. She turned it over with her nose, sniffing it to see if it were worth taking home. She decided that it was.

Along and long the road she limped, the kitten dangling from her unloving mouth, the dead leaves whirling about her, as though they would bury her, the icy ruts biting her paw.

But the clouds had broken and the Indian-summer sun was leaping out. As she hobbled into her own yard her fur was warm and dry on her back. She laid the kitten beside the other and gave herself up to suckling them. And as they drew life from her, her love went out to them. She made soft trilling noises to them, threw her forelegs about them, lashed her tail about them, binding them close. She licked their fat bodies and their blunt heads till they shone.

Then suddenly a noise in the kitchen galvanized her. She leaped up, scattering the sucklings from her nipples. It was the rattle of a stove lid she had heard. She ran up the steps and meowed at the back door. It opened and the cook let out a scream of joy.

"Harriet! Harriet! Harriet's here!"

Pat ran to meet her, putting his paw on her back. She arched herself at him, giving a three-cornered smile. The cook ran to room after room, telling the news. The Boyds came from room after room to welcome Harriet, to marvel at her return.

"She must have come early last night," said the cook, "for she's had kittens in the tool shed.

"Well, they'll have to be drowned," said Mr. Boyd.

Harriet could not eat her bread and milk for purring. The purring sang in her throat, like a kettle. She had left her saucer and went to Mr. Boyd and thrust her head into his hand.

"Just listen how she purrs!" said Mrs. Boyd. "I've always said she was an affectionate cat."

⚜

THE   GENTLE   CAT

MINNA   MINNA   MOWBRAY

BY *Michael Joseph*

AMONG ALL MY CATS, past and present, Minna Minna Mowbray was an outstanding personality. Except to a connoisseur of cats Minna was not physically impressive. She was a short-haired tortoiseshell tabby, with tiny white paws to watch her piquant white face. Her head was small but beautifully shaped. The rather large ears were grey, and streaks of orange fur ran down between her amber eyes and on either side to the under part of her delicate jaw, forming a regularly designed tortoiseshell frame for her white face. A flash of coral pink was visible when she opened her dainty mouth.

QUITE AT HOME. *From Art Journal, London*

Her teeth were white and strong. The under part of her body was
pure white and even in the soot and grime of London this was
nearly always spotlessly clean. At kitten time it was dazzlingly white.
This part of her was domestically known as her "ermine." When
she was feeling particularly sociable, certain favoured members of
the household were permitted, sometimes even encouraged, to mas-
sage it gently.

Minna was small, as cats go, but exquisitely proportioned. All
her movements were graceful. She would sit upright, with her tiny
forepaws close together, her long, rather full tail coiled round. Her
favourite position for sleep was a crouch, the hind legs drawn up
close and head resting on the outstretched forepaws which she
converted into cushions by turning them inwards. Sometimes she
preferred to lie on her side, legs oustretched luxuriously at queer
angles. Various attitudes I learned to recognize as meditative (often
assumed, this one), ecstatic, proud (both these when kittens were
on view), majestically indignant (accompanied by business with
tail), enquiring (as when she wanted to know what I was eating—
this was primarily curiosity, for as often as not she rejected after
close scrutiny the morsel I offered her) and leave-me-alone-please.
This last was indicated by a haughty turning aside of her head;
if this failed she would calmly turn her back, and if *that* gesture
had no effect she would walk off with the air of an offended
dowager.

Like her mother, Lady Dudley, she had no voice, her vocal chord
being partially paralyzed. Oddly enough—for such a physical defect
is presumably not hereditary—her kittens seldom cried, except when

they were very young. Minna opened her mouth when, for instance, she wanted a door opened, but no sound emerged. When she was greatly agitated about something a faint squeak was audible if you listened carefully. She could purr loudly enough but did not purr often. She could also swear, in delicate but determined fashion, but this again was reserved for special occasions.

Minna Minna Mowbray was a gentle cat. She never attempted to scratch a human. Babies and small boys could do what they liked with her. Like all self-respecting cats she disliked rough handling but she never attempted retaliation. If her tail were pulled or her long, sensitive whiskers touched she showed displeasure by asking silently to be allowed to go.

Contrary to expert advice, Minna wore a collar—an elegant green collar with an identity disc and two brass bells. A collar, I have heard, is undesirable because it may catch in the spikes of railings or the branches of a tree, but in my experience this risk is negligible if a cat is trained to a collar when very young. It is possible that a grown cat may so resent the introduction of a collar that he will try to drag it off and thereby injure himself, but I have never heard of an instance.

Minna was proud of her collar and plainly enjoyed wearing it. She put the bells to practical use, whenever she wanted to be admitted to a room, by shaking her head outside the closed door. She never worried if she were late for breakfast, knowing that the tinkle of her bell would cause the door to be opened. Sometimes when she rang outside the door I delayed, for the satisfaction of hearing her tinkle imperiously repeated. And with what an air of affronted majesty she stalked into the room if she had been thus kept waiting! Custom brought her to the dining-room at breakfast time, not hunger, for as often as not she turned up her aristocratic nose at the fish or milk offered her.

Minna also learned to summon her kittens by sounding her bells. When the babies got to the exploring stage and escaped from the maternal eye in house or garden Minna recalled them by an agitated peal. They usually answered the summons promptly but Minna would continue to ring until they did.

Minna could silence her bell as effectively as she could ring it. Not a sound was to be heard when she stalked a bird. What a waste of time it is to "bell the cat" with the intention of suppressing natural instincts!

The real owner of my house in those days was Minna. She walked about with the manner of a landed proprietor surveying his domain; on the whole proud, but reserving the right to be critical. The day nursery and the kitchen were her favourite rooms. The dining-room and what my family insisted on calling "the study" were frequently patronized. Her appearances in other rooms were rare, with the exception of my bedroom in the winter, when warm milk was usually to be coaxed from me last thing at night.

When she was younger the bathroom enchanted her. She soon discovered it to be a magic, fascinating and deliciously dangerous place with a queer contraption which was often filled with water. As a kitten, Minna used to insist on walking round the edge of the bath when there was water in it, balancing precariously at the rounded corners. Running water fascinated her and she would play with a dripping tap for hours. Her mother, and some of Minna's own kittens, shared this fondness for running water: and so did my favorite Siamese, Charles. Micky Jos, one of Minna's most spirited kittens, had a passion for water and thoroughly enjoyed being soaked to the skin. But when she was grown up, with matronly responsibilities, Minna seldom played with water. It was beneath her dignity.

Another forsaken attraction in her middle age was the piano. As a kitten she took a great interest in it. As soon as it was opened she would jump on the keyboard. A series of spirited discords marked her progress from bass to treble and back again. She much preferred the bass, possibly because the deeper volume of sound or the stronger vibration took her fancy. But as she grew up Minna tired of the piano and took no notice of it.

Minna had a curious aversion to whistling. If I tried to whistle (it is not one of my accomplishments) Minna was at once agitated and tried to stop it by putting her paw on my lips. So long as I continued she behaved as one would expect an operatic tenor to behave within hearing of a mouth organ. It was not often that I outraged Minna's artistic susceptibilities, but, when I did, her agitation was intense.

Flowers had a curious attraction for Minna. She could never resist nibbling at them. Spring flowers particularly; if not prevented she would drag daffodils and tulips to the ground for the aesthetic satisfaction of sampling their flavour at her leisure. It was not that she required vegetable diet, for grass, which cats eat regularly when they can get it, was easily accessible. Minna's taste for flowers was not utilitarian.

If there was one thing Minna disliked more than any other it was preparation for a journey. As soon as suitcases were produced she made a prompt and plaintive appearance on the scene. Her agitation always increased when packing began. She would sit mournfully looking on while cupboards and drawers shed their contents, every now and then making a timid and reproachful attempt to interfere with our progress. Even the perfunctory packing of a suitcase for a week-end disturbed her. As for the wholesale removal of the family during the summer, that was a terrible ordeal. On one occasion, when boxes and cases were being brushed as a preliminary to their annual excursion, Minna, shaking her bell in protest, disappeared downstairs, to reappear a few minutes later with Peter, our wire-haired terrier. And then the pair of them sat gazing lugubriously at the signs of departure.

Minna, like most cats, disliked travelling. She had a very commodious basket (I was always annoyed by people who called it a dog basket) and entered it with a poor grace. Poor dear, she knew what was coming. However comfortably the basket was lined, the taxi jolted her up and down and the noise of passing traffic frightened her. The ignominy of being deposited on the platform of a railway station was bad enough, but worse was to follow. The train was the climax of the torture.

It was only when Minna was with me in a railway carriage that the sensation of being cooped up in a swiftly-moving box oppressed me. To the more sensitive creature who was my cat the jolting, swaying movement of the small compartment which carried us so swiftly and mysteriously to an unknown destination must have been a paralysing torture. It was only then that I realized how uncomfortable even the most modern railway carriage is. Poor Minna! She would emerge timidly from her basket, grateful for release, but terrified of the unknown. Even in her fear curiosity compelled her to climb for a view of the rushing landscape. A glimpse was enough, and down on to the floor she would spring, crouching and panting, her little pink tongue hanging from her mouth like a signal of distress.

Only once do I remember Minna facing a railway journey with equanimity—and that, I am sure, was more apparent than real. On that occasion Minna was the proud mother of five kittens, who had also to be transported. The booking-office clerk stared when I told him I had six cats with me. When I added that they were infants in arms and enquired if there were any reduction on account of either age or quantity, or both, he grinned comprehendingly. I was mad, of course. He gave me one ticket and took my half-crown with cheerful tolerance. I betook myself and my cat basket off hastily before he could change his mind.

Minna, evidently determined to conquer her fears for the sake of her kittens, was remarkably self-possessed. She submitted without anxiety to imprisonment in the basket and made no fuss when it was lifted into the taxi and dumped on the floor. Not until the train was speeding southwards and she was allowed the freedom of the carriage did she betray her usual agitation. And then, I observed, only when she was well clear of the basket and its tiny occupants. On the seat beside me, snatching a furtive look out of the window from time to time, Minna went through the familiar performance of crying silently, appealing to me with a troubled paw to bring the dreadful and mysterious train to a standstill. But she had one eye all the time on the basket below and, at the first whimpering sound she was back again, comforting her babies with placid, maternal purring.

Minna was always an exemplary mother. But cats vary considerably in this respect. I have already mentioned Meestah, an earlier kitten of Lady Dudley's and therefore a half-sister to Minna. Meestah was worse than neglectful. Her nomenclature, by the way, was based on an Arab word meaning "to hide," for she had a strange habit of hiding away in odd corners. Meestah eventually found the outer world a better hiding-place and after several prolonged absences she one day hid herself for good and, to my sorrow, for I was very fond of her, she never came back.

Meestah was so long before she became a mother that we began to think she would escape the inevitable fate of a female cat, but one day the family arrived—two beautiful kittens. Meestah was most resentful. She would have nothing to do with them. All our coaxing was of no avail. Fortunately this was when I had fourteen cats. About nine of them were females and the kitten problem was rapidly becoming serious. But, luckily for Meestah's kittens, another of my large cat family accommodatingly had kittens just then and as the litter was small we were able to add Meestah's offspring to the new nursery. This met with the complete approval of both mothers. Meestah was enormously relieved. That, so far as I am aware, for she disappeared not very long after, was her sole venture into motherhood. How my Minna must have disapproved of her!

Minna adored having kittens. Indeed, a certain cynical member of my family once remarked that it was her life's work. Her kittens were invariably beautiful and never commonplace. Tortoiseshell tabby, orange, and prettily marked black and white were the usual arrivals, and there were often black flecked with bronze, and kittens mottled distinctively which I am at a loss to describe. Sometimes they were long-haired but usually they inherited the smooth, short-haired coat of their mother. Lest it be thought that I was prejudiced in their favor I must add that Minna's kittens excited admiration even in people usually indifferent to cats.

With kittens arriving in regular batches it may seem surprising that the problem of their disposal seldom arose. I would have liked to keep them all; but my family had other ideas.

There were two good reasons why we had no surplus kittens. One was that the demand exceeded the supply. Not that the supply was not plentiful! I had a "waiting list" for kittens, with the requirements of my friends noted in detail. The fame of my Minna's kittens spread far and wide. Her offspring grew into handsome cats in households all over the country. As my work brought me into touch with a large number of authors, several of her kittens were transferred to literary ownership. Other kittens went to more modest family circles. Our milkman was a regular customer. He had been rather unlucky with his kittens and we cheerfully replaced them. The fishmonger begged for one which captivated him; and the little orange tabby which went to the greengrocer's wife was the recipient of so much affection that I am sure he did not begrudge the others the natural advantages of their respective establishments.

The other reason was rather amusing. Several times we resolved to keep for ourselves a particularly charming kitten. There was

Dinah, a fluffy, sentimental and very attractive young lady whom we brought from the country when we went to live in Regent's Park. I was especially fond of Dinah; whenever Minna held herself aloof—and that was often—Dinah could be depended on to stay purring blissfully on my knee. Dinah was as affectionate as she was decorative.

Not long after our arrival in London Dinah was reported missing. The usual frantic search followed, with no result. Imagine my feelings. Dinah's virtues were magnified with the passing days and, when at last I had to admit there was no longer any hope of finding her, my loss seemed irreparable. I can write of my lost Dinah in this lighthearted way on account of what followed.

One Sunday morning, some weeks later, someone looking out of a window said, "Isn't that Dinah?" I must explain that the back of our house faced the backs of a crescent of other houses, with small gardens abutting on each other. In these gardens were trees and on a low-lying bough there was a cat. It certainly did look like Dinah.

I ran down to the garden and, climbing on to the wall, made my way along until I was close enough to identify the cat. It *was* Dinah. She watched me coming and when I called her name looked down at me with mild interest. I noticed, with relief, that she had evidently been well fed and cared for. If she recognized me she did not show it. Balancing precariously, I tried to coax her down. Dinah took no notice. So, feeling rather foolish, I retired, in the vain hope that she would follow.

Then I had an inspiration. Dinah might have transferred her affections to another human being, but what about her mother? I dashed into the house, picked up Minna and returned to the garden wall. To reach the tree I had to pass along the tops of several garden walls, on some of which my neighbors had erected trellis-work, wire and such-like impediments. With Minna doing her best to escape it was no easy matter to negotiate these obstacles but, apart from blacking my hands and face and tearing my trousers on a nail, I completed the journey safely. I was confident that Dinah would eagerly come down as soon as she saw Minna; and that Minna would be overjoyed to find her lost baby.

I held Minna up in my arms, balancing on tiptoe, so that the two cats could see each other face to face. Dinah looked down on us with surprise, as if to remark what a strange world this was, with human beings performing antics with other cats on the tops of walls. Her innocent eyes looked at Minna with an expression which clearly said, "I don't know you, madam, and I don't want to know you." Minna, on the other hand, recognized her offspring at once. Was she overjoyed? Did she utter the crooning call, half purr, half squeak, with which she had always summoned her kittens? Not she. She spat viciously and began to swear under her breath, in a suppressed note of unmistakable feline hate. She kept it up in a steady crescendo until I lowered her on to the wall and let her go: and then she sprang to the ground, lashing her tail with fury.

At the time I was amazed at this unmotherly behavior. Dinah was still a kitten and only a few weeks before had been the apple of her mother's eye. It was inconceivable that she could have become a stranger in so short a time. I knew that grown cats fail to recognize their parents and *vice versa*, but there was Minna behaving in a way most unnatural and offensive.

Later, I became suspicious. It dawned on me that there was something odd about these disappearances of favorite kittens. Whenever we tried to keep one of a litter, it invariably left us before it was many months old. Everyone who has had anything to do with cats knows how distressed the mother cat is when a kitten is lost or taken away, especially if it is the sole survivor of a litter. Now, it struck me as curious that Minna showed no anxiety when these mysterious departures occurred. We all searched high and low, but Minna was quite unconcerned.

It was when Fowey vanished that my suspicions were confirmed. Fowey (named after the Cornish seaport) was a mischievous orange rascal with china-blue eyes, the throatiest purr I have ever heard, an insatiable appetite and absurd fluffy paws which contrasted oddly with the dainty and aristocratic white feet of his mother. He was an intelligent and charming kitten and everyone made a great fuss of him.

When Fowey was about three months old, Minna took him for long walks. On one occasion I discovered them in a field by the railway a long way from the house. No doubt these expeditions were a source of delight to little Fowey, who wanted to see the world, but there seemed to me to be something sinister about them.

One day mother and son left the house together, Fowey as usual prancing with delight at the prospect of yet another expedition into the fascinating unknown. I watched them go, and there was a queer look in Minna's eye, a look which I can only describe as wicked. There was an evil resolution in that look. Maybe it was only my fancy but it was enough to make me ask at once for Fowey when I returned home that evening. My fears were realized; Minna was there, smirking triumphantly, I fancied, but Fowey was missing.

The days went by and Fowey did not return. We searched in vain. When I asked Minna she looked up at me with an expression so blandly innocent that I am sure she understood perfectly well what I was talking about. Now there is no doubt whatever in my mind that what happened was this. Minna took Fowey to some unfamiliar, deserted spot and there turned round and attacked her unsuspecting offspring. Most probably she said something like this to him:

"Look here, young Fowey (*bang*) you understand this (*scratch*). I'm the only cat wanted in Their house (*biff*) and I'm not (*scratch*) going to have you on the premises. (*Bite, scratch, bang.*) You go and find a home of your own. (*Spit.*) You're not wanted, d'you hear me?" (*Bang, spit, bite, scratch and general fireworks.*)

No wonder poor Fowey beat a retreat like all the others! He reappeared a few weeks later in one of the gardens at the back; and I discovered that he was lording it over one of the houses in the neighbouring crescent. He had grown into a magnificent cat with a long coat (carefully brushed, I was glad to note) and a huge plume of a tail which I could see daily fluttering in the trees when I was shaving in my bathroom. He was, to judge by appearances, a happy cat and played joyously in the gardens most of the day. But he never came into ours.

Minna was an expert in the art of getting her own way. I can recall only two occasions when she was defeated and then I think she allowed herself to be. The first occasion was the little matter of Peter's basket.

Peter belonged to my wife before I knew her, and, incidentally, there were times when that dog made me feel as a second husband must feel when his wife describes the virtues of his predecessor. Who is this interloper? Peter seemed to say. Well, when Peter became part of the new ménage the basket came along too, but in the excitement of meeting Minna Minna Mowbray and the consequent revolution in his habits and ideas of home life, Peter apparently forgot about the basket.

My wife was upset. She said that Peter was so intelligent he wouldn't go to sleep anywhere but in his basket. (That was before she knew the change Minna could produce.) So it came about that Peter slept—I suspect uneasily—on the mat outside her bedroom door. Then one day my wife said, "Poor Peter! No wonder he looks unhappy. He hasn't got his basket." So the basket was dug out of the pile of miscellaneous kit which was awaiting disposal in the new house, and was ceremoniously put outside the door for Peter's accommodation. I rather liked the look of it and reflected aloud, to my wife's indignation, that my Minna Minna Mowbray could just do with a basket like that.

Peter wagged his stump, looked intelligent and barked. That night be occupied the basket according to plan. We knew something was wrong (from Peter's point of view) when he scratched at the door the next morning about an hour before his usual time. He came in with the air of an ill-used dog, his stump registering dejection.

We had not long to wait for the explanation. Shortly after tea Minna Minna Mowbray stalked upstairs and leisurely installed herself in the basket. By the time we turned off the wireless and went upstairs to bed she was coiled up fast asleep (or ostensibly so) while Peter, squatting on the landing, regarded her balefully from a discreet distance.

That was the beginning of the basket war. The old Trojan War, the Hundred Years War and the Great War faded into insignificance. Our household was promptly divided into two factions—the pro-Peterites, led by my wife, and the pro-Minnaites, which was me. The cook thought it was too bad, the parlourmaid echoed, "Poor Peter." It is true the postman grinned unsympathetically when he heard about it, but he and Peter are traditional enemies, so that he was more anti-Peter than pro-Minna.

The fact that numbers were against her did not daunt my Minna. Her tiny stature was deceptive. In action she could give points to any Amazon. So that Peter's fugitive attempts to regain possession of his sleeping quarters are scarcely worth recording. Except perhaps the day when, bloated with tea and Dutch courage, he made a spirited attempt to get in while Minna dozed peacefully on the cushion. The battle was swiftly over; and Peter emerged from the regions of the coal cellar only after an interval of two days and much coaxing.

Then other and more important domestic affairs took precedence over the Minna-Peter feud. While the rest of the household talked of other things it rumbled on in a state of trench warfare, with Minna securely dug in and Peter making occasional raids across No-man's-landing. Indeed, we all regarded the basket war as a permanent feature of our domestic life.

Actually it lasted for just over two years. Armistice was declared only when our baby daughter Shirley crawled out of the bedroom door, seized Minna by the scruff of her furry neck, neatly ejected her and solemnly climbed into the basket.

Peter was present at the ceremony and (presumably) gave a loud doggy guffaw. Minna withdrew with dignity. She then turned the day nursery into her sleeping quarters and Peter retired to the kitchen. The basket was "reconstructed" after the war and for a long time was occupied by a teddy bear, a musical duck and a woolly rabbit. There was peace in our time.

The other occasion when Minna graciously surrendered was the advent of Charles O'Malley, my Siamese cat. I have written another book about Charles and I shall not say much about him here; although readers of that book may understand my feeling that this is Hamlet without the Prince of Denmark.

Charles O'Malley was the first Siamese I had had. Minna Minna Mowbray was furious when I brought him home and always looked upon him as an intruder. It was quite clear that she would never forgive me for adopting another cat. As for Charles himself, Minna at first swore and spat vigorously at his approach. But she soon decided to tolerate him and after a fortnight or so the two cats were drinking peaceably from the same saucer. Charles, as a ten-weeks-old kitten, was enormously impressed by Minna Minna Mowbray. No amount of bad language or threats deterred him from the pursuit of her tail but it was several weeks before Minna permitted him to play with her.

Charles O'Malley was aristocratically bred, and looked it. With his sapphire-blue eyes, delicate cream coat, chocolate-pointed ears, feet, tail and "mask," he was a truly handsome creature.

There are differences between Siamese and other cats, apart

from their shape and colouring. The Siamese voice is quite distinctive. When Minna first heard Charles's raucous squeak (for I expect
that is how she would have described it) she visibly shuddered.
Siamese cats have the reputation of being ferocious fighters; they
are certainly stronger than ordinary cats. I do not think they are so
graceful when walking or jumping. Indeed, Charles would land on
his feet with a thud which was positively canine. Siamese are exquisite animals, however; sensitive, intelligent and responsive.
Charles O'Malley (whom I confess I adopted partly to annoy
Minna, who had been treating me very cavalierly at the time) was
indeed a most lovable and charming cat and as readers of his story
will know, he was destined to become my best loved cat.

However, no despot ever ruled his kingdom with more certainty
of getting his own way than Minna Minna Mowbray did the house
which we then lived in. It was a benevolent tyranny, this rule of
Minna's; often amusing, never malicious, always sure and precise.
She was clearly a believer in the divine right of cats, exercising her
power with due regard to the niceties and obligations of her position.

To the uninitiated it may appear that I was merely foolish about
my cat. However, I was not Minna's only subject. She bossed everyone in the house, with the exception of my little daughter Shirley,
who occasionally did a bit of bossing herself. But Minna was quite
happy about that. Shirley was privileged to stroke her fur the wrong
way, to play with her tail and to carry her round the nursery suspended at all sorts of queer angles. I fancy that Minna rather
enjoyed it all. Shirley was very fond of her and if Minna was acci-
dentally hurt when they were playing together—this rarely happened, for Shirley knew she must be careful—the ensuing ceremony
of contrite apology on the part of one and the gracious forgiveness
of the other was amusing to watch.

When Minna had kittens Shirley was a privileged visitor from
the time of their birth. Minna allowed her to stroke them, knowing
that Shirley would only touch them with a gentleness appropriate
to the occasion. As soon as the babies reached the romping age
Shirley was in her element. The nursery was transformed into an
arena, in which young tigers leaped and raced swiftly in all directions, with Shirley's attempts at pursuit interrupted by her gurgles

of excited laughter. Minna used to look on quite happily at these performances.

Like all cats who are happily accommodated in a human household Minna was a docile creature. But she insisted on having her own way. She would observe, with well-bred interest, my wife's painstaking preparations to provide her with a comfortable and secluded bed for her kittens. A large cardboard box, of the kind she loved, carefully lined with successive layers of newspaper, tissue paper and soft linen, and placed in one of her favourite cupboards, which was conveniently warm, well ventilated and discreetly dark —this was dutifully prepared at certain times by one of us, my wife, Nannie or myself. Whoever prepared her bed, however comfortably made and conveniently placed it might be, we could be sure of one thing—Minna would not use it.

Minna deceived several generations of interested cooks and house-parlourmaids by her tactics on these occasions. It was her custom to inspect at intervals the box or basket which had been so thoughtfully made ready for her, even to occupy it for forty winks every now and again, as if to advertise her satisfaction. Many a beaming domestic servant announced the good news that "Minnie is very pleased with her new box." But these premature expectations were invariably disappointed. Minna knew what she was about. The attention of our expectant domestic staff being thus publicly drawn to a particular spot, Minna had her kittens elsewhere.

In this respect most cats, I believe, behave in the same independent way. Is it yet another survival of jungle instinct, this hiding away from prying eyes at important times? Or merely a gesture of independence, a rejection of our human proprietorship, a challenge to man and his stupid ways? Minna, although intensely secretive about her plans, made no further attempt at concealment when her kittens were born. She was then embarrassingly anxious that they should be seen and admired. In this I think she may have differed from other cats who, reasonably enough, do not like to be disturbed for some days. Minna, however, scorned further camouflage. She unmistakably invited us to pay our respects to the new arrivals. Nor did she object to their being touched. Our praise was clearly to her liking; she would purr loudly if we admired the little, squealing, almost invisible babies.

Naturally enough she would resent it if we overstayed our welcome, or if any stranger should presume to intrude on her privacy. And what a calamity if there should be any attempt to move her family! In that event, as soon as the coast was clear, Minna would remove them methodically, one by one, to what she obviously trusted would be a place less liable to disturbance. She was quite capable of registering a protest if disturbed by strangers; this usually took the form of depositing her kittens under the cover of my bed. There were times when I arrived home to find the house in a state of agitation because Minna and her kittens had disappeared. Nearly always they were to be found huddled together at the end of my bed comfortably asleep under the warm and sheltering darkness of the eiderdown.

Minna brooked no interference in her private affairs. At an early age she began to take an active interest in the opposite sex and all our well-meant efforts to influence her in the direction of a more lady-like modesty were frustrated. In other words, if the doors were shut she climbed out of a window. Nor were our attempts to find her a worthy husband any more successful. Whether the so-called attraction of opposites is responsible or not, it is a lamentable fact that Minna invariably chose the most disreputable gentleman friends. Any ugly, one-eyed, torn-eared tom cat seemed to have an irresistible attraction for our Minna Minna Mowbray.

In her early days I had great ambitions for her. I studied the interesting advertisements of cat-breeders and made all sorts of wonderful plans for her matrimonial future. Alas! an Earl's Court garden proved my undoing, or rather hers. I am fond of cats, even scallywag tom cats, but that neighbourhood swarmed with them. I have never felt the same way towards Earl's Court since.

From the very beginning Minna seemed determined to outdo all the great lovers of history. As I have remarked, a tom cat had only to be an ugly brute in order to qualify as one of Minna's suitors. The uglier they were, the more eligible they appeared to be. She had, I remember, a disgraceful passion for an old roué with a lacerated tail, fractional ears, a permanently closed left eye and a pronounced limp. At his approach Minna behaved in a shameless and otherwise indescribable fashion. On such occasions I used to pretend she was not my cat.

When we were living in Surrey we did our best to reform her.

It was not successful. Within a few days of our arrival the news had spread in some mysterious fashion that a new and comely lady cat had taken up her residence and that she had a decided preference for experienced lovers. Somehow Minna had made it known to the cats of all Surrey (and part of Sussex, too, I fancy) that she liked to choose her followers from the ranks of the veterans and middle-aged. She had no use for boy friends, it appeared.

We discovered this, and were considerably humiliated thereby, when we introduced her to a young orange cat from a neighbouring house. As soon as we set eyes on this cat, we decided that here was an ideal husband for Minna. He was a strikingly handsome cat, young and, so far as we could see, perfectly eligible. Minna, however, thought not. She promptly spat at him in a most unladylike way. Our candidate let us down badly. He fled for his life. After that we left Minna to her own devices—and to the reprobate toms of the neighbourhood.

To look at Minna Minna Mowbray as she sat demurely on the arm of my chair, her little white paws set neatly together in a modest pose, you would never imagine that she favoured the toughs and tramps of the tom cat world. In every other respect she was fastidious to the point of absurdity. She would refuse to drink from a saucer that was not spotlessly clean; would spend hours industriously making her toilet, until every hair was in its proper place; insisted on her milk being at exactly the right temperature; and objected to being touched, making a pretense of exquisite discomfort if I happened to stroke her when she didn't feel like it or to lay hands, however gently, on any part of her sensitive anatomy. Yet, ten minutes later, she could be observed (if you cared to gaze on the unedifying spectacle) in the garden below, being rolled playfully about in the mud by a cave-man lover from the slums of Camden Town.

JENNIE'S LESSONS TO PETER
ON HOW TO BEHAVE LIKE A CAT

BY *Paul Gallico*

O NCE ABOARD, Jennie's experience and knowledge of ships
stood her in good stead. She called for the point-to-point method
of procedure again, for she was particularly anxious not to encounter
any human beings before the ship had cast off, and while she herself could melt and blend with the shadows in corners and behind
things, she was worried over the conspicuousness of Peter's snow-
white coat. But she followed her nose and her instincts as well as
her memory of the other steamships on which she had served and
soon was leading Peter down a narrow companionway that led to a
small dining-saloon and thence to the galley.

Tea was long since over, all of the crew and officers were on
deck engaged with the cargo and preparations for leaving, and
Jennie counted on finding that part of the ship deserted. She was
right. The galley fires were out and there was no immediate sign
of cook or sculleryman. Also no doors were shut anywhere, which
gave Jennie further indication of what kind of craft it was, and
she led him from the galley through the pantry to the small storeroom where the immediate supplies were kept. At the end of this
room was a doorway and a narrow iron staircase that descended to
another passageway, on one side of which was the refrigeration
room and on the other a large dry-stores enclosure where the ship's
supplies in bulk were kept—sacks of flour and beans and dried peas,
tins of fruit and vegetables, boxes of biscuits, tea, coffee, and so on.

The slatted door to this also stood wide open. It was dark, but an
electric light burning far down the passageway shed sufficient light
so that with their acute vision they soon accustomed themselves
and could see their way about the boxes and cartons and barrels as
well as though it were broad daylight.

CATS IN MAPLE. Gui-
seppe Macri. *Courtesy
The Contemporaries,
New York*

And it was there in the storeroom, well concealed behind a case
of tinned tomatoes, that Peter saw and missed his first mouse, revealing what might have been a fatal weakness in their plans. It
had never dawned on him, and Jennie too had quite neglected to
think about it and take into consideration that, for all his looking
like and appearing to be a cat and learning to behave like one, Peter
had not the faintest idea how to go about the difficult and important
business of catching a mouse. Indeed, it was only through a lucky
break that at the last moment more cargo arrived and the *Countess
of Greenock* did not sail that night, nor the next night either, and
that they were able to remedy their deficiency at least partly, for,
superstition or no, a cat that proved itself wholly unable to catch
marauding rodents might have received short shrift aboard such a
craft.

The awkward discovery came when Jennie called Peter's attention to a little scratching, nibbling sort of noise from the other side
of the storeroom, whispering: "Ssh! Mouse! There he is over by the
biscuit box. Let's see you get him."

Peter concentrated, staring through the gloom, and there indeed
he was, just edging round the corner of the large tin marked
"HUNTLEY & PALMER LTD., READING," a long, grayish chap with a

greedy face, impertinent whiskers, and beady black eyes.

Peter was so anxious to show off to Jennie what he could do as a cat if given the chance that he hardly even set himself to spring, or paused to measure the distance, the obstacles and the possible avenues of escape open to the mouse. Without a moment's thought or plan, he launched himself through the air in one terrific pounce, paws spread wide, jaws open to snatch him.

There was of course no mouse there when Peter landed.

And not only that, but his teeth clicked together on empty air, there was nothing beneath his paws, and in addition, having miscalculated his distance, or rather not having calculated it at all, he gave himself a nasty knock on the head against the side of the tin box, all of which did not help the feeling that he had made a perfect fool of himself.

But while the mouse had saved itself momentarily, it also committed a fatal error by failing to dodge back behind the tin. Instead, gripped by panic, it emitted a squeak and went the other way, and the next instant, like a streak of furred lightning, Jennie had hurled herself through the air, her front paws, talons bared and extended, striking from side to side in a series of short, sharp, stunning hooks, even while she was in passage. The blows, as she landed, caught the mouse, knocking him first to one side, then back to the other, dazed and bewildered, then tossed him up in the air and batted him a couple before he came down at which point Jennie seized him in her mouth and it was all over before Peter had even so much as recovered his balance as well as from his confusion.

"Oh dear," Jennie said, dropping the mouse. "I hadn't thought of that. Of course you wouldn't know how. Why should you? But we *shall* be in a pretty pickle if we're caught here before you know something about it. And I don't know how much time we shall have. Still—"

Peter at last found his tongue and emitted a cry of anger and mortification. "Goodness," he said, "isn't there *anything* I can do? Does *everything* have to be learned?"

"It's practice really," Jennie explained. "Even *we* have to keep practicing constantly. That, and while I hate to use the expression —know-how. It's like everything else. You find there's a right way and a wrong way. The right way is to catch them with your paws, not your mouth, and of course the preparation is *everything*. Look here, I'll show you what I mean."

Here she crouched down a few feet away from the dead mouse and then began a slow waggling of her hind quarters from side to side, gradually increasing the speed and shortening the distance of the waggle. *"That's* what you must try, to begin with," she explained. "We don't do that for fun, or because we're nervous, but to give ourselves motion. It's ever so much harder and less accurate to spring from a standing start than from a moving one. Try it now and see how much easier it is to take off than the other way."

Peter's rear-end waggle was awkward at first, but he soon began to find the rhythm of it—it was almost like the "One to get set, two to make ready, and *three* to go" in foot-racing, except that this was even better because he found that what Jennie said was quite true and that the slight bit of motion did start him off the mark like an arrow.

Next he had to learn to move his paws so that, as he flew through the air and landed, they were striking left, right, with incredible speed, a feat that was much more difficult than it sounds since he could not use his paws to land on, but had to bring up his hind part in time while lashing out with the front.

His second mouse he missed by a hair's breadth due to over-anxiousness, but Jennie praised his paw-work and spring, criticizing only his judgment of distance and haste. "You rarely lose a mouse by waiting just a little longer," she explained, "because a mouse has a one-track mind and will keep on doing what it started out to do provided it isn't disturbed; and if it is disturbed, it will just sit there and quake, so that you have all the time in the world really. . . ."

But his third mouse Peter caught and killed, one-two-three, just like that. Jennie said that she could not have done it better herself, and when Peter made her a present of it she accepted it graciously and with evident pleasure and ate it. But the others they saved because Jennie said that when they came to be discovered, it would be a good thing to have some samples of their type of work about them.

And so, for the rest, Peter practiced and hunted busily, and Jennie advised him to keep the mouse alive and in the air as long as possible, not to torture it, but to gain in skill and accuracy and train his muscles to react swiftly at the slightest movement.

It was the second night before they sailed that Peter awoke to an uncomfortable feeling. There was a new and unpleasant odor in the storeroom, one that tended to make him a little sick. And suddenly from a far corner he saw glowing two evil-looking red eyes. Before he could stir he sensed through his whiskers that Jennie was awake too; and for the first time using this means of communication with him so that there should not be a sound, she warned: "Rat! It is serious, Peter, and very dangerous. This is something I cannot teach you or help you with. You'll just have to watch me and try to learn as best you can. And, above all, now whatever happens, don't move a muscle, don't stir, and don't make a sound, even if you want to. Now remember. I'm off."

Through the shadowing gloom Peter watched the stalk, his heart thumping in his chest, for this was different from the gay, almost light-hearted hunt of mice. Jennie's entire approach and attitude were those of complete concentration—the carriage of her body, the expression of her head, flattened forward, the glitter in her eyes, and the slow, fluid, amazingly controlled movement of her body. There was a care, caution, and deadly earnestness about her that Peter had never seen before, and his own throat felt dry and his skin and mustache twitched nervously. But he did his best to hold himself rigid and motionless as she had told him, lest some slip of his might bring her into trouble.

The wicked red eyes were glowing like two hot coals now, and Peter's acute hearing could make out the nasty sniffling noises of the rat, and the dry scrabbling of its toes on the storeroom floor. Jennie had gone quite flat now and was crawling along the boards on her belly. She stopped and held herself long and rigid for a moment, her eyes intent upon her prey, measuring, measuring. . . .

Then, inch by inch, she began to draw herself up into a little ball of fur-covered steel muscles for the spring. The rat was broadside to her. She took only two waggles, one to the left, one to the right, and then she was in the air aimed at the flank of the rat.

But lightning-fast as she was, the rodent seemed to be even faster, for his head came around over his shoulder, and his white teeth were bared in a wicked slashing movement and Peter wanted to shout to his friend: "Jennie, *look out!*" but just in time he remembered her admonition under no circumstances to make a sound, and he choked it down.

And then he saw what seemed to him to be a miracle, for launched as she was and in mir-air, Jennie saw the swift movement of the rat and, swifter herself, avoided the sharp ripping teeth; and making a turn in the air, a kind of half-twist such as Peter had seen the high divers do in the pool at Wembley one summer, she landed on the back of the rat and immediately sank her teeth in its spine just below the head.

Then followed a dreadful moment of banging and slamming and scraping and squealing and the sharp snick of teeth as the rat snapped viciously and fought to escape, while Jennie hung on for dear life, her jaws clamping deeper and deeper until there was a sharp click and the next moment the rat hung limp and paralyzed and a few seconds later it was all over.

Jennie came away from it a little shaken and agitated, saying: "Phew! Filthy, sickening beasts! I *hate* rats—next to people. . . . They're all unclean and diseased, and if you let them bite you anywhere, then *you* get sick, for their teeth are all poisoned, and sometimes you die from it. I'm always afraid of that."

Peter said with deep sincerity: "Jennie, I think you are the bravest and most wonderful person—I mean cat—I ever saw. *Nobody* could have done that the way you did."

For once, Jennie did not preen herself or parade before Peter, for she was worried now since it was she who had coaxed him into this adventure. She said: "That's just it, Peter. We can't practice and learn on the rats the way we did on the mice, because it's too dangerous. One mistake and—well, I don't want it to happen. I *can* show you the twist, because you have to know how to do it to avoid the slash of theirs, but the spring, the distance, the timing, and, above all, just the exact place to bite them behind the neck to get at their spines—well, you must do it one hundred per cent right when the time comes, and that's all there is. If you get them too high on the head, they can kick loose or even shake you off. Some of the big fellows weigh almost as much as you do, and if you seize them too far down the back they can turn their heads and cut you."

"But how will I learn, then?" Peter asked.

"Let me handle them for the time being," she replied, "and watch me closely each time I kill one. You'll be learning something. Then if and when the moment comes when you have to do it yourself, you'll either do it right the first time and never forget it thereafter or—" Jennie did not finish the sentence but instead went into the washing routine, and Peter felt a little cold chill run down his spine.

When they were finally discovered, it was some seven hours after sailing, as the *Countess of Greenock* was thumping her slow, plodding way down the broad reaches of the Thames Estuary. When the cook, an oddly triangular-shaped Jamaican Negro by the name of Mealie, came into the storeroom for some tinned corned beef, they had a bag of eight mice and three rats lined up in lieu of references and transportation. Three of the mice were Peter's, and he felt inordinately proud of them and wished there could have been some way whereby he might have had his name on them, like autographing a book perhaps—"Caught by Peter Brown, Storeroom, *Countess of Greenock*, April 15, 1949."

The Negro grinned widely, increasing the triangular effect, for his face and head were narrower at the top than at the bottom. He said: "By Jominy dat good. Hit pays to hodvertise. I tell dat to Captain," and forthwith he went up on the bridge, taking Jennie's and Peter's samples with him. It was the kind of ship where the cook did go up on the bridge if he felt like having a word with the captain. There he told him the story of finding the two stowaways and then added: "But by Jominy they pay possage already. Look you dat!" and unrolling his apron, showed him the fruits of their industry.

The captain, whose name was Sourlies and who was that rare specimen, a fat Scotsman, looked and felt ill and commanded Mealie in no uncertain language to throw the mess over the side and go back to his galley. It was the beginning of his time of deep unhappiness anyway, for he hated the sea and everything connected with it and was reasonably contented only when in port, or near it, or proceeding up and down an estuary or river with plenty of land on both sides.

He carried this queer notion to the point of refusing even to dress the part of a ship's captain, and conducted the affairs of the *Countess of Greenock* wearing a tweed pepper-and-salt business suit with a gold watch chain across his large expanse of stomach and a mustard-colored fedora hat or trilby with the brim turned up all around.

As Mealie was leaving, however, he did decree that inasmuch as the cats seemed to have got aboard and appeared inclined to work

their passage, they might remain, but told him to shift one of them
to the fo'castle as the men had been complaining of the rats there.

Mealie took his time going aft and told his story and showed the
bag to everyone he met, with the result that there arrived back in
the storeroom quite a committee, consisting of Mr. Strachan, the
first mate, Mr. Carluke, the second, Chief Engineer McDunkeld,
and the bo'sun, whose name appeared to be only Angus.

They held a meeting, the gist of which Peter tried to translate
rapidly for Jennie's benefit, and before they knew it, the two
friends found themselves separated for the first time, Jennie being
sent forward to live with the crew and Peter retained, chiefly
through the insistence of Mr. Strachan, in the officers' quarters.

Jennie had only time to say to Peter: "Don't worry. We'll find
ways to get together. Do your best. And if you come across a rat,
don't hesitate and don't play. Kill!"

Then the bo'sun picked her up by the scruff of the neck and
carried her forward.

❧

Using the smooth sides of a huge packing case as a practice
ground, Peter learned the secret of the double jump-up, or second
lift; or rather, after long hours of trial with Jennie coaching, it
suddenly came to him. One moment he had been slipping, sliding,
and falling back as he essayed to scale the perpendicular sides, and
the next he had achieved it, a lightning-like thrust with the hind
legs, which somehow this time stuck to the sides of the case and
gave him added impetus upwards, and thereafter he could always
do it.

Jennie was most pleased with him, for as she explained it, this
particular trick of leaping up the side of a blank wall without so
much as a crack or an irregularity to give a toe-hold was peculiar to
cats, and it was also one that could be neither wholly explained,
demonstrated, or taught. The best she was able to tell him was:
"You *think* you're 'way to the top, Peter. You just know you are
going to be able to do it, and then you can."

Well, once the old *Countess* had taken a bit of a roll in the
trough of a sea, and that helped Peter a little and gave him confidence. And the next time he felt certain he was going to be able to
do it and he did.

Jennie was endlessly patient in teaching Peter control of his body in the air for she maintained that few things are of so much importance to cats. With her he studied the twist in mid-air from the spring so that, once he had left the ground, he could change his direction almost as in flying, and Peter loved the sense of power and freedom that came to him when he turned himself in the air like an acrobat, or a high diver, and this he practiced more than anything else. And he had to learn, too, how to drop from any normal height and twist in falling so that he would always land on his feet; and soon, with Jennie's help, he became so expert that he could roll off a case no more than a yard from the ground and still, turning like a flash, whip round so that his four paws touched the deck first, and that without a sound.

But their free time was not all devoted to hard work and practice. There were quiet hours when they rested side by side on a hatch coaming and Peter would ask Jennie questions—for instance, why she always preferred to perch on high things and look down— and she would explain about the deep instincts that survived from the days millions and millions of years ago when no doubt all cats were alike in size and shape and had to learn to protect themselves to survive. To escape the dangers that lurked on or near the ground from things that crawled, slithered, or trampled, they took to living high up in rocky caves, or perched along branches of trees where they could look down and see everything that approached them.

In the same manner, Jennie explained, cats liked to sleep in boxes, or bureau drawers, because they felt completely surrounded on all sides by high walls, as they were deep in their caves, and therefore felt relaxed and secure and able to sleep.

Or again, Peter would say: "Jennie, why when you are pleased and happy and relaxed, do your claws work in and out in that queer way? Once back home—I mean when we lived in the warehouse—I noticed that you were moving your paws up and down, almost as though you were making the bed. I never do that, though I do purr when I am happy."

Jennie was lying on her side on the canvas hatch cover when Peter asked that question, and she raised her head and gave him a most tender glance before she replied: "I know, Peter. And it is just another of those things that tell me that in spite of your shape and form, you are really human, and perhaps always will be. But maybe I can explain it to you. Peter, say something sweet to me."

The only thing Peter could think of to say was: "Oh, Jennie, I wish that I could be all cat—so that I might be more like you."

The most beatific smile stole over Jennie's face. Her throat throbbed with purring, and slowly her white paws began to work, the claws moving in and out as though she were kneading dough.

"You see?" she said to Peter. "It has to do with feeling happy. It goes all the way back to our being kittens and being nursed by our mothers. We cannot even see at first, but only feel, for when we are first born we are blind, and our eyes open only after a few weeks. But we can feel our way to our mother's breast and bury ourselves in her soft, sweet-smelling fur to find her milk, and when we are there, we work our paws gently up and down to help the food we want so much to flow more freely. Then when it does, we feel it in our throats, warm and satisfying; it stops our hunger and our thirst, it soothes our fears and desires, and oh, Peter, we are *so* blissful and contented at that moment, so secure and peaceful and— well, just happy. We never forget those moments with our mothers. They remain with us all the rest of our lives. And later on, long after we are grown, when something makes us very happy, our paws and claws go in and out the same way, in memory of those early times of our first real happiness. And that is all I can tell you about it."

Peter found that after this recital he had need to wash himself energetically for a few moments, and then he went over to where Jennie was lying and washed her face too, giving her several caresses beneath her soft chin and along the side of her muzzle that conveyed more to her than words. She made a little soft crooning sound in her throat, and her claws worked in and out, kneading the canvas hatch cover faster than ever.

But likewise during the long days of the leisurely voyage, and particularly when they were imprisoned in Dartmouth Harbor for two days by pea-soup fog, there was mock fighting to teach Peter how to take care of himself should he ever find himself in any trouble, as well as all the feline sports and games for one or two that Jennie knew or remembered and could teach him, and they spent hours rolling about, growling and spitting, locked in play combat, waiting in ambush to surprise each other, playing hide-seek-and-jump-out, or chasing each other madly up and down the gangways and passages below deck, their pads ringing oddly on the iron floors of the ancient *Countess,* like the hoofs of tiny galloping horses.

And here again Peter was to learn not only that were there method and strict rules that governed play as well as the more serious encounters between cat and cat but that he needed to study as well as practice them with Jennie in order to acquire by repetition the feeling of the rhythms that were a part of these games.

Thus Jennie would coach him: "I make a move to attack you, maybe a pass at your tail, or a feint at one of your legs; raise your left paw and be ready to strike with it. That's it. That makes me think twice before coming in. No, no, Peter, don't take your eyes off me just because I've stopped. Be ready as long as I am tense. But you've got to *feel* it when I've changed my mind and relaxed a little. You can drop your left paw, but keep watching. There! *I've* looked away for a moment—now *wash!* That stops everything. I can't do anything until you've finished except wash too, and that puts the next move up to you and it's your advantage."

Most difficult for him was the keeping of the upper hand by eye and body position and acquiring by experience the feeling of when it was safe to relax and turn away to rest, how to break up the other's plans by washing, luring and drawing the opponent on by pretending to look away and then timing his own attack to the split second when the other was off balance and unprepared for it, and yet not violate the rules, which often made no rhyme or reason to him at all.

None of these things Peter would have done instinctively as a boy, and he had to learn them from Jennie by endless repetition. Often he marveled at her patience as she drilled him over and over: "Crouch, Peter. Now sit up quickly and look away. . . . *Wash!* Size up the situation out of the corner of your eye as you wash. I'm waiting to jump you as soon as you stop washing. Then turn and get ready. Here I come. Roll with it, onto your back. Hold me with your forepaws and kick with the hind legs. Harder—harder. . . . No, stay there, Peter. I'm coming back for a second try. Chin down so I can't get at your throat. Kick. Now roll over and sit up, paw ready, and threaten with it. If I blink my eyes and back away, *wash.* Now pretend you are interested in something imaginary. That's it.

MINETTE WASHES.
Gottfried Mind

If you make it real enough you can get me to look at it, and when I do, then you spring!"

Jennie had a system of scoring these bouts, so many points for buffets, so many for knockdowns and roll-overs, for break-aways and washes, for chases and ambushes, for the amount of fur that flew by tufts to be counted later, for numbers of back-kicks delivered, for bluffs and walk-aways, feints and ducking, with bonuses for position and length of time in control, and game plus one hundred points called any time one maneuvered into position to grip teeth on the throat of the other.

And gradually, almost imperceptibly at first, the scores drew nearer level and soon Peter found himself winning regularly over Jennie in the training ring they had arranged among the crates and boxes in the forward hold. And when this happened and Peter won almost every time, none was prouder and happier over it than Jennie. "Soon," she said with satisfaction, "you'll be cat through and through."

And yet when the tragedy happened, it was just as well that Peter was not all cat.

In a way it began when Peter caught his first rat. The *Countess of Greenock* was plowing the Irish Sea 'twixt the Isle of Man and the Cumberland coast, close enough inshore so that one could see the peaks of the Cumbrian Mountains inland, shining in the sun. The ocean was flat calm and glassy and the only cloud in the sky was the one made by the black smoke poured forth by the *Countess,* which owing to a following breeze over the surface, she carried along with her over her head like an untidy old charwoman shielding herself from the sun with an old black cotton umbrella. They were on the reach between Liverpool and Port Carlisle on the

Scottish border and Captain Sourlies was in a great hurry to make
it before nightfall. That was why the *Countess* was under forced
draft, emitting volumes of soft-coal smoke and shuddering from the
vibrations of her hurrying engines.

Peter had an appointment with Jennie on the after deck at six
bells of the early afternoon watch, or three o'clock, for he had
quickly learned to tell the ship's time from the strokes of the bell
struck by the lookout on the bridge. This was always a kind of
do-as-you-please time aboard the *Countess,* for then Captain Sourlies would be taking his afternoon nap in his cabin, Mr. Carluke,
torn from his latest literary composition, which he was calling *The
Bandit of Golden Gulch,* was on duty on the bridge, and everybody
else followed his hobby or loafed by the rail or snoozed in the sun.
And since Mr. Strachan, the first mate, still had a badly aching arm
from the stitches taken in it, his dummy lurked in a corner in
disgrace and the red-haired mate on this day was yarning with Mr.
Box, the carpenter, about an episode that had happened to him in
Gibraltar during the war and as proof produced an 1890 Queen
Victoria copper penny that he had happened to be carrying on his
person at the time of the adventure.

Jennie was already dozing in the soft spring sunshine, squatted
down atop the stern rail. She. liked to perch there because it was
fairly high and gave her an over-all view, and also to show her
superiority, for everyone was always prophesying that some day she
would be knocked or fall off from there into the sea. But of course
there never was a cat more certain or sure-footed than Jennie
Baldrin.

Peter awoke promptly at ten minutes to three—he found that he
could now awake at exactly any time he desired—and made a rough
toilet with his tongue. He stretched and strolled casually from the
lower storeroom, which was his quarters and which it was also his
job to keep clear of vermin. Up to that moment there had been only
mice, which Peter had kept down quite handily.

He should have smelled the rat long before he saw it, but
although his smell senses were feline and quite sharp, his mind
was still human and he had been thinking that he must tell Jennie
about a member of the black gang, a stoker who fed the furnace,
who was such an admirer of Winston Churchill that he had a
picture of the former Prime Minister tattooed on his chest, cigar

and all. And so he had not been alert. When he saw the rat he was in a very bad position.

The beast was almost as large as a fox terrier and it was cornered in a small alcove made by some piled-up wooden cases of tinned baked beans, from which several boxes had been removed from the center. Also it was daylight, Peter wasn't stalking, and the rat saw Peter at the same time that Peter saw the rat. It uttered an ugly squeal of rage and bared long, yellow teeth, teeth that Peter knew were so unclean that a single scratch from them might well poison him beyond help. And for the first time he really understood what people meant by the expression "fight like a cornered rat," or rather he was about to understand. For in spite of the fact that Jennie had warned him never to go after a rat except when it was out in the open, he meant to attack this one and prove himself.

He was surprised to find that now in this moment of danger he was not thinking of lessons he had learned, or what he had seen or heard or what Jennie had said, but that his mind seemed to be extraordinarily calm and clear and that, almost as though it had always been there ready and waiting, his plan unfolded itself in his mind. It was only much later he found out that this was the result of discipline, study, patience, and practice that he had put behind him at Jennie's behest.

His spring, seemingly launched directly at the foe, appeared to be sheer folly, and the rat rose up on its hind legs to meet him head on, slashing at him viciously. But not for nothing had Peter learned and practiced the secret of continuing on up a smooth wall from a single leap from the floor. A split second faster than the rat, his fore and hing legs touched the slippery sides of one of the piles of cases for an instant and propelled him high into the air so that the flashing incisors of the rodent, like two hideously curved yataghans, whizzed between his legs, missing him by the proverbial hair's breadth.

The extra impetus upwards now gave Peter the speed and energy to twist not half but the whole way around in a complete reverse and drop onto the back of the rat to sink his own teeth deep into its spine just behind the ears.

For one dreadful moment Peter felt that he might yet be beaten, for the rat gave such a mighty heave and surge and lashed so desperately to and fro that Peter was thumped and banged up against the sides of the boxes until he felt himself growing sick and dizzy and no longer certain whether he could hold on. And if once he let go, the big fellow would turn on him and cut him to ribbons.

In desperation he set his teeth with all his might and bit, one, two, three times, hard. At the third bite he felt the rat suddenly stiffen. The swaying and banging stopped. The rodent kicked twice with its hind legs and then was still. It never moved again. Peter unclamped his aching jaws and sat down quickly and did some washing. He was badly shaken and most emphatically needed to recover his composure.

Nevertheless it was exactly at six bells that he came trotting onto the after deck carrying the rat in his mouth, or rather dragging it, because it was so large that when he held it in the middle, its head and tail hung down to the deck. It was so heavy that he could barely lift it. But of course he managed because he simply had to show it off to Jennie and anyone else who happened to be around.

It was Mr. Box who saw him first and let out a yell: "Blimey, looka there! The white un's caught a bloomin' helephant."

Mr. Strachan also gave a shout, for Peter passed quite close to him and the rat dragged over his foot, causing him to jump as though he had been stung. The cries brought several deckhands over on the run to see. They also woke up Jennie Baldrin.

She had not meant to fall so soundly asleep, but the peaceful sea and the warm afternoon sun had lulled her deeper than she had intended, and now the sudden cries sent alarms tingling down her spine. And when she opened her eyes they fell on Peter and his rat and in the first confusion she was not certain whether the rat was carrying Peter or vice versa, whether it was alive or dead, whether Peter was still engaged in fighting it. The sound of running feet added to her confusion, and she recoiled from the unknown and the uncertain and the thought of possible danger to Peter.

But there was no place to recoil to from her precarious perch on the ship's rail, and with an awful cry, her four paws widespread, and turning over once in the air, she fell into the sea and was swept away in the white salt froth of propeller wash.

"Cat overboard!" a deckhand cried, and then laughed.

"Good-by, pussy," said Mr. Box. "Arskin' for it, she was, perched up there loike that."

Mr. Strachan stared with his mouth open.

The sailor who had been a hermit said to Peter: "There goes yer pal, Whitey. Ye'll no see Coptain Sourlies tairnen his ship aboot to rrrrrrescue a wee puss baldrin."

But Peter was no longer there. There was only a white streak of fur as he dropped the rat, leaped to the rail, and from it, long and low, shot straight into the sea after Jennie.

(*Ed. note: Jennie and Peter were saved, needless to say, and continued their travels.*)

It was only half true that Peter wanted to go home. For boy and cat were becoming so intermingled that Peter was not at all certain any longer which he really was.

More than once during his voyage aboard the *Countess of Greenock* and the subsequent adventures Peter had thought of his mother and father and Scotch Nanny and wondered how they were, if they were missing him, and whether they had any explanation for his mysterious disappearance. For certainly none of them, not even Nanny, who had been right there at the time, could be expected to guess that he had changed suddenly from a boy into a snow-white tomcat under her very eyes almost and had been pitched out into the street by her as a stray.

He thought it was probable that they would have notified the police, or perhaps, believing that he had run away, placed an advertisement in the "Personal" columns of the *Times* saying: "Peter: Come home, all is forgiven—Mummy, Daddy, and Nanny," or possibly it might have been more formally worded: "Will anyone who can give information as to the whereabouts of Master Peter Brown, vanished from No. 1A Cavendish Mews, London, W.C. 2, kindly communicate with Colonel and Mrs. Alastair Brown of that address. Reward!"

But, in the main, when he thought of those at home he did not believe that he was much missed except by Nanny, who of course had been busy with him almost from morning until night, leaving out the hours when he was at school, and now that he was gone would have nothing to do. His father was away from home so much

of the time that except for their occasional evening romps he could
hardly be expected to notice the difference. And as for his mother—
Peter always felt sad and heavy-hearted when he thought about his
mother, because she had been so beautiful and he had loved her
so much. But it was the kind of sadness that is connected with a
memory of something long ago. Looking back to what life had been
like in those now but dimly recollected days, he felt certain that
his mother had been a little unhappy herself at first when he was
missed, but then, after all, she never seemed to have much time,
and now that he was gone, perhaps it would not have taken her
long to get used to it.

Really it was Jennie who had come more and more to mean
family to him and upon whom he leaned for advice, help, companionship, trust, and even affection. It was true she talked a great
deal and was not the most beautiful cat in the world, but there was
an endearing and ingratiating warmth and grace about her that
made Peter feel comfortable and happy when they slept coiled up
close to each other, or even when he only looked at her sometimes
and saw her sweet attitudes, kindly eyes, gamin-wise face, and soft
white throat.

The world was full of all kinds of beautiful cats, prize specimens
whose pictures he had seen in the illustrated magazines during the
times of the cat shows. Compared with them, Jennie was rather
plain, but it was an appealing plainness he would not have ex-
changed for all the beauty in the world.

Nor was it his newly acquired cat-self that was seeking a return
to Cavendish Mews in quest of a home, though to some extent the
cat in him was now prey to curiosity about how things were there
without him and what everyone was doing. But he knew quite
definitely that his mother and father were people who had little
or no interest in animals and appeared to have no need of them and
hence would be hardly likely to offer a haven to a pair of stray cats
come wandering in off the streets—namely, Jennie and himself.

Peter's suggestion that Jennie accompany him on a trip home
to Cavendish Mews was perhaps more than anything born out of
the memory that when he had been unhappy and upset about their
treatment of Mr. Grims at the time of their first encounter with
him, *she* had managed to interest and distract him by proposing the
journey to Scotland. When he saw her sunk in the depths of grief

and guilt over the fate of the poor old man, Peter had plucked a
leaf out of her book of experience in the hope that it would take
her mind off the tragedy and particularly what she considered her
share in it. By instinct he seemed to have known that nothing
actually would have moved her from the spot but his expression of
his need for her.

Anyway, it was clear after they had set out for Cavendish Mews
that she was in a more cheerful frame of mind and anxious to help
him achieve his objective.

It is not easy for cats to move about in a big city, particularly
on long journeys, and Jennie could be of no assistance to Peter
in finding his way back to Cavendish Mews, since she had never
lived or even been there and hence could not use her homing
instinct, a kind of automatic direction-finder that communicated
itself through her sensitive whiskers and enabled her to travel
unerringly to any place where she had once spent some time.

Peter at least had the unique—from a cat's point of view—ability
to know what people around him were saying, as well as being able
to read signs, such as for instance appeared on the front of omni-
buses and in general terms announced where they were going. One
then had but to keep going in that direction and eventually one
would arrive at the same destination or vicinity. In his first panic
at finding himself a cat and out in the street, Peter had fled far from
his home, with never any account taken of the twistings and turn-
ings he had made. He was quite familiar with his own neighborhood, however, and knew if he could once reach Oxford and Regent
streets he would find his way. But when it came to the lore of the
city and knowing how to preserve one's skin whole, eat, drink, and
sleep, Jennie as usual proved invaluable.

En route he learned from her all the important things there were
to know about dogs and how to handle them—that, for instance,
he must beware of terriers of every kind, that the average street
mongrel was to be despised. Dogs on leashes could be ignored even
though they put up a terrific fuss and roared, threatened, growled,
and strained. They only did it because they *were* on the leash,
which of course injured their dignity, and they had to put up a
big show of what they would do if they were free. They behaved
exactly the same when sighting another dog, and the whole thing,

according to Jennie, was nothing but a lot of bluff. She, for one, never paid the slightest attention to them.

"Never run from a dog if you can control it," she admonished Peter, "because most of them are half blind anyway, and inclined to be hysterical. They will chase anything that moves. But if you stand your ground and don't run, chances are he will go right by you and pretend he neither sees you nor smells you, particularly if he has tangled with one of us before. Dogs have long memories.

"Small dogs you can keep in their places by swatting them the way we do when we play-box, only you run your claws out and hit fast and hard, because most of them are scared of having their eyes scratched and they don't like their noses clawed either, because they are tender. Here, for instance, is one looking for trouble and I'll show you what I mean."

They were walking through Settle Street near Whitechapel, looking for a meal, when a fat, overfed Scotty ran barking from a doorway and made a good deal of attacking them, barking, yelping, and charging in short rushes, with an amount of snapping its teeth, bullying, and bravado.

Jennie calmly squatted down on the pavement facing the foe with a kind of humiliating disinterest, which he mistook for fear and abject cringing and which gave him sufficient courage to close in and risk a real bite at Jennie's flank. Like lightning flashes her left paw shot out three times, while she leaned away from the attack just enough to let the Scotty miss her. The next moment, cut on the end of the nose and just below the right eye, he was legging it for the cover and safety of the doorway, screaming: "Help! Murder! Watch!!"

"Come on," Jennie said to Peter. "Now *we've* got to move out. You'll see why in a minute." Peter had long since learned not to question her, particularly about anything that called for split-second timing, and he quickly ran after her out of range, just as the owner of the dog, a slatternly woman, evidently the proprietress of the dingy greengrocery, came out and threw a dishpanful of water after them, but missed, thanks to Jennie's wisdom and speedy action.

"I'm out of practice," Jennie said with just a touch of her old-time showing off for Peter. "I missed him with my third. Still— They'll run off screaming for help, and if you stay around you're likely to catch it, as you saw, though not from *them*.... And you don't always have to do that. Quite often they've been brought up with cats or are used to them and are just curious or want to play, and come sniffing and snuffling and smelling around with their tails wagging, which, as you know, means that *they* are pleased and friendly, and not angry or agitated or nervous over something, as it does with us. Then you can either bear up under it and pretend not to notice it, or try to walk away or get up on top of something they can't reach. I, for one, just don't care for a wet, cold, drooly nose messing about in my fur, so I usually give them just a little tap with the paw, unloaded, as a reminder that we are after all quite totally different species and their way of playing isn't ours."

"But supposing it's a bigger dog," Peter said, "like the ones in Glasgow."

Jennie gave a little shudder. "Ugh!" she said. "Don't remind me of those. As I told you then, any time you see a bull terrier, run, or, better still, start climbing. But a great many of the others you can bluff and scare by swelling up and pretending to be bigger than you actually are. Let me show you. You should have been taught this long ago, because you can never tell when you are going to need it."

They were walking near Paternoster Row in the wide-open spaces created by the bombs before St. Paul's Cathedral, and Jennie went over a low coping and into some weeds and fireflowers that were growing there. "Now," she said, "do just as I do. Take a deep breath—that's it, 'way in. Now blow, but hold your breath at the same time. Hard! There you go."

And, as she said, there indeed Peter went, swelling up to nearly twice his size, just as Jennie was, all puffed out into a kind of lopsided fur ball. He was sure that he was looking perfectly enormous and quite out of plumb, and he felt rather foolish. He said as much to Jennie, adding: "I think that's silly."

She answered: "Not at all. You don't realize it, but you really looked quite alarming. It's sort of preventive warfare, and it makes a good deal of sense. If you can win a battle without having to fight it, or the enemy is so scared of you that he won't even start it and goes away and there is no battle at all, that's better than anything. It doesn't do any harm, and it's always worth trying, even with other cats. For in spite of the fact that you know it's all wind and fur, it will still give you the creeps when someone does it to you."

Peter suddenly thought back to Dempsey and how truly terrifying the battle-scarred veteran of a thousand fights had looked when he had swelled up and gone all crooked and menacing on him.

"And anyway," Jennie concluded the lesson, "if it shouldn't happen to work, it's just as well to be filled up with air, because then you are ready to let out a perfect rouser of a battle cry, and very often that *does* work, provided you can get it out of your system before the other one does. A dog will usually back away from that and remember another engagement."

In the main, on this walk across a portion of London, Peter found cats to be very like people. Some were mean and small and persnickety and insisted upon all their rights even when asked politely to share; others were broad-minded and hospitable, with a cheery, "Certainly, do come right in. There's plenty of room here," before Jennie had even so much as finished her gentle request for permission to remain. Some were snobs who refused to associate with them because they were strays; others had once been strays themselves, remembered their hardships, and were sympathetic. There were cantankerous cats always spoiling for a fight, and others who fought just for the fun of fighting and asserting their superiority; and many a good-natured cat belonging to a butcher, or a pub, or a snack bar or greengrocer would steer them toward a meal, or share what they had, or give them a tip on where to get a bite.

Also Peter learned, not only from Jennie, but from bitter experience, to be wary of children and particularly those not old enough to understand cats, or even older ones with a streak of cruelty. And since one could not tell in advance what they would be like, or whether they would fondle or tease, one had no choice, if one was a London stray, but to act in the interest of one's own safety.

This sad piece of knowledge Peter acquired in a most distressful manner as they threaded their way past Petticoat Lane in Whitechapel, where a grubby little boy was playing in the gutter outside a fish-and-chips bar. He was about Peter's age, or at least the age Peter had been before the astonishing transformation had happened to him, and about his height, and he called to them as they hurried by: "Here, puss. Come here, Whitey. . . ."

Before ever Jennie could warn him or breathe a "Peter, be careful!" he went to him trustingly, because in a way the boy reminded him of himself and he remembered how much he had loved every cat he saw in the streets, and particularly the strays and wanderers. He went over and held up his head and face to be rubbed. The next moment the most sharp and agonizing pain shot through his body from head to foot so that he thought he would die on the spot. He cried out half with hurt and half with fear, for he did not know yet what had happened to him.

Then he realized that the boy had twined his fingers firmly about his tail and was pulling. *Pulling* HIS *tail.* Nothing had ever hurt him so much or so excruciatingly.

'Nah, then," laughed the boy, nastily, "let's see yer get away."

With a cry of horror and outrage, and digging his claws into the cracks in the pavement, Peter made a supreme effort and managed to break loose, certain that he had left his tail behind him in the hand of the boy, and only after he had run half a block did he determine that it was still streaming out behind and safely attached to him.

And here Peter discovered yet another thing about cats that he had never known before. There was involved not only the pain of having his tail pulled, but the humiliation. Never had he felt so small, ashamed, outraged, and dishonored. And all in front of Jennie. He felt that he would not be able to look at her again. It was much worse than being stood in a corner when he had been a boy, or being spoken to harshly, or having his ear tweaked or knuckles cracked in front of company.

What served to make it endurable was that Jennie seemed to understand. She neither spoke to him sympathizingly, which at that moment Peter felt he would not have been able to bear, nor even so much as glanced at him, but simply trotted alongside, minding her own business and pretending in a way that he was not there at all, which was a great help. Gradually the pain and the memory began to fade, and finally, after a long while, when Jennie turned to him and out of a clear sky said: "Do you know, I think it might rain tonight. What do *your* whiskers say?" he was able to thrust his mustache forward and wrinkle the skin on his back to the weather-forecasting position and reply:

"There might be a shower or two. We'd better hurry if we want to reach Cavendish Square before it starts. Oh, look there! There's the proper bus just going by now. We can't go wrong if we keep in the same direction."

It was a Number 7, and the sign on the front of it read: "Oxford Street and Marble Arch."

"For Oxford Street crosses Regent, and then comes Princes, and if we turn up Princes, we can't help coming into Cavendish Square," Peter explained, "and then it's only a short step to the Mews and home."

Jennie echoed the word "home" in so sad and wistful a voice that Peter looked at her sharply, but she said nothing more, and proceeding quickly by little short rushes from shop door to shop door, as it were, the two soon had passed from Holborn through New Oxford into Oxford Street and across Regent to Princes, where they turned up to the right for Cavendish Square.

❖

THE DISILLUSIONED CAT

LOVE ADVENTURES OF A FRENCH CAT

BY *P-J. Stahl*

First Letter: MINETTE TO BÉBÉ.

"What will you say, my dear Bébé, on receiving this letter from your sister supposed to be dead, for whom you have doubtless wept, as one who is almost forgotten.

"Forgive me, my sister, for supposing that you can ever forget me, although we live in a world where many more than the dead are forgotten.

"First of all I write to tell you I am not dead, that my love for you is as strong as ever, and that I am still animated by the hope of one day rejoining you, alas! my sister, that day may be far distant.

"This evening I thought about our good mother, who was always so kind and careful of our toilet, whose delight it was to watch the flicker of the fire-light on our glossy, silken coats, and to train us in the paths of domestic peace, virtue, and sobriety. I was touchingly reminded of our simple family-life, with its happy days, and inno-cent frolic, all hallowed by the light of love. Yet the brightness of that light of true hearts casts many dark shadows across my path, shadows of regret for neglected ministries of tenderness to my mother who is now perhaps no more. Above the sentiment that prompts me to write, is the desire to make a regretful confession of the circumstances which separated me from the dear ones at home.

"Silently I took up the pen, and the result is before you. I am bending over my task by the dim light of an alabaster lamp, care-fully shaded from the eyes of my sleeping mistress.

"Although I am rich, Bébé, I would rather be poor and happy! Oh, my mistress is waking. I must quickly say good-bye. I have barely time to roll up my letter and push it under the cover of a chair, where it must remain till daybreak. When it is finished I will forward it by one of our attendants who is now waiting on the terrace. He will bring me your reply.

"My mother! my mother! tell me all about her.

"YOUR SISTER."

"P.S.—Place confidence in my messenger, he is neither young nor handsome, neither a Spanish Grandee nor a rich Angora, but he is devoted and discreet. He found out your address. He loves me and would do anything for me, so he has become my courier. He is a slave! Do not pity him; the chains of love are his fetters.

"You must address your letters to Madam Rosa Mika, that is the name I am known under here.

"My mistress is certainly waking up, she sleeps badly, and I dread discovery.

"Again, adieu! In all this scribbling you will recognise more of the heart than the hand of your sister."

❦

Second Letter: BÉBÉ TO MINETTE.

"MY DEAR MINETTE,—I thought I should go mad on reading your letter, my joy knew no bounds, and indeed it was shared by all. One would willingly see all one's relations die, if they all came to life again like you. Ah, Minette, your departure caused us great grief. Were you forced to leave us so long in doubt? If you only knew how everything is changed here since you left. To begin, your mother is deaf and blind, and the poor old creature passes her days at the door, without even uttering a complaint. When I wished to tell her you were still alive, I could not make her understand, and she could neither read nor see your letter. Her many troubles have told sadly upon her. After you left, she searched everywhere in vain for you, and the loss seems to have undermined her health and left her the wreck I describe.

"Do not grieve too much, old age no doubt must take the lion's share of blame. Besides, she sleeps, drinks, and eats well; and there is always plenty in the cupboard, as I would rather starve than let her want.

"Our young mistress has lost her mother, so she is more unfortunate than we are, as she has lost everything, except her pretty figure, which does not change.

"It was necessary to leave the little shop in Murais; to give up the ground floor, and all at once mount to the attic, and to work from morning to night, and from night till morning sometimes. But, thank heaven, I have a sure foot, good eye, and am a capital hunter.

"You touchingly remark that you are rich, and would rather sacrifice wealth for happiness. I do not clearly see how I can complain of being poor. How funny you are! you dine at a polished board, off gilded plates, and goodly fare. One would think from your way of putting it, that by stinting one's self of food, one gets what riches cannot buy. Some wise cat will no doubt prove before long, that poverty is the cure for all evils. Seriously, do you believe that fortune impairs happiness? If that is your creed, become poor at once, ruin yourself! Nothing is easier than that, live by your teeth if you can. Tell me what you think of it. Complain of being unhappy, but not of being rich, for we who are poor are no strangers to misery. I scold you as your elder sister ought to do, so forgive me.

"Do you not know that Bébé would only be too happy to be of some use to you? Do not keep me waiting for another letter. I begin to fear you have been seeking happiness where it can never be found. Of course you will hide nothing from me. Ease your heart and write down your griefs on your perfumed paper, as you proposed. Adieu, Minette, adieu! This is enough, it is the hour for our mother's meal, and it is yet running about in the loft. Things are not going on well there, the mice are clever, and every day seems to develop new instincts of cunning. We have feasted so long on them, they begin to notice it. My neighbour is a cat, not a bad specimen, were he not so original. He dotes on the mice, and pretends that some day there will be a revolution when mice will be able to hold their own against cats.

"You see I am right in profiting by the peace we now enjoy, hunting at will in their grounds. But do not let us talk politics!

"Adieu, Minette.

"Your messenger is waiting. He refuses to disclose your address. Shall we soon meet each other?

"Your sister till death,

"BÉBÉ."

"P.S.—I own your old courier is very ugly. For all that, when I saw what he brought, I kissed him with all my heart. You should have seen him bow when he presented the letter from Madam Rosa Mika. Were you out of your mind Minette when you adopted such a name? Was Minette not a charming name for a cat so white as yourself? As I have no more paper, I conclude."

A Starling had the misfortune of upsetting a bottle of · ink over Minette's reply to Bébé, so that several pages of the letter are illegible. The loss of these passages, however, does not interfere with the narrative. The missing matter is indicated by dotted lines.

❧

Third Letter: MINETTE TO BÉBÉ.

....."Do you remember the doll given to us by our mistress, which soon became a subject of discord. How you used to scratch me. Oh dear! I almost feel my back bleeding when I think of it. How I used to complain of you to my mother when you so persistently called me a story-teller, but I got no satisfaction. It is from this point, this little wrong, that all my miseries sprang? Indignant at repeated miscarriages of justice, I resolved to fly from

you and seek a happier home. Ascending to the roof, the heaven
of cats, I viewed the distant horizon, and determined to wander
to its furthest limit. The prospect for a kitten so young was not
tempting. I foresaw many dangers to which I would be exposed
in making my way into strange lands. I remember. . . . I seemed
to hear choirs of voices in the air—

" 'Do not cry, Minette,' whispered a voice—no doubt that of my
evil genius—'the hour of your deliverance approaches. This humble
dwelling is an unworthy shelter for one born by nature to adorn the
halls of a palace!'

" 'Alas,' replied a voice softer and more musical—that of my conscience—'You mock me, sir, I am a lowly maiden, a palace is no
place for me!'

" 'Beauty is queen of the world,' continued the first. 'You are
extremely beautiful, therefore you are queen! What robe is whiter,
what eyes brighter than yours!'

" 'Think of your mother,' said the pleading voice. 'Can you forget
her? Can you forget your sister Bébé?'

" 'Bébé makes you her slave, and your mother does not love you.
You are a child of misfortune. You have been reared by chance.
Chance is your foster-mother. You are alone indebted to chance.
Come, Minette, come, the world is before you. Here is misery and
obscurity, yonder, riches and fame!'

"My good angel in vain tried to picture a future of darkness and
despair. The love of finery took possession of my heart and sealed
my doom!

"The voice became more and more irresistible, and I blindly
followed its commands.

"I had fallen into a faint, but when I became conscious, judge
my surprise to find that my charmer was no illusion. Before me
stood a young cat gazing tenderly down on me.

"Ah, Bébé, he was handsome! and his eyes sparkled with the
flame of kindling love. He was the ideal cat of whom we sing when
gazing on the moon veiled by the city smoke. At last, in a high-
pitched rapturous voice, he exclaimed, 'Divine Minette, I adore
thee.' I felt my tail expand at his audacity, but my heart expanded
as if in unison, for I already felt that he was mine. Soon he settled
down, his gaze riveted upon my face. You ought to have seen how
humbly he begged for a single glance from me. How could I

MINETTE GOES TO
THE DEVIL. J. J.
Grandville. *From
"Love Adventures of
a French Cat"*

refuse his request, he who, perhaps, had rescued me from the terrible death of a fall from the tiles.

"If you had only heard his eloquence, Bébé. I confess I felt flattered and puffed up with pride, and saw myself prospectively arrayed in all the finery he promised to lay at my feet; lace, collars, jewels, and a superb ermine muff. This last gift brought me into great trouble.

"I was naturally indolent—he pictured to me a life of ease, with its soft carpets, velvet and brocade cushions, arm-chairs, sofas, and all sorts of fine furniture. He assured me that his mistress—an ambassador's wife—would be delighted to receive me whenever I cared to visit her, and that all the collection which made her apartments a magazine of curiosities was at my disposal.

"Oh, it was delightful to dream of being waited on so; I would have a maid, and my noble mistress would serve me.

" 'We are called domestic animals,' he said, why, it is impossible to say. What position do we fill in a house? Whom do we serve and who serves us, if not our masters? He assured me I was simply perfect, in tones so musical, that I heard the old landlady below screaming with delight. I said I felt lonely, and he swore eternal fidelity—Oh! how he did swear—and promised a life of cloudless joy. In a word I was to become his wife, and the ambassador's titled cat.

"What more need I add. I followed him and thus became Madame de Brisquet.

❧

Fourth Letter: FROM THE SAME TO THE SAME.

"Yes, Bébé, Madam de Brisquet.

"Pity me, Bébé, when I write this name it seems to me to contain the whole story of my misery, condensed and sublimated, yet I have imagined myself happy in the possession of wealth, honour, and his affection. Our entrance into the hotel was a real triumph, even the ambassador opened his window to receive us. The lady pronounced me the most beautiful creature she had ever seen, and after exhausting her store of agreeable flatteries, she rang for her people, told them all to respect me, and committed me to the care of her lady-in-waiting. I was at once named the queen of cats, the fashionable beauty, by all the most renowned Angoras in Paris. My husband was proud of my success, and I looked forward to a lifetime of happiness.

"O Bébé, when I recall all this, I often ask myself how it is I have any heart left.

"My honeymoon lasted fifteen days, after which I discovered that Brisquet had no real love for me. In vain were his assurances that his affection had not changed—I was not to be deceived. But love desires what is impossible, and is after all satisfied with very little. Even when all tokens of affection were at an end, I felt I still loved him, and would not believe that love so sincere awakened no kindred flame in his heart.

"Remember this, Bébé, there is nothing more transient than the love of cats. Far from being pleased at my constancy, Brisquet became impatient with me.

" 'I cannot understand,' he exclaimed angrily, 'why love, the most gay and agreeable pastime of youth, should become the most serious, absurd, and bothering business of our maturer years.'

"I abandoned my mother and sister, because I loved you! I, I—wept!

"My grief only hardened his heart, he became cruel, even brutal, and I, who had rebelled against my poor mother's neglect, bent under his oppression, and waited, hoping for brighter days. But time is a pitiless monster, and teaches us many a hard lesson we would rather not learn. Time may also be likened to a good physician, who, after many days heals the deepest wounds. I became calm, feeling that the last ember of my unrequited love had been rudely stamped out; and I forgave him.

"Brisquet was one of those who love themselves better than all the world, and who are easily elated by anything that flatters their vanity. He was a true disciple of the school of gallantry, whose doctrines are framed to please, without the troublesome sentiment of love. Their hearts have two doors which open almost simultaneously, the one to let you in, the other to kick you out. Naturally, Brisquet while ceasing to care for me, had found another dupe. Fortune had furnished a singular rival, a Chinese creature from the province of Peichihli, who, soon after she had landed, set all the cats in Paris in a ferment. This gay intriguer had been imported by the manager of a theatre, who wisely foresaw that a Chinese cat would create a tremendous sensation among the Parisians.

"The novelty of this last conquest pricked the self-love of Brisquet, while the drooping ears of the foreigner did the rest. Not long after he announced his intention of leaving me.

" 'I found you poor, I leave you rich. You were despairing and knew nothing of the world, now, your instinct has been sharpened by experience. You owe all to me; thank me, and let me go.'

" 'Go,' I said, 'I ought never to have loved you,' and he left me.

"His departure lifted a load from my heart. I no longer cared for him. O Bébé, if I could only have forgotten all, and become a kitten again.

"It was about the time of Brisquet's disappearance that I renounced the world, and refused to quit my apartments. Under the able tuition of my mistress, I soon perceived that there was more probability in the fable of the cat transformed into a woman, than one would suppose. In order, therefore, to while away the time, I took to the study of human nature from our point of view. I resolved to put together my observations in the form of a little treatise, entitled, 'History of a Woman, as a Caution to Cats; by a Votary of Fashion.'

"Should I find an editor, this important work will soon see the light. Bébé, I have no heart to write more. Oh, that I had, like you, remained poor, and never known the pain of luxurious misery. Bébé, I have decided to return to the loft to rejoin you and my dear mother, who, perhaps, after some time may know me again. Do not deter me, I will work, I will forget all the pomp and vanity of riches. Adieu! I hope to leave for home to-morrow."

Fifth Letter: BÉBÉ TO MINETTE.

"As I have just received and perused your long, sad letter, I can only say, that I am ready to welcome you home. Your story was read through a mist of tears. Although, as I say, I am ready to receive you, for your own sake, I entreat you to remain where you are. Think well before plunging into poverty, and exchanging the sentimental misery of your position for the real woes of want. Remain where you are, for beneath the richly-laden boards of the great, you can never feel privation. You can never feel the savage instinct that causes your poor relations at home to fight for the foulest refuse.

"Mark well my words, Minette. There is only one overwhelming type of misery in the world, and that is, born of poverty. I need say nothing to prove that our lot is a sad one. The masons have just left the loft, where they stopped up every mouse-hole, and transformed our happy hunting-grounds into howling wastes of bare timber and plaster. My mother, who knows nothing of all this, is dying for a meal. I have nothing to give her, and I have tasted nothing for days.

"BÉBÉ."

"P.S.—I was begging the privilege of hunting in the neighbours' preserves, and have been driven from their roofs and spouts. Keep your sorrows, you have leisure to weep over them, and over the sad lot of your poor sister and mother.

"It is said no one dies of hunger in Paris—we shall see!"

Sixth Letter: BÉBÉ TO MINETTE.

"We are saved! a generous cat has come to our aid. Ah, Minette, how joyous it is to come to life again!

"BÉBÉ."

Seventh Letter: FROM THE SAME TO THE SAME.

"You do not reply, Minette. What is the reason? Ought I to excuse you? I have great news, I am going to be married. I have consented to wed our deliverer. He is elderly and fat, but very good. I feel certain you will approve of the step. His name is Pompon, a nice name which suits him well. It is, besides, a good match, he is a well-fed cat. You see my education has led me to view this union in a plain practical way. Write soon, lazy one!

"BÉBÉ."

Eighth Letter: (*written in pencil*).
FROM MINETTE TO BÉBÉ.

"While I write to you, Bébé, my maid—the one kept for me by my mistress—is engaged in making a linen bag, when finished I will be thrust into it, it will be sewn up, and I shall be carried off by the footman and thrown into the river.

"This is to be my fate.

"Do you know why, Bébé. It is because I am sick, and my mistress, who has the most superfine feelings, dreads the sight of suffering and death. 'Poor Rosa Mika,' she said, 'how she is changed!' and in a sad voice gave the fatal order, 'Be sure to drown her well, do not have her suffer pain.'

"Ah, Bébé, what do you say now? Do you still envy my miseries? My illness prevented me from writing. Adieu.

"Bébé, in a few minutes all will be over.

"MINETTE."

You know the history of my married life, would you wish me to begin again?

As for Bébé, her lot in life was a happy one, only marred by the death of her mother, who expired in her arms while blessing her daughter.

Pompon proved a devoted husband and father, for Bébé soon became the mother of a numerous family of little Pompons and Minettes.

Epilogue.

"We are happy to say that poor Minette is not dead, a telegram has just been handed to us intimating that she escaped as if by a miracle the sad end which menaced her.

"Both mistress and maid died suddenly before the fatal bag was finished. Their death is an event most unaccountable, unless it was brought about to meet the exigency of this romantic tale. Minette, by means best known to the author of this faithful history, soon recovered, and was restored to her sister, with whom she lived happily for many years, enjoying neither riches nor poverty. Minette's tranquillity was broken for a time by the news that Brisquet had first associated himself with a desperate gang of nocturnal serenaders, and ended his midnight exploits and his life by falling from a roof into the street. Bébé seeing Minette a lonely widow, was filled with compassion, and tried to persuade her to wed one of the friends of Pompon. All her efforts were vain. Minette remained unmoved, saying, 'One only loves once. There are those for whom I might die, but with whom I must refuse to live. Besides, my resolution is taken—I shall end my days in widowhood.' "

THE CAT THAT WAS FEY

BY *Arthur Stanley Riggs*

SECOND OFFICER HENDERSON had the duty when Peter came aboard.

The rusty, wheezy, foul smelling tramp *Calyx* lay alongside the Shrub Terminal Stores loading machinery for Callao. A week before she had come in from Iloilo and Manila with a full cargo of copra—and copra bugs. Between the bugs that were everywhere, even in the java, and the gritty cinders and dust from her poor steam coal, there was reason enough for Mr. Henderson's dark mood. Nothing the war had done to him as a BM/2c under an unfit young skipper compared with this. He sat in the opened door of the charthouse sucking on a dead pipe and staring at the starboard gangway without seeing anything. Then *he* hove in sight.

"Holy St. Peter!" exclaimed the Second, shivering.

Marching with complete assurance up the gangway was the animated skeleton of what at second appraisal proved to be somewhat like a cat. He was as desolate and disreputable in appearance as the ship he was invading. Once evidently black, his fur was so matted, dirty, touseled and gouged out in spots that the washboard of ribs down each side made him something for a caricaturist's delight. His tail rose into a perfect question mark astern; the knot on its tip marked clearly some adventure with a door. One ear had been chewed into complete distortion; the other was ragged but cocked well forward.

The expression on his scarred, wicked and hungry face defied anything Mr. Henderson could find on his tongue. Straight up the gangplank without haste or hesitation, straight along the welldeck, up the ladder and straight to Mr. Henderson he came. A foot away he paused. Man and cat eyed each other in appraising silence. "Miaouw!" finally remarked the animal, and set a tentative paw against Mr. Henderson's near leg.

71

A deep sigh escaped the man. He could feel the sharp claws against his own tough hide. His relief was genuine. "Holy St. Peter," he murmured. "Cat, I swear you're real! I'm not—not just seein'—."

Two calculating green eyes peered anxiously at the shaken Second Officer, and from the scrawny throat of the creature came a harsh sound like an echo of the *Calyx's* gears grinding ominously in a quartering sea. Five needle sharp claws pricked gently a trifle deeper.

"Hah! Purr at me, will ye? An' hungry! Well, come along, fellah. Ought to be somethin' in the galley y' c'n eat."

There was. Cook Swensen and Second Officer Henderson watched amazed as the starveling snatched and gulped, choked and bolted, until his ribs bulged and he could not down another bite. He sighed profoundly as he backed away from his plate, his tail flicking. Slowly he came to Henderson, fixed him with unblinking eyes, rubbed against his leg and purred again, more grindingly than before. The cook grumbled.

"Likely he ain't et good f'r a week. S'pose we'll have to feed him now till we shove off. I git him the grub, and the beggar thanks you!"

"Sure. That's all right. He come to me first. I knew where the grub was an' brung him here. Y' know, Cookie," he added, transfixed by one of his rare ideas, "we ain't got no cat since Nig jumped ship in Manila. I think this here beauty's a-goin' with us."

Swensen looked sourly at the over-stuffed animal already half asleep at Henderson's feet. "If he's a ratter we c'n use him all right. Stores are so full o' them big brown devils boarded us in Iloilo we won't have no stores pretty soon. Cat!" he barked, bending over and shaking a thick finger at him. "Go git me a rat. Show some gratitude. Pay for your dinner!"

With dignity the stray rose, flexed his muscles, gave the cook a green glare and vanished. Swensen chuckled. "Goo'bye, pussy! Smart lad. He got me aw ri'. That's the last we'll see of him."

Mr. Henderson shook his head. A searching look through the galley port discovered no signs of life down the long pier, and though he should have been topside, he settled down again and he filled his pipe. The match he lighted never reached the tobacco.

Egyptian Bronze Cat. Ptolemaic Period. *Courtesy The Metropolitan Museum of Art*

As he raised it, in staggered the cat, his jaws firmly clamped on a still struggling monster rat almost as large as himself. Scornfully he dropped it at Swensen's feet, gave it the *coup de grâce* with one ferocious crunch, crossed to Mr. Henderson and gazed up for approval.

"Holy St. Peter!" gasped that officer, burning his fingers.

Swensen laughed. "Some name y' got yourself, pussy!"

Gently the dazed Henderson took him on his muscular lap. Peter liked it. The man's legs were softer than dock planks, and warm and dry. The man's caressing hand was not too clumsy or heavy. Peter squirmed into a comfortable position, closed his eyes and again purred raucously. Both men stared at him silently. Henderson dropped his pipe and made no effort to pick it up. Too many hitherto unimagined things were stirring in his hardened soul to make even a pipe of importance. At last he said, a trifle huskily: "Cookie, this here's the first time anybody ever thought I was

somethin'. Never a soul since I was confirmed, until a cat—an'
Gawd, what a cat! But now . . . Say, this Peter's my cat. Him an'
me, just him an' me. I can beat the ears off'n anybody says no."

"Includin' me?" gibed the burly Swensen.

"Includin' you, an' the Skipper, an' Mr. Blain!"

"The First, he don't like cats. He'll kick the guts outa him."

Mr. Henderson lowered his face over the drowsy animal and
tweaked an ear. "Hear that, Peter? You sheer off whenever the
First Officer heaves in sight."

One green eye opened. Peter yawned prodigiously and turned
his head under his paws. Mr. Henderson approved. "Don't try to
tell me animals don't think an' can't savvy talk. Didn't he go git
you the rat you ast for? We'll be the lucky ship with him aboard."

Exactly how lucky did not appear for some time. Mr. Henderson
felt sure Peter knew all the answers, and his behavior was such
that even the dour Mr. Blain failed to aim a single kick at him.
Certainly the rats were no longer a nuisance. But when, the day
before sailing, the owners picked up a good additional freight for
Havana, Peter came to Mr. Henderson as soon as he knew of the
change in orders, and protested vehemently.

Something was wrong, but what it could be the bewildered
Henderson could not imagine. The extra freight was harmless
enough; a deckload of sugar mill grinding machinery and the copper tubing for some rum stills. Nothing in that to worry about.
And the change in course from the Old Bahama Channel and
Mona Passage to the Yucatán Channel was nothing—only about
six, seven hundred miles farther to Colón. Unless—. He suddenly
wondered what courses the Old Man would order.

Peter continued objecting, his battle scarred face grim. He
watched the deck load stowed and lashed, battened in with special
timbers that secured it against anything but sheer disaster, and
miaouwed his disapproval in tones so ominous everybody who
heard them shuddered. "Murphy," a Polish oiler with a name so
unpronounceable the ashcats had promptly dubbed him "Irish" and
then "Murphy," crossed himself and shivered. Chief Engineer Mac-
Nab, sober for the moment because he was overhauling his ram-
shackle engines, also heard, and wagged his gray head.

"Trrouble be a-coomin', an' the beastie kens it weel. 'Tis fey he is. Betterr we a' watch oot. Peterr," he said gently to the uneasy cat, "coom tell ut me, a guid Scot, an' fey like yersel. Be ther' ony pixies wi' yon machinery?"

Peter rubbed against his legs and purred, but there was no conviction in the harsh rattle of his throat. Mr. Henderson, who was supervising the stowage, laughed sourly. "Pixies or no, Peter'll smell it afore it strikes, Chief. Him an' me are mates. I'll be waitin' for his warning. You just give us steam."

Chief MacNab grunted and vanished below. When the fasts were cast off a few hours later and the *Calyx* wheezed out into the stream, her engines were in better condition than they had known for a long time. The engine and fire-rooms, however, were not comfortable. The bridge was even less so. Old Captain Grant, a Scot like the Chief, and equally bibulous, confided his worries to the pilot who took the ship to sea.

"A beastie, a domned, worrthless, pierrheid-joomper of a strray cat, to upset a whole ship's coompany like he's doin'! Firrst thing ye know the whole blurry lot'll get rreligion. Whoosh! Aiblins they'll even stop off the'r whuskey. I'm no so guid as a navigator masel; the Firrst, he can't find any fix wi'in aboot a degree, the Second's not much betterr—him that claims yon beastie," pointing at the uneasy Peter, maintaining a sharp lookout forward—"an' ma Chief's soberr forr the firrst time in yearrs! He's got real steam on her this time. Arrrgh!"

The trim pilot snickered. "Looks like you'll have to keep sober yourself this trip, Captain," he grinned.

"Aye, that wull I, wi' such a lot o' maunderrin' ijits. An' that Peterr!"

A light southwest breeze, the barometer high, and only a touch of groundswell sped the rheumatic *Calyx* on her course to Havana. That Peter was a veteran seafarer was immediately evident. He had his sea legs, he showed his familiarity with the devious bowels of a ship, and he grew fat and clean and glossy, but not lazy. In his brilliant green eyes there was a concentration, a strange appearance of seeing beyond the visible. He talked a lot to Mr. Henderson, who worried a lot because he could not understand cat speech.

The men quickly forgot their initial forebodings, stuffed Peter outrageously, laughed at him, teased him with rough good humor, and complained only that he hated his job as much as any of them. Eat a rat he would not. And torment one he would not. Tigerish in his attack, he finished the vermin as quickly as possible and dropped each still warm carcass beside the nearest man and miaouwed fiercely if it were not hove overside promptly.

A day in hot and sticky Havana was enough to get rid of the deckload of machinery and tubing, and the *Calyx* wheezed out to sea again, squared off for about 86° west, and churned along at her best eight knots without a cloud in her sky. Captain Grant breathed more easily. Only Peter, Henderson and MacNab continued alert. When they had made sufficient westing and turned sharply southeast on the Old Man's order to save coal by threading the maze of banks and islands between them and the Panama Canal, Mr. Henderson did not need Peter's irritable restlessness to warn him of the danger.

There were islands and shoals all the way from Swan, past Old Providence right down to Colón. He pored over his charts, checked his plotting and fixes under Peter's warning gaze, and sweated freely. Occasionally the cat descended to the engineroom and tried to tell Chief MacNab something that not even the old Scot was fey enough to understand. But he always managed to have a bit of steak or liver somewhere about, and Peter accepted the titbit graciously.

Nothing happened. The voyage droned on under perfect conditions. Swan was sighted and passed safely to port. Thus far the navigation was correct. Ahead lay Old Providence and before that a series of reefs and cays, Christmas Eve, and a falling barometer. His fears gone now that the voyage was so well advanced and everything so apparently well in hand, Captain Grant gave permission for a mild celebration of the holiday.

"Peter," asked Mr. Henderson apprehensively, as the cat leaped to his table and stared down at the much soiled chart the Second was studying, "is this it? What will it be: snorter, shoals, leak, collision, Christmas—what?"

"Miaouw," replied the animal in his most beseeching tone. He set a paw firmly on the chart, but Henderson, however superstitiously he believed in the cat's prescience, could not make up his mind whether the paw's position denoted anything or was a mere gesture.

The barometer went slowly, steadily down, but there was nothing to indicate that a snorter, one of those terrific winds that develop Caribbean hurricanes, was in the making. Chief MacNab reported his domain in perfect order, the carpenter tested his wells and found nothing by way of leakage. Reluctantly, for Henderson had begun to consider himself distinctly important since Peter appeared to rely upon him so completely, surrendered his fears for the moment and entered into the Christmas jollifications as heartily as anyone. With everything secure, and no banks or cays to beware of for at least another twelve hours, the old *Calyx* gave herself over, fore and aft, above and below decks, to the sort of roistering that has sent many a stout ship to Davy Jones.

By the time a staggering hand made eight bells midnight, and Christmas was upon them, Captain Grant was in a happy fog partly slumber, largely Jamaica rum, the Chief was snoring in stentorian gasps and gurgles, the watch on deck was "singing" in the lee of the forward starboard lifeboat, Mr. Henderson was unable to focus his sextant to get a star sight, and Peter was snarling at him, switching his tail and venting strange sounds, half miaowing, half growls. In the fireroom the coal passers were over-firing, and the *Calyx's* rusty stack belched like a small volcano.

Steadily the old bucket rolled along, a fine bone in her teeth, doing better than her accustomed speed, while the drowsy quartermaster at the wheel kept only half an eye on the card. At five bells the horizon began to close in, wet and thick as a blanket.

In fifteen minutes all Mr. Henderson could see as he laid his sextant away was the glare of two green lights dead ahead: Peter's reproving eyes. He laughed, with a hiccup, and began mechanically to check his dead reckoning with his last position. Four days and nights had passed since they left Havana, and they must be getting very close to the 80th meridian and a change of course.

Before he could determine anything, Peter was upon him with a wicked miaouw. Sharp claws pressed through his trousers deep into his leg. He looked down. The cat stiffened, tense in a listening attitude. Again he laid a paw on the officer's leg, purred as loud and harsh as his throat permitted, stopped, and again took the listening pose.

"What ye want, Peter?" queried the startled Henderson, slightly sobered. "I don't hear anything. What it is?" The thought of fire flashed into his mind, and he turned to inspect the old-fashioned telltale on the after bulkhead of the charthouse. Tubes clear; not a sign of anything. He called the engineroom; nothing there.

Again Peter pressed close, and this time drove his claws deep, miaowing horribly. He sprang up on the chest abaft the wheel and stared out ahead, his head cocked to one side, every nerve and muscle tense. Henderson stared at him, then searched the wet fog blanket ahead. Except for the faintly bright spot aloft forward where his running light was evidently burning, there was nothing. And then, with the cat almost in hysterics, he, too, heard it.

At intervals out of the soggy darkness came a long, low, soul chilling snore. It sounded like all the giants of all time rolled into one, rasping out a troubled dream of terror and destruction. As he leaped at the wheel and spun it hard over before the astonished quartermaster could wake up enough to know what he was doing, Henderson saw that every hair on Peter's back was stiffly erect.

Under the stress of the sudden turn, the old *Calyx* careened wildly in the heavy swell, groaned in every plate and rivet, and thrust her blunt nose into a sea that all but capsized her. A thunderous crash and clatter from the galley told of crockery tossed about by the lurch. Everything not secured carried away. In an instant the ship was wide-awake. Up from his bunk ran Mr. Blain, barefoot and with only his pajama trousers on, crying out to know what was wrong.

"Roncador Reef!" gasped Henderson, completely sober and more frightened than the rest. "Roncador, the Old Snorer! We just missed it. I got the wheel over just in time. Listen!"

Again and again through the fog came that ominous gurgling, gasping warning as the seas thrust through the vast hole in the reef at tide level, sucking air in with them to make the blood freezing snore that set men to crossing themselves and mumbling prayers of thanks for their salvation. One touch of the thin-sided old tramp on those jagged rocks, and the *Calyx* would have become a ghost. "Phoooo!" breathed Mr. Blain at last.

Chief MacNab had burst furiously in a moment before. Now he was as scornful as only a Scots engineer can be of navigators. "Ye rruint me wi' yer twisty hellum," he growled. "Crracked ma bed-plate, an' nearr took ma low pressure ingine off the strruts. Rroncadorr, is ut? Losh, Peterr," he said to the now quiet beastie, stroking his head, "if I didna keep ma ingines betterr than they topsides keep the'r navigation, whaur'd we a' be the noo?"

Peter arched his back, rose, turned as if to go below, thought better of it. Jumping down from the chart chest, he walked deliberately over to the binnacle, sniffed, pawed at something just forward of it, and came to Henderson with a heavy seaman's knife in his mouth. Before anyone could speak, the quartermaster cried out sharply. "Sir! Look! We were three points off course! That knife!"

Henderson stood with it in his hand, looking at it dumbly. Blain and the Chief stared. It was the Skipper's knife, evidently dropped after he had shaved off some plug to fill his pipe. Nobody spoke. Peter finally said softly: "Miaouw—ouw!"

Everyone but Henderson went out. Hastily he checked his plot, ordered half speed, set the new course. Satisfied that he had done everything he could, he looked at Peter, again comfortably sprawled on the bulkhead chest. For a long moment the man stared. Then he went over and knelt, taking the drowsy cat in his arms. His voice was shaky as he whispered, but the fear was out of him. "Peter! Peter! You saved the ship. You've—made me."

Soberly enough the *Calyx* anchored in Colón harbor, took her Canal pilot aboard, and soon was fast to the electric mules that would tow her through the Gatun locks. Mr. Blain was on the bridge, Mr. Henderson in the bows, Chief MacNab at the throttle below. Peter was everywhere. He purred at Mr. MacNab and was brusquely ordered out of the engineroom; he disdained Captain Grant, who stood beside the Canal pilot, and dropped down to Henderson, who did not notice him for a moment. The Canal auxiliary crew had his entire attention. Inch by inch the *Calyx* was nosing into the great lower lock.

Peter eyed the proceedings approvingly, calculated the side walls, and finally placed a paw against Henderson's leg. Without taking his eyes from the Canal men, the Second stooped and took the cat in his arms. This was as it should be. Peter purred and flicked his battered tail about. Made fast to the mules ahead, alongside and astern, the ship rose slowly as the lock filled, until her bridge was level with the central pier. Peter struggled, jumped from Henderson's grasp and leaped upon the ship's rail.

Poised there, he calculated the distance between himself and land, turned his head enough to give Henderson a loud, farewell hail, and with a prodigious leap, landed safely. Everyone shouted. Peter gave the ship one last searching survey, turned and marched away, tail erect. His work was done; he was back home.

THE   CRIMINAL   CAT

MACAVITY: THE MYSTERY CAT

BY *T. S. Eliot*

Macavity's a mystery cat: he's called the Hidden Paw—
For he's the master criminal who can defy the Law.
He's the bafflement of Scotland Yard, the Flying Squad's despair:
For when they reach the scene of crime—*Macavity's not there!*

Macavity, Macavity, there's no one like Macavity,
He's broken every human law, he breaks the law of gravity.
His powers of levitation would make a fakir stare,
And when you reach the scene of crime—*Macavity's not there!*
You may seek him in the basement, you may look up in the air—
But I tell you once and once again, *Macavity's not there!*

Macavity's a ginger cat, he's very tall and thin;
You would know him if you saw him, for his eyes are sunken in.
His brow is deeply lined with thought, his head is highly domed;

Two CATS. Gerhard Marcks. Woodcut. 1921. *The Museum of Modern Art, New York, gift of Mrs. Donald B. Straus*

His coat is dusty from neglect, his whiskers are uncombed.
He sways his head from side to side, with movements like a snake;
And when you think he's half asleep, he's always wide awake.

Macavity, Macavity, there's no one like Macavity,
For he's a fiend in feline shape, a monster of depravity.
You may meet him in a by-street, you may see him in the square—
But when a crime's discovered, then *Macavity's not there!*

He's outwardly respectable. (They say he cheats at cards.)
And his footprints are not found in any file of Scotland Yard's.
And when the larder's looted, or the jewel-case is rifled,
Or when the milk is missing, or another Peke's been stifled,
Or the greenhouse glass is broken, and the trellis past repair—
Ay, there's the wonder of the thing! *Macavity's not there!*

And when the Foreign Office finds a Treaty's gone astray,
Or the Admiralty lose some plans and drawings by the way,
There may be a scrap of paper in the hall or on the stair—
But it's useless to investigate—*Macavity's not there!*

And when the loss has been disclosed, the Secret Service say:
"It *must* have been Macavity!"—but he's a mile away.
You'll be sure to find him resting, or a-licking of his thumbs,
Or engaged in doing complicated long division sums.

Macavity, Macavity, there's no one like Macavity,
There never was a Cat of such deceitfulness and suavity.
He always has an alibi, and one or two to spare:
At whatever time the deed took place—MACAVITY WASN'T THERE!
And they say that all the Cats whose wicked deeds are widely
    known
(I might mention Mungojerrie, I might mention Griddlebone)
Are nothing more than agents for the Cat who all the time
Just controls their operations: the Napoleon of Crime!

THE DEAF CAT

LITTLE WHITE KING

BY *Marguerite Steen*

SPRING VANISHED WITH THE BLOSSOM, and summer loitered
imperceptibly into autumn. The sycamores clung to their
leaves, then, in two or three sudden gusts, let them down on the
lawns. He found a new delight: that of following the gardener as
he swung the arc of the broom across and across the grass. Sometimes he became a white windmill, a catherine-wheel of silver,
cutting indescribable capers among the dry brown flakes that broke
into confetti on his back, his flanks and the banner of his tail.
Always addicted to the mower, he helped to give the lawns their
last cut of the year.

All who had known him from his infancy remarked upon the
burgeoning of his beauty, during those autumnal weeks. 'In standing water' between kitten and cat, his adolescence, like that of the
human animal, had a poignancy of its own, which one knew must

vanish when his transformation was complete. He had grown enormously; from the tip of his nose to the base of his tail he was already longer than the Black One, although not quite so tall. The tail had lost the very last of its pale golden trace, and was broader than the broadest ostrich plume. His feet no longer seemed too big for his body, and had garnished themselves with a set of powerful nails, more like jade than ivory, which he still employed too often on upholstery, but never on those who played with him. If, by misfortune, they missed their mark—the piece of ribbon or paper or string we were trailing for him—and registered on human flesh, it was never his intention; the torn hand, offered in place of the toy, was patted with a pad of velvet.

He was very imperious; very definite and autocratic in his requirements. He really needed a vassal, dedicated to his service alone: to shut and open doors, give him a drop of milk, dry his paws when he had been out in the rain, find the ping-pong balls he always batted into the most inaccessible places, or carry him on a shoulder. Although it was easy to say he was 'always eating' (a couple of mouthfuls at a time), no thickness developed in the soft, elastic body, no hardness in the tender bones. To lift him was still like lifting a muff. I wondered how long the sweet sensation would last. He must harden, grow sinewy, develop the rangy stride of the male and the predatory head of the hunter. Of one thing I was glad: the loss of his sex had not affected his vocal cords; his cry, his purr still had the richness of the entire.

One thing in particular endeared him to me: his almost benign attitude towards birds. Full of interest and curiosity, he stalked them, but never—at least in my sight—attempted to kill them. He followed the foolish feathered things through grass or border, flattening himself, watching with sparkling eyes, but never, apparently, with lethal intent. He appeared to extend to them the innocent attention he gave to all small moving objects—leaves, butterflies or shadows. He leapt, he struck. If the blow had ever landed, one can hardly doubt that primitive instinct would have asserted itself; but somehow, for all his agility, he always missed, and, missing, lost interest in the game.

The same with field mice. Never having had to hunt for his food, he was content to give them a pat or two, and could seldom be troubled to follow them when they escaped into the long grass.

I must confess to feeling rather badly about this: something like a
mother whose small boy fails to distinguish himself in the field of
sport; but consoled myself by reflecting on his many gifts and graces,
which more sportsmanlike cats could not rival. I remembered one
of my little North Country queens, a loving little party, who almost
every morning brought me in a cold, dead mouse, which she laid
on my pillow and nozzled affectionately up against my ear, in case
I should overlook it; it was a compliment with which one could
dispense—and one which might well have occurred to le Petit Roi
if he had been a mouser. I had been spared something—if only the
sight of mutilated little bodies, which, vermin though they be, give
me a horrid pang.

When winter declared itself, with fogs and frosts and raw, cheerless mornings, he spent more time indoors, making still closer
acquaintance of the human beings who guarded his simple life.

He had no specially favored spot for his repose; sometimes it was
at the head of the stairs, close to a radiator. Sometimes it was on
the dining-room hearthrug, in front of the Pither stove, or on one
of the Napoleon chairs in the corners of the fireside. On sunny
mornings it was in the deep alcove of a little window, between a
Frank Dobson model of a child's head and the sun-warmed glass.
Sometimes it was the dressing stool in front of my looking-glass,
with the electric stove behind him. At night, when we gathered
in the parlor, it was the back of a couch, or under the flounce of
a chair. Unlike the Black One, he did not care for cushions, or
any too-yielding surface; I had learned, when he came on my bed,
to push back the eiderdown and make a little flat space for him on
the mattress, where, after conducting his toilet, he settled to sleep.

One thing he had in common with the Black One: a mania for
the social life. Christmas, with an influx of guests, was bliss—from
the dinner party on Christmas Eve to the Twelfth Night cocktail.
It was not only a wild and whirling time of tinsel and cellophane,
sparkles and ribbons, things that went bang and flashed (his first
experience of drawing-room fireworks brought him near swooning
point with ecstasy); but he was the center of attention—the Snow
King, the Winter King, le petit roi Noël!

He received tributes with dignified reserve, resisted some foolish
attempts to interest him in his Christmas cards and, sated at last
with pleasure, folded his paws under his chest, to watch the go-

ings-on. His best Christmas present, a mechanical mouse, he played with on Christmas Eve, showing, I fear, more politeness than enthusiasm, and thereafter abandoned. Human beings, with their strange and unpredictable antics, were more fun than a clockwork mouse. His aloofness made the Black One's eager friendliness and her readiness to show off her few self-taught tricks appear—alas—almost fulsome.

He and the Black One had arrived, by then, at 'an understanding.' It was his doing, not hers. But she, with all her elderly ways, her natural anxiety to retain the first place in my affection, was not proof against a little pink muzzle that lifted itself to hers, the soft persistence of his approach, the warmth and comfort of that silver fleece on a winter night. They had begun occasionally to share an armchair: the Black One reluctant, taut, drawn into herself and stiff with resistance, he folded calmly, seemingly immovable, but encroaching little by little on her space, on the woollen scarf that belonged to her, until their limbs were touching. The Black One flung agonized glances at me: 'Must I bear this?' I nodded. The Black One sighed and accepted the all but imperceptible contact. She drew the line, however, on the one occasion he attempted to wash her. What?—a miniature poodle with four champions in her pedigree—submit to being washed by a cat? She bit him, for once, in earnest—and justifiably; and the lesson did him no harm. He sat, blinking offendedly; but, in that respect, he sinned no more. Even when he chewed the tassels on her ears, he showed, thereafter, a certain awareness of the 'thus far and no farther'—which he was keen enough on claiming for himself.

As the days darkened, and there was little to tempt him out of doors, he developed a regime of his own. In the mornings he shadowed Alice about her household duties. Sometimes on her shoulder, sometimes under her arm, he helped her to dust, to sweep and polish—pouncing with delight on the duster, taking flying leaps on to the tops of cupboards or dressers; finally settling on plate-chest or sideboard, his tail curled round his toes, admiring his own reflection in the shining surface. When he endangered something fragile or precious with his antics, Alice's reproachful 'Bert!' was an endearment. When I picked him up in my arms, and, instead of giving him the spanking he had earned, called him 'My white tom kitten!' his struggles and flounces to escape were tolerated for the sake of his perfect beauty.

One of the things most beguiling, to cat-lovers, is the intractibility of a cat, its blank refusal of coercion, its refusal to surrender the least part of its spiritual independence even to those for whom it has learned to care. No one who does not understand and accept this is fit to have the guardianship of a cat. Only one cat of my acquaintance, a Mrs. Bertha Mocatta, was amenable to physical punishment; but Mrs. B. was a gorgeous old tavern harridan who took from her owner the cosh she constantly earned as merely one of the courtesies of everyday existence, and was capable to her last sinful breath of fighting back. Idolizing the hand that obliged her to behave herself, Mrs. B. was one of the immortals; for some time after her demise, her presence was (literally) felt in the studio over which she ruled after her previous owners gave up the local in which she was raised. Her ghost would still be around, I think, but for the establishment of her successor, the gentle Mrs. Laura Chevely, against whom ghostly teeth and ghostly talons cannot prevail.

It may have been noticed that I use the word 'guardianship' in preference to 'ownership,' of a cat. 'Ownership' implies authority over body and soul. A dog, in its devotion, will, of its own free will, accept this authority; a cat, never. This independence is offensive to people who do not care for cats: I have never been able to understand why. I can no more see why one should assume possession over an animal than over a human being.

Now that winter had come, le Petit Roi's afternoons were passed in sleep, unless a brief gleam of sun enticed him out of doors, or the northerly gale, fluttering the dead leaves, tempted him to fling himself about the lawns. He would visit our neighbors, trotting across their grass, lifting his little head, uttering his beguiling Prr-rr-oo, and wave his tail in acknowledgment of a caress, before leaping up their pergola, or on the garage roof, or into the pear tree, where he stood out on a branch, noble as a ship's figurehead, breasting the gale; or, up on the ridge tiles, allowed himself to be blown into a white chrysanthemum by the wind.

His communications with those who shared the house with him now notably increased their range. When he looked up and observed 'Prr-rr-oo,' he was not asking for food, or to go out, or to be

STUDIES FOR A PICTURE OF CATS. Henriette Ronner

played with. It was 'I am here'; or 'Where have you been?' or simply 'Take notice of me.' Often he came and sat beside me, on the arm of chair or sofa, purring so loudly that the Black One would rouse and lift her head in astonishment.

He discovered the miracle of the fires; tempting as they were, he was very sensible about them. For all the comfort they gave him, he was careful not to singe his coat or the restless plume of his tail. And, cosy as he found them, he would withdraw himself—though with an air of protest—if the person he wished to be with was not sitting near the fire.

In one manner he was implacable, and, as the evening wore on, impatient. He must have his games. Useless to offer him his ping-pong balls, his string with the rabbit's tail on the end of it, his crumpled bits of silver paper or the bells that swung on the Black One's collar and lead. He flatly refused to play by himself. He sulked, set up a protestant yowl; leapt on the card table, to scatter aces and kings and queens, and to pat the pencil of the score card on to the floor. Dismissed as a nuisance, he set out on a gloomy progress over chairs, tables and sofas; he deliberately attacked the screen of cordobès leather, or the newly covered couch—anything that was precious and would bring some one leaping to check his ill behavior.

There was nothing for it but to play with him; to rush up and down stairs, trailing a scarf, or the Black One's lead. The game hurtled from room to room; he crouched under beds, to leap out with a wild pat at our ankles; he flung himself prone in affected exhaustion belied by the wild, dark brightness of his eyes. Sometimes the exhaustion was real, and he submitted to being thrown over one's shoulder like a white tippet, and rocked backwards and forwards, purring quietly—until, at the moment one fondly believed he was falling asleep, he would take a bound like a flying squirrel, and the game was on again.

One day shortly after Christmas he had a shock.

At twilight, I opened the back door to let him out, and as he took a cautious step on to the porch, the air around him filled itself with white feathers. The whirling whiteness took him by surprise; he drew back, then, losing his head completely, turned round and flew straight up into my arms. I laughed and held him, and walked out with him on to the path. The snow fell on him and me, and because I was holding him he recovered his confidence, and presently leapt lightly down and went to his accustomed place on the border. But for once he did not linger. It was too cold. He flashed past me, rushed to the dining-room fire, and began hurriedly to lick the cold wetness that had settled on his coat.

Next morning, sitting on the bench at my bedroom window, he looked out on a strange world: a scene of whiteness, glittering with sun. He was fascinated. Presently he called to be let out, and slid on to the back porch, which had been swept clear, and was already warmed by the eastern sun. He sat there, taking in the altered aspect of his familiar surroundings. After watching le Petit Roi gazing at the greenness which overnight had been translated into whiteness, I have no doubt that cats know about color. He was baffled and impressed.

The flagged path that leads down under the archway and out into the lane had also been swept, and, at his own leisure, he trotted down it, for another view of this strange, white scene.

Meanwhile, the Black One had gone for her morning walk. She had known many snows and, on the whole, enjoyed them. Her minute feet, hardly bigger than birds' claws, sank into the cold softness, she rubbed her muzzle in the snow and came up with white moustaches and fringes of white on her ears. As le Petit Roi sat there, under the archway, she returned up the lane.

He rose on his toes; he blew himself out into a white balloon; he spat—for the first time in his life. He swayed back into a defensive arc, as IT came by: a black and yellow IT, familiar, yet horribly strange. The Black One, in her daffodil-yellow sweater which he had never seen before, horrified him. He slapped out a paw. The Black One stood still and stared. He hunched himself, let out a slow, protracted growl, and spat again. The Black One, impressed, walked up for a closer view of this strange conduct on the part of one who, so far, had never been anything but amiable.

His eyes blackened and enlarged themselves, his pink mouth, wide open, dragged back at the corners, held in his breath. Then, with a gasp, he recognized the Black One, and shot like an arrow for the kitchen door. Shaking the snow from her fringes, the Black One galloped after him. They hunched at each other in front of the dining-room stove, then spent ten minutes smelling each other all over from head to tail, as though meeting for the first time.

That was the week he discovered the possibilities of the Knole couch. The last, most lovely picture of the Little King is of a long white arm, reaching between the back and the slung end of the couch; of a snow-white head, mad with gaiety, and a pair of ruby-red eyes blazing from shadow at the evening paper, rolled up and poked into the space between cushions and wall for him to snatch at.

It was round about that time that I wrote in my diary:

'Of all the cats that have owned me, there has never been one like my white tom kitten, for sweetness, intelligence and affection. Hearing is very unimportant, after all.'

SENTIMENTALITIES

BY *Colette*

CHARACTERS

KIKI-THE-DEMURE, an Angora tabby.
TOBY-DOG, a brindled French bull-dog.
HE ⎫
SHE ⎭ courtiers.

The steps in full sun. It is the hour of the after-lunch siesta. TOBY-DOG *and* KIKI-THE-DEMURE *are lying on the burning stone. There is a Sunday silence, but* TOBY-DOG, *tormented by the flies and his heavy lunch, is not asleep. With his hind-quarters splayed out like a frog's, he wriggles on his stomach over to* KIKI-THE-DEMURE, *whose striped fur is motionless.*

TOBY-DOG Are you asleep?

KIKI-THE-DEMURE *purrs faintly*

TOBY-DOG Are you even alive? You look so flat anyone might take you for an empty cat's-skin.

KIKI-THE-DEMURE *(in a languid voice)* Leave me ...

TOBY-DOG You're not ill, are you?

KIKI-THE-DEMURE No ... leave me alone. I'm asleep. I can't even remember whether I have a body. Oh what torment it is to live with you! I've had my meal and it's two o'clock. Do let's sleep.

TOBY-DOG I can't. There's a thing like a ball in my stomach. It'll move down all right, but it takes time. And oh my goodness, these flies, these flies! The mere sight of one of them makes my eyes start out of my head. However do they manage it? Here am I all jaws bristling with terrible teeth (can't you hear them snapping?) and yet the dratted creatures escape me. Why do they always go for my ears, my soft dark tummy and my burning truffle of a nose? There! there's one now, right on my nose, d'you see? How on earth can I catch it? I'll try squinting. Are there two of them now? No, only one ... no, two. I toss them up like a lump of sugar but all I catch is emptiness. I feel quite worn out. I loathe the sun and the flies and every blessed thing! (*He groans.*)

KIKI-THE-DEMURE (*sitting up, his eyes pale from sleep and the light*) Well, you've succeeded in waking me up. That's just what you wanted, isn't it? My dreams have fled. As for those flies you're trying to catch, I was hardly aware of their irritating little feet on my thick fur. Every now and then I could feel the sleek and silky grass of my coat shiver into a ripple under a caress that barely touched it. But you never can do anything discreetly. You have to impose your vulgar joy on everyone, and when you're sad you groan like a third-rate actor. Take yourself off, you mountebank!

TOBY-DOG (*bitterly*) If it was only to say that to me that you waked up ...

KIKI-THE-DEMURE (*correcting him*) That you waked me up.

TOBY-DOG I was feeling wretched and I wanted someone to help me with an encouraging word.

KIKI-THE-DEMURE I don't know any digestive verbs. When I think that, of us two, I'm supposed to be the difficult one! Just consider yourself for a minute and see how we compare. The heat exhausts you, hunger maddens you, cold paralyses you ...

TOBY-DOG (*vexed*) It's because I'm so sensitive.

KIKI-THE-DEMURE Say rather, so uncontrolled.

TOBY-DOG I won't say any such thing. As for you, you're an outrageous egotist.

KIKI-THE-DEMURE Maybe. But neither you nor the Two-Footed Ones have the faintest idea what true egotism, the egotism of Cats, really means. They use the word indiscriminately for our instinct of self-preservation, our modest reserve, our dignity, and our weary resignation when we realise it's no use expecting them to understand us. Perhaps, Dog, unrefined though you are, since you have no prejudices, you can understand me better? The Cat is a guest and not a plaything. I really don't know what the world is coming to! Why should the Two-Footed, He and She, be the only ones who have the right to feel sad or rejoice, to scrape their plates clean, to grumble and infect the whole house with their ill-humour? I too have my whims, my moments of sadness, a variable appetite and times when I turn my back on the world to be alone with my own thoughts.

TOBY-DOG (*taking it all in carefully*) I'm listening but it's rather difficult to follow you, because you talk so clever and a bit above my head. But I must say you astonish me. Do They ever oppose your changing moods? You meow: They open the door for you. You curl up on that precious paper that He spends his time scratching: He merely shifts along and leaves the soiled page to you. You saunter off, wrinkling your nose and jerking your waving tail, obviously on the look-out for mischief: She watches you and laughs, and He announces: "Off on the war-path." Well then, what are you complaining about?

KIKI-THE-DEMURE (*insincerely*) I'm not complaining. Anyhow, psychological subtleties will always be beyond you.

TOBY-DOG Don't speak so fast, I must have time to take things in. It seems to me . . .

KIKI-THE-DEMURE (*teasing him*) Don't hurry, it might upset your digestion.

TOBY-DOG (*deaf to the irony*) You're quite right, it might. I'm finding it difficult to express myself to-day. Now I've got it! It seems to me that, of us two, you're the one that's spoilt; and yet it's you who complain.

KIKI-THE-DEMURE Dog logic! The more I'm given, the more I expect.

TOBY-DOG I think that's bad manners.

KIKI-THE-DEMURE No it isn't. I have a right to everything.

TOBY-DOG Everything? Then what about me?

KIKI-THE-DEMURE There's nothing you lack, is there?

TOBY-DOG Well, I wouldn't say nothing. Often when I'm at my happiest, I suddenly feel like crying, my eyes grow misty and my heart pounds. While the anguish lasts I want to be sure that every living thing loves me, that nowhere in the world is there a sad dog behind a door, and that nothing nasty will ever happen.

KIKI-THE-DEMURE (*mockingly*) And then what nasty thing does happen?

TOBY-DOG Oh dear, you don't have to ask! It's always just at that moment that She arrives, carrying a yellow bottle with that horror swimming about in it ... you know ... the castor oil! How heartless and unreasonable She seems then! She grips me between her strong knees, forces my teeth apart ...

KIKI-THE-DEMURE   You should clench them tighter.

TOBY-DOG   I'm afraid of hurting her. And then I taste that sickly slime on my shuddering tongue. I choke and spit, my poor face puckers with anguish—and it's ages before the torture has any results. You've seen me after it, dragging myself dejectedly along with my head down, listening to the filthy gurgling of the oil in my stomach, and then hiding my shame in the garden.

KIKI-THE-DEMURE   You don't hide it very well!

TOBY-DOG   Well, I haven't always got time!

KIKI-THE-DEMURE   Once when I was little, She wanted to purge me with oil. I scratched and bit her so hard that She never tried again. She almost thought for a moment She was holding the devil in her lap. I coiled myself into a spiral, belched fire, multiplied my twenty claws by a hundred and my teeth by a thousand, and then vanished as if by magic.

TOBY-DOG   I would never dare behave like that. I love her, you see. I even love her enough to forgive her the bath-torture.

KIKI-THE-DEMURE   *(interested)*   Do you really? Tell me what that feels like. The mere sight of what She does to you when you're in the water gives me the shivers.

TOBY-DOG   I don't wonder! Listen then, and pity me. Sometimes, after She's got out of her tin tub wearing nothing but that sweet hairless skin of hers which I like licking—very respectfully of course—She doesn't at once put on again those other skins of cloth and linen. She pours in more hot water, throws in a brown brick smelling of tar and says: "Toby!" As soon as I hear that my soul quails within me and my legs give way. I'm blinded by something glittering and wavering on the surface of the water; it looks like a window all out of shape. She seizes my poor limp body and plunges me in ... help! help! After that I know no more. My one hope is in her, I fix my eyes on hers, while something warm and tight clings all round me, like another skin on my skin.

Oh that foaming brick, that smell of tar, and the water that stings my eyes and nostrils and fills my drowning ears! She warms to the job and pants and laughs as She cheerfully scrubs me. Then at last comes the rescue, when She fishes me out by the scruff of my neck, while my paws beat the air in an effort to get back to life. After that comes the rough towel and the warm blanket where I feebly convalesce.

KIKI-THE-DEMURE (*really upset*) Pull yourself together.

TOBY-DOG That's all very well, but just describing it's enough to . . . I say, though, wait a moment! You sit there taking a mocking interest in my misfortunes, but didn't I see you one day stretched out on a washstand, while She bent over you with a sponge in her hand?

KIKI-THE-DEMURE (*very embarrassed, his tail swishing*) That's a very old story. My plus-fours had got dirty and She wanted to clean them. But I soon convinced her that the sponge made me suffer horribly.

TOBY-DOG What a liar you are! She didn't believe you, did She?

KIKI-THE-DEMURE Well . . . not all the time. It was my own fault. Lying there flat on my back I looked like a lamb on an altar offering up its innocent stomach, its terrified but forgiving eyes. Through the thickness of my fluffy trousers I was just faintly aware of something chill, then nothing more! Terror seized me, I was afraid I'd lost all power of feeling. My rhythmic wailings rose and fell—you know what a powerful voice I've got—then rose again like the roar of the sea. I did all my imitations: the little calf, the child being whipped, the cat on the tiles, the wind under the door; and gradually got so carried away with my own singing that long after She'd finished polluting me with cold water I was still moaning, with my eyes turned up to the ceiling, while She laughed tactlessly and cried: "You're as deceitful as a woman!"

TOBY-DOG (*with feeling*) That *was* a bit hard!

KIKI-THE-DEMURE I was sore with her about it for a whole afternoon.

TOBY-DOG Oh yes, you know how to sulk all right. I never can. I just forget injuries.

KIKI-THE-DEMURE (*drily*) And you lick the hand that chastises you. Oh yes, we all know that!

TOBY-DOG (*falling into the trap*) I lick the hand that . . . Yes, you put it perfectly. What a very nice expression!

KIKI-THE-DEMURE   It isn't my own. You'll never die of dignity. Really, sometimes I'm ashamed of you. You love everyone indiscriminately, and no matter how you're snubbed you take it lying down. Your heart's like a public garden, open to all, and commonplace.

TOBY-DOG   It's nothing of the sort, you ill-bred thing. You think you know everything, but you simply don't understand my good manners. Frankly now, would you have me snap at the ankles of his friends, and hers, pleasant well-dressed people who are strangers to me, but who know my name and pull my ears in such a friendly way?

KIKI-THE-DEMURE   I detest new faces.

TOBY-DOG   I don't care for them either, whatever you may say. I only love . . . Her and Him.

KIKI-THE-DEMURE   And I love Him . . . and Her.

TOBY-DOG   Oh yes, I've known for a long time which was your favourite. There's a kind of secret understanding between Him and you.

KIKI-THE-DEMURE   (*with a rapt, mysterious smile*)   An understandstanding . . . yes, that's it. Secret and shy and deep. He spends his time making mouse-squeaks on the paper, and rarely speaks. He's the one to whom I've given my reluctant heart, my precious cat's heart. And with never a word said, He has given me his. This exchange has filled me with a private bliss. Now and again I feel the stirrings of that strange capricious instinct to dominate which cats and women know; and then I test my power over him. So when we're alone it's for his benefit that I slant my ears forward in the diabolical way that means I'm about to spring on to his scratching-paper. And when my paws go pad-pad-padding among the pens and the scattered letters, it's just to attract Him. The persistent meowing which means I want to be let out—what He laughingly calls "The Hymn to the Door-knob" or "The Prisoner's Lament"—is all for Him too. But beyond everything else, for Him alone is the tender gaze of my thrilling eyes, which dwells on his bent head until his own gaze, grown aware of it, seeks and meets mine in a souls' encounter so tensely awaited and so sweet that I close my eyelids in exquisite shame. But as for Her, She's too restless. She often jostles me or waves me in the air, gripping two of my paws in each hand, or strokes me till

She's all wrought up herself. She laughs out loud about me too, and imitates my voice too well.

TOBY-DOG (*roused to indignation*) I think you're very hard to please. Of course I love Him because He's kind and pretends not to see my mistakes, so that He won't have to scold me. But She! To me She seems the dearest and most beautiful thing in the world, and the hardest to understand. Her step enchants me and on her changing look depend my happiness and my sadness. She's like Destiny, She never hesitates. Even torments, at her hands ... you know how She teases me?

KIKI-THE-DEMURE   Yes, roughly.

TOBY-DOG   No, not roughly; subtly. I never know what's coming. This morning, for instance, She bent down as if She were going to speak to me, but instead She lifted the flap of my little elephant-ear and gave a shrill cry which pierced to the bottom of my brain.

KIKI-THE-DEMURE   How vile!

TOBY-DOG   Was it kind? Or cruel? I'm still not sure. It made me so nervous that I spun madly round in circles. Nearly every day the whim takes her to make me do what She calls "the fish": She holds me in her arms and squeezes my sides to suffocation point till my mouth opens silently like the mouths of carp when they drown in the air on dry land.

KIKI-THE-DEMURE   That's her all over.

TOBY-DOG   Then all of a sudden a miracle happens and I'm free and alive again, thanks to her will alone. How beautiful life seems to me then! And how I chaw the hand hanging at her side, and the hem of her dress!

KIKI-THE-DEMURE (*with contempt*) What a jolly game!

TOBY-DOG   All the good things that happen to me, and all the bad things too, come from Her. She's my sharp torment and my one sure refuge. When I'm terrified and bury myself in Her, my heart pounding, how gentle her arms are and how cool her hair on my forehead. Then I'm her "black baby", her "Toby-Dog", her "little sweety-pie". To soothe me She crouches on the floor until She's as small as I am, or lies down flat so that I'm maddened by the sight of her face below mine, lying framed in her hair with its good animal smell and a whiff of hay in it too. How can I resist Her then? My passion overflows, I nuzzle her with my quivering truffle, searching for a pink crunchy ear-lobe—Her ear!—and when I've found it I chew it until She can no longer bear the tickling and calls out: "Toby, that's terrible! Help, help, this dog's eating me!"

KIKI-THE-DEMURE Wholesome pleasures, crude and simple . . . And after that, off you go to make love to the cook.

TOBY-DOG And you to the cat at the farm.

KIKI-THE-DEMURE *(shortly)* None of that, if you please. That concerns no one but me . . . and the little cat.

TOBY-DOG A fine conquest! You ought to be ashamed of yourself, a cat only seven months old!

KIKI-THE-DEMURE *(excited)* An unripe fruit, a wild berry, that's what she is! And no one shall steal her from me. She's as slender as a pea-stick . . .

TOBY-DOG *(aside)* Lewd old thing!

KIKI-THE-DEMURE With her body balanced on lanky legs, she has the uncertain gait of a virgin. Hard work in the fields where she hunts field-mice, shrew-mice and even partridges, has hardened her muscles and saddened her childish face a little.

TOBY-DOG She's ugly.

KIKI-THE-DEMURE Not ugly at all! But she's certainly strange, with her goatish nose and its pink nostrils, and those large furry ears of the country cat. Often the bright gaze of her slanting eyes, the colour of old gold, slithers into a fascinating squint. How madly she flies from me, thinking she's terrified when she's only shy! I, on the other hand, stalk slowly past, looking quite indifferent, wrapped in my splendid robe whose stripes dazzle her. She'll come to heel all right, that lovesick little Cat! And then, all restraint thrown to the winds, she'll writhe under me like a white scarf!

TOBY-DOG Well, have it your own way. As things are here, all that love business leaves me comparatively cold. What with physical exercise and my responsibilities as a watchdog, I never even think of spooning.

KIKI-THE-DEMURE *(aside)* Spooning! A commercial traveller, that's what you are!

TOBY-DOG *(frankly)* And besides, I don't mind telling you . . . Well, the fact is that I am, as you see, very small, and by an extraordinary but very real piece of bad luck everyone I meet hereabouts is a young giantess. That bitch at the farm—you know, the big mongrel she-devil with the yellow eyes—would be quite ready to take me on; she never says no. She's as fast as they make 'em, but all the same she's a good sort with an exciting smell, and she has a kind of coarse and haggard charm, too, rather like a gentle she-wolf's, with those hungry looks of hers . . . But alas! I'm too small . . . I know several others too in the houses round here. There's a placid Great Dane who towers over me like a cliff, a sheep-dog who never has time because of her job, and a highly-strung setter who's given to biting suddenly, though her wild eyes show she has a hot nature. . . . Alas, alas, it's better not to think about it! It's really too exhausting to come home worn out and unsatisfied and toss with fever all night. Forget it.

She and He are all that matter to me, and I love them with a devout and troubled passion which lifts me to their level, and is enough in itself to fill my heart and my days. And now, Cat, my scornful friend, whom all the same I love and who loves me, the hour of the siesta is nearly over. Don't turn away your head! That peculiar modesty of yours makes you try to hide what you call weakness and what I call love. But d'you think I'm blind? Lots of times when I've been coming back to the House with Her, I've seen your triangular face at the window light up and smile at my approach. By the time the door was opened you'd already put on your cat-mask again, that pretty Japanese mask of yours with the slit eyes. . . . Can you deny it?

KIKI-THE-DEMURE (*determined not to hear*) The hour of the siesta's nearly over. The conical shadow of the pear-trees on the gravel is growing longer. All our sleep has vanished in words. You've forgotten the flies and your uneasy stomach and the heat quivering over the fields. The lovely drowsy day is ending. Already the air begins to stir and wafts down to us the scent of the pines, whose trunks are melting into transparent tears.

TOBY-DOG Here She comes. She's got up from her cane armchair and stretched her graceful arms, and I can read the promise of a walk in the way her dress moves. Can you see Her, behind the rose-bushes? She's breaking a leaf of the lemon-tree with her nail, and now She's crumpling it and sniffing it . . . I'm all hers. Even with my eyes shut I'm aware of Her presence.

KIKI-THE-DEMURE Yes, I see Her. She's quiet and gentle—for a moment. But what matters to me is that soon He'll leave his paper and follow Her. He'll come out calling to Her: "Where are you?", and then He'll sit down, exhausted, on the bench. To honour Him I shall get up politely and go and fray the leg of his trousers with my claws. Then, both of us equally happy and silent, we shall listen to the day closing. At the hour when my night-seeing eyes grow large and dark and begin to read mysterious Signs in the air, the scent of the lime-tree will become almost sickly sweet. Later, far away behind the crest of the mountain, a serene blaze will light up the sky, a sphere of gleaming mist, rosy in the ash-blue of the night. The dazzling blade of the new moon will spring out of this luminous cocoon and sail through the heavens, cleaving the clouds. Then will come the time for sleep. He will take me up on his shoulder and, as this is not the season for love, I shall sleep on his bed, close to his feet which never disturb my rest. But the first light will find me quivering with youth again, sitting facing the sun, pearled by the dew with a silver halo which makes me appear to be indeed the God that once I was.

THE LONELY CAT

THE BEST BED

BY *Sylvia Townsend Warner*

THE CAT HAD KNOWN MANY WINTERS, but none like this. Through two slow darkening months it had rained, and now, on the eve of Christmas, the wind had gone round to the east and instead of rain, sleet and hail fell.

The hard pellets hit his drenched sides and bruised them. He ran faster. When boys threw stones at him he could escape by running; but from this heavenly lapidation there was no escape. He was hungry, for he had had no food since he had happened upon a dead sparrow, dead of cold, three days ago. It had not been the cat's habit to eat dead meat, but having fallen upon evil days he had been thankful even for that unhealthy-tasting flesh. Thirst tormented him, worse than hunger. Every now and then he would stop, and scrape the frozen gutters with his tongue. He had given up all hope now, he had forgotten all his wiles. He despaired, and ran on.

The lights, the footsteps on the pavements, the crashing buses, the swift cars like the monster cats whose eyes could outstare his own, daunted him. Though a Londoner, he was not used to these things, for he was born by Thames' side, and had spent his days among the docks, a modest useful life of rat-catching and secure slumbers upon flour sacks. But one night the wharf where he lived had caught fire; and terrified by flames, and smoke, and uproar, he had begun to run, till by the morning he was far from the river, and homeless, and too unversed in the ways of the world to find himself another home.

A street door opened, and he flinched aside, and turned a corner. But in that street, doors were opening too, every door letting out horror. For it was closing-time. Once, earlier in his wanderings, he had crouched in by such a door, thinking that any shelter would be better than the rainy street. Before he had time to escape, a hand snatched him up and a voice shouted above his head. "Gorblime if the cat hasn't come in for a drink," the voice said. And the cat felt his nose thrust into a puddle of something fiery and stinking, that burned on in his nostrils and eyes for hours afterwards.

He flattened himself against the wall, and lay motionless until the last door should have swung open for the last time. Only when someone walked by, bearing that smell with him, did the cat stir. Then his nose quivered with invincible disgust, his large ears pressed back upon his head, and the tip of his tail beat stiffly upon the pavement. A dog, with its faculty of conscious despair, would have abandoned itself, and lain down to await death; but when the streets were quiet once more the cat ran on.

There had been a time when he ran and leaped for the pleasure of the thing, rejoicing in his strength like an athlete. The resources of that lean, sinewy body, disciplined in the hunting days of his youth, had served him well in the first days of his wandering; then, speeding before some barking terrier, he had hugged amidst his terrors a compact and haughty joy in the knowledge that he could so surely outstrip the pursuer; but now his strength would only serve to prolong his torment. Though an accumulated fatigue smouldered in every nerve, the obdurate limbs carried him on, and would carry him on still, a captive to himself, meekly trotting to the place of his death.

He ran as the wind directed, turning this way and that to avoid the gusts, spiked with hail, that ravened through the streets. His eyes were closed, but suddenly at a familiar sound he stopped and stiffened with fear. It was the sound of a door swinging on its hinges. He sniffed apprehensively. There was a smell, puffed out with every swinging-to of the door, but it was not the smell he abhorred; and though he waited in the shadow of a buttress, no sounds of jangling voices came to confirm his fears, and though the door continued to open and shut, no footsteps came from it. He stepped cautiously from his buttress into a porch. The smell was stronger here. It was aromatic, rich, and a little smoky. It tickled his nose and made him sneeze.

The door was swinging with the wind. The aperture was small, too small for anything to be seen through it, save only a darkness that was not quite dark. With a sudden determination the cat flitted through.

Of his first sensations, one overpowered all the others. Warmth! It poured over him, it penetrated his being, and confused his angular physical consciousness of cold and hunger and fatigue into something rounded and indistinct. Flooded with weariness, he sank down on the stone flags.

Another sneezing-fit roused him. He jumped up, and began to explore.

The building he was in reminded him of home. Often, hunting the riverside, he had strayed into places like this—lifty and dusky, stonefloored and securely uninhabited. But they had smelt of corn, of linseed, of tallow, of sugar; none of them had smelt as this did, smokily sweet. They had been cold. Here it was warm. They had been dark; and here the dusk was mellowed with one red star, burning in mid-air, and with the glimmer of a few tapers, that added to the smoky sweetness their smell of warm wax.

His curiosity growing with his confidence, the cat ran eagerly about the church. He rubbed his back against the font, he examined into the varying smell of the hassocks, he trotted up the pulpit stairs, sprang on the ledge, and sharpened his claws in the cushion. Outside the wind boomed, and the hail clattered against the windows, but within the air was warm and still, and the red star burned mildly on. Over against the pulpit the cat came on something that reminded him even more of home—a wisp of hay, lying on the flags. He had often seen hay; sometimes borne towering above the greasy tide on barges, sometimes fallen from the nosebags of the great draught horses who waited so peacefully in the wharfingers' yards.

The hay seemed to have fallen from a box on trestles, cut out of unstained wood. The cat stood on his hind legs, and tried to look in, but it was too high for him. He turned about, but his curiosity brought him back again; and poising himself on his clustered paws he rocked slightly, gauging his spring, and then jumped, alighting softly in a bed of hay. He landed so delicately that though the two kneeling figures at either end of the crib swayed forward for a moment, they did not topple over. The cat sniffed them, a trifle suspiciously, but they did not hold his attention long. It was the hay that interested him. A drowsy scent rose out of the deep, warm bed as he kneaded and shuffled it with his forepaws. This, this, promised him what he had so long yearned for; sound sleep, an enfolding in warmth and softness, a nourishing forgetfulness. He paced round in a small circle, burrowing himself a close nest, purring with a harsh note of joy. As he turned he brushed against a third figure in the crib; but he scarcely noticed it. Already a rapture of sleepiness was overcoming him; the two kneeling figures had done him no harm, nor would this reposing one. Soon the bed was made to his measure. Bowing his head upon his paws, he abandoned himself.

Another onslaught of hail dashed against the windows, the door creaked, and at a gust of wind entering the church the candle-flames wavered, as though they were nodding their heads in assent; but though the cat's ears flicked once or twice against the feet of the plaster Jesus, he was too securely asleep to know or heed.

❦

DANGER—CRAZY CATS

BY *Murray Robinson*

As one who has long been a pushover for cats, I should like to offer a packet of color-fast, preshrunk advice: If a stray kitten bounds out of nowhere when you're taking a walk, mews piteously, and rubs a soft shoulder against your leg, flee to the hills until the danger is over.

What danger, you ask? The danger of stopping to console the furry little conniver, of course. Because, if you make that mistake, you're hooked; not for life, but for nine lives, all his, and he'll make sure they're nine fat lives—at your expense.

I speak out of a vast experience. I've fallen time and again for this feline stratagem of finding a comfortable home and a good provider. And it's only a sample of the infinite variations a cat can play on the man-who-came-to-dinner theme.

But don't get me wrong. I love cats and have never regretted a moment of my long bondage to them. Well, hardly ever. I shouldn't have given you the above advice, either. It was written in a pique after the latest skirmish with Willie, my family's current cat.

Willie maintains it isn't polite for me to read a newspaper in his august presence, and possibly he's right. He shows his displeasure by jumping up and planting himself between my eyes and the paper. If this isn't effective, he shreds the paper with a swipe of his claws.

I usually don't mind, but this time he ripped up the racing entries just when I had spotted a real good thing. I protested. He offered rebuttal, and finally one of us left the room. It was I, of course, and the last thing I saw was Willie in full possession of my easy chair, which happens to be his favorite, too. He had probably planned the whole episode to that end.

So disregard my advice. Go get yourself stuck with a cat and support him in a manner to which he'll soon accustom you. Your pay-off will be the chance to study at close range a nonpaying guest who's a genius at getting his way—and who has rocks in his head. A fascinating combination, I assure you.

My own love for cats may be due, in part, to the fact that the innately haughty beasts have usually made a play for me at first sight. They don't do that with everyone, you know, and the implied flattery must have gone to my head.

Cats have displayed the same affinity for my wife, who recalls that, as a little girl, she had no trouble dressing them in dolls' clothes and wheeling them through the park in a toy carriage. They wouldn't hold still for the other kids. And Willie, then a sprawling kitten about six weeks old, followed my son home from a ball-field a half-mile away to declare himself in. Cats just seem to attach themselves to us, and we've never been without at least one.

The best way to enjoy a cat to the fullest, I think, is to let him adopt you. He wants it that way. If you buy a cat, or get one on the rebound from a friend, he may learn to tolerate and even like you, but there's always the chance that he may secretly resent you because he wasn't consulted on the custody arrangements.

For this reason, I've never bought a cat. Well, there's another reason, too. It's that pedigreed cats, or "fancies," always give me a feeling of inferiority, what with their regal beauty and delicate air. So I've limited my admiration for Persian, Siamese, Burmese, Manx, and Abyssinian cats to just looking at them.

My favorite is what the uninformed rudely call the alley cat. Actually, this is the American short-hair—a cat of sterling character, independent spirit, unlimited resourcefulness, and charming lunacy when given his head, the way I've always done. I allow my cats to express themselves, never interfere with their romances, and raise them with dogs to broaden their outlook.

Speaking of charming lunacy brings me back to Willie, now two and one-half years old; a slim, handsome, gold tomcat with white vest and gloves. There are said to be 21,000,000 cats in the United States, and I claim Willie is the wackiest of the lot.

Willie had a normal kittenhood, which means he did no more than his share of trying to climb the walls and getting stuck in drainpipes. He was taught his manners by another cat in the house by the name of Amber, four years old at the time Willie mooched his way in. They looked so much alike that the whisper went around they were father and son. Could be, but it was never proved.

Willie's education was furthered by Laddie, a gentle wire-haired terrier who died last year at the age of 13, and who showed infinite patience in handling the shenanigans of first Amber and then Willie. Under such respectable auspices, Willie should have grown up to be a real All-America cat, even though Amber did teach him to eat spaghetti with marinara sauce. But I have to tell the truth: Willie is nuts.

He fancies himself a great fighter, but he isn't at all, and he sports a practically permanent scratch on one side of his nose to prove it. Trouble is, he has never developed a defense for a hard left jab.

When he makes ready to go out of an evening (our house is on the city outskirts, with a big backyard and plenty of safe roaming space beyond), he goes through an impressive routine, like a fighter warming up in his corner.

First, he stretches, then pokes a few practice jabs and hooks at our puppy, Kim, a goofy little beagle we fervently pray will outgrow *his* silliness. And then he finishes up by sharpening his claws on a small rug near the door long ago written off as expendable. We'd feel awful if Willie lost a fight because we didn't let him hone his talons.

The ritual completed, we let Willie out. There's silence for a few minutes, then a sudden outbreak of fearsome caterwauling— and Willie is back on the window sill, urgently seeking re-entry. We let him in, swearing under his breath. Either a new cut is visible on the side of his nose or the old one has been reopened. Willie has again been a sucker for the left jab of a feline foe.

Along with his mistaken notion that he's a championship fighter, Willie imagines himself a mighty hunter, and he feels driven to produce evidence of his prowess—a characteristic of most cats. One day last fall he proudly brought home a field mouse and called loudly to come see.

Willie purred happily as the citation was read to him. I picked up the deceased mouse, a wee beastie indeed, and gave it decent burial beyond the back fence. Next day, Willie was back with another trophy of the hunt. It was the same battered mouse. He had dug it up when the second day's hunt went poorly and tried to pass it off as a fresh kill.

Another day, he came home with a bluejay in his mouth. Recalling the havoc I had seen a pair of those belligerent birds raise with a big tomcat earlier in the year, I suspected Willie was again trying to pass off a stiff. One of the neighbor's children verified my suspicion. The bluejay had been lying dead in the street and Willie had just picked it up.

But the biggest fraud our addled cat tried to pull came the day he leaped up on the window sill with a chicken foot in his mouth. His eyes were huge green disks, glowing with triumph. He had obviously filched it from a butcher shop, yet sought credit for snaring a hen.

Tomcats are rated high in the romance department, but I don't know about that Willie. Mitzie, a neighbor's pretty little tabby, has been trying to make time with him for months. But my reluctant Romeo chases her out of the yard in a pet, the bell on her collar jingling wildly as she flees to the safety of her own domain.

I figure this is a good break for Willie. If Mitzie ever stood her ground and started throwing left jabs at him, he'd be disgraced for life.

One final instance of Willie's aberrations, but this is one which endears him to us because it seems based on the cheerful belief that somewhere the sun *must* be shining and things just *can't* be bad all over. We love him for this and wish everyone could feel the same way he does.

Willie the Optimist wakes from a nap and wants out. He walks to the front door and politely states his case. I open the door, and Willie sticks one dainty paw across the threshold. Whoa! It's raining. He pulls back into the house. Does that end the episode, often repeated during the past two years? No, because Willie has a brilliant idea. He leads the way to the back door, chirping cheerfully that while it's raining out front, the sun is probably shining in the backyard.

The back door is opened. Willie peers out. More rain. He pulls back again, thinks for a moment, then trots eagerly to a front window and hops up on the sill, figuring it can't be raining everywhere. I open it for him—and raindrops pelt his tender pink nose. Then he tries a back window. Still more rain. By this time, he recalls the front door. That's when I draw the line. Once around to a customer. Willie just shrugs and goes back to sleep.

Second only to Willie in my crazy-cat album—and this is a photo finish—was a gray cat with tremendous white whiskers. This one— we named him Chauncey—walked up to the house boldly one afternoon and counted himself in.

His first departure from the cat norm was a mighty whooping which seized him almost every hour on the hour. This would startle Mac—a wonderful little Scottie who had welcomed Chauncey to his bed and board with all the dignity of his breed—and cause his sharp ears to flutter. A visit to the veterinarian was indicated.

The doctor kept Chauncey under observation a few days, then called us in. "This cat of yours," he pronounced, rather testily, I thought, "is in a heck of a fix. He's allergic to cat fur!"

Chauncey was in no position to hock his fur coat or otherwise jump out of his skin, so he had to make the best of it. He soon found he got a lot of sympathy, and even extra sardines, which he adored, whenever he went into the whooping bit, and began getting them every half-hour. Chauncey was an opportunist.

He took full advantage of Mac's good nature and used the Scottie's shaggy coat for claw-sharpening exercise without once drawing a protest. He insisted on going along whenever I walked Mac. Possibly under the delusion that he, too, was a dog, he used the trees the same way Mac did, to the amazement of the oldest inhabitants.

The strange cat invented a game in which Mac was an unwitting patsy. When we neared home from a walk, the Scottie was allowed off his leash to run free up a long walk to the porch. Chauncey took to racing him up the walk and porch steps, winning easily every time.

Bored by these hollow victories, Chauncey devised a handicap system. He'd give the dog a head-start, increasing it each day until the cat would win only by inches. One day he overestimated himself. He drew the handicap so fine that Mac beat him to the wire by a whisker.

Losing this close one enraged Chauncey, and he cuffed the Scottie all over the porch. Next day, he cut out the handicap and beat the dog from scratch by yards. Then he went back cautiously to giving Mac a head-start—but never again one big enough to leave the result in doubt.

Chauncey was a highly accomplished mouser, but something usually spoiled his triumphs. One evening he caught a tiny mouse in the attic. I had instructed him early in his career to take his catches outside. He was a smart one. All you had to do was hold the door open for him and out he'd go, mouse and all.

Well, on this occasion, I heard the wailing signal the cat always made on scoring a catch, and I hurriedly opened the back door for him. Chauncey was close behind me and traveling fast with his mouse. Suddenly, there was a crash—and Chauncey was out cold on the floor, the mouse escaping in the confusion. I had neglected to open the screen door, and Chauncey had hit it head-on.

Early one morning, Chauncey became a very temporary hero. We were awakened by his plaintive wailing in the kitchen, where he and Mac had their bed. I went downstairs to see what the trouble was. The kitchen was full of gas pouring from two open jets. on the range. With a final wail, Chauncey swooned. I turned off the jets and opened the door to the yard. Sturdy little Mac waddled out under his own power. I had to carry Chauncey out.

"Just think of it," I said to my wife, 'if it hadn't been for Chauncey, we might all have been asphyxiated. Chauncey is a hero."

"Some hero!" she replied. "Who do you think turned on those gas jets but that dumb cat?" She was right.

When we sold this house, we tried taking Chauncey with us to live in an apartment a mile away. There was an elderly lady to see us off. She was loaded with advice on cats. "Smear his paws with butter before you start out for your new place," she said. "Otherwise, he'll find his way back here."

So we buttered Chauncey's paws and drove him over to our new quarters. He gratefully licked off the butter and asked for more. When it wasn't forthcoming, he muttered something, leaped out a window, and scurried right back to our old house. Fortunately, the new owners took him in. I still wonder, as a matter of science, if he'd have found his way back if he hadn't licked the butter off his paws.

Amber, who helped raise Willie before passing away last year, once starred in a performance which, I imagine, still has the older feline set wagging their heads in disbelief. When he was about a year old, we looked out the back window of our present house one day and did a double-take. Amber was lying listlessly in a corner of the yard under a faucet, from which water was dripping slowly on his head. All around him, in solemn conclave, sat a dozen older cats studying him with scientific absorption.

Hours later, they were still there. So was Amber, his little golden brow sopping wet. We tiptoed through the hushed circle of older cats and carted our seemingly daft Amber off to the doctor. We told him what he'd been up to.

"He has a fever," the doctor explained, "and he was just trying to cool his hot head under the faucet."

It developed that the cat was suffering from leucopenia, a blood disorder. "Better give him up," we were advised, but we demurred. We've never yet given up on a pet, intensely disliking the mawkish "Put him to sleep." The doctor shrugged and said we might try a diet of corn syrup and orange juice on the cat. We did, and his peaked little face was covered with the goo for weeks—but he recovered.

Cats are the cleanest of all domestic animals. With them, the business of washing is not only a necessity; it is a pleasure, an exercise, and takes on, in most cases, an almost religious intensity.

While their generally accepted diet consists of raw meat or a good grade of prepared cat food, cats, like human beings, have strange food preferences. One of my cats is so crazy about cantaloupe he will even eat the rinds. A neighbor who is a backyard gardener tells me he has had to give up growing tomatoes, because his Maltese tom raids the vines and devours the tomatoes as fast as they ripen. I've even heard, without verification, that some cats have a taste for olives! A friend of mine owns two cats, both from the same litter. Both prefer the same type of meat, but one will eat it only raw, while the other insists it must be cooked. My friend is convinced that this is due not to their preferences, but to their determination to let him know who's the boss.

In these days of tension, human beings can learn a great deal about relaxation from watching a cat, who doesn't just lie down when it is time to rest, but pours his body on the floor and rests in every nerve and muscle. We can also learn much from him about patience and determination. Once a cat's mind is made up you can't change it or its purpose. He will keep at you, using every wile he has until he gets his way, sticking with it sometimes even for days.

One of the things I've learned about cats is their willingness to share with friends—an unexpected streak of generosity in animals supposed to be selfish loners. This was demonstrated strikingly one evening by one of our first cats, a big, timid tom named Barney. At mealtimes his big head was always framed in the kitchen window, and if I were off on urgent business at the time, he'd come running when my wife called.

This evening, Barney's food was ready, but he was nowhere in sight at the window, so my wife called him. However, instead of Barney leaping gracefully into the kitchen, there lumbered in the ugliest old tomcat my wife had ever seen; a tramp with torn ears, matted coat, and bleary eyes. But he had a congenial smirk on his face and uttered a jovial growl as he waddled over to eat Barney's dinner.

The lady of the house was so astonished, she froze near the window, and her first panicky thought was that the big bum had done our Barney in. But she heard a reassuring sound from the yard below. It was Barney, sitting contentedly under the window and talking up to her in an excited chirrup. "He was telling me," she said later, "that he had brought a friend home for dinner."

Smoky, a beautiful Maltese tom who adopted us one day, also displayed this generous streak—but he knew when to stop. He fell in love with a homeless but immaculate black tabby who fled at the sight of a human yet looked as plump and sleek as any house cat.

I often watched Smoky coax his girl-friend out from the hedges in back of our house and try to show her how to climb to the high kitchen window. He would do it himself, then talk to her encouragingly, but she never could muster the courage to try it. We often fed Smoky in the backyard, and he'd call to her to come join him.

Quite suddenly, the black tabby disappeared from the scene. One night, during a thunderstorm, we heard a kitten yowling in the yard. I went out with my flashlight and, under a hedge I found a tiny jet-black kitten. I brought her into the house and we fed her with an eye-dropper. Smoky came into the kitchen, glowered at this sudden threat to his sovereignty, and went upstairs to brood. The next day was bright and sunny, and we put the kitten out

CATS. Jean Louis Gericault. *Courtesy Louvre, Paris*

into the yard in a little box for some fresh air. Smoky, who had been sunning himself, jumped up and disappeared down the driveway into the street. A half-hour later we saw him running up the driveway again, but he wasn't alone. At his side was the wild black tabby, and he kept chattering to her all the way into the backyard.

Strong as the female's maternal instinct was, she couldn't overcome her fear of humans. She held back, but kept calling urgently to the kitten in the box, obviously her kitten. We left the mewing infant in the box and went into the house. The black cat at once ran to the box, picked the kitten out in her mouth, and went off with her.

When she had disappeared, Smoky strutted into the house leering triumphantly. His strategy was simple and effective. Figuring we might have been tempted to keep the kitten, he had gone off to some secret rendezvous with the mother cat and told her the terrible things that were happening to her baby.

He had been willing to share his home with the black tabby, but not with her kitten!

One of the most generous cats I ever met was a female who had been taught by her owner to hammer on the back door when she wanted in or out. That worked fine, until the cat broadened her acquaintance. Apparently, she informed her new friends that the groceries were pretty good at her house, led them one by one to the back door, and taught them how to knock.

"Now, when I hear a knocking," the owner told me, "I never know whether it's my cat or whether, when I open the door, six strangers will walk in."

We once had a seductive female cat named Boots who first charmed us into taking her in and then proceeded to charm all the toms for miles around. Perhaps some of her allure was due to a strange yen she had for vitamin pills of a certain brand. She practically lived on them and such strange items of feline diet as cake and carrots.

When she gave birth to a litter of four perfectly matched striped kittens, she became a tender, solicitous mother, but only long enough to see them established in our house. Then she reverted to her playgirl ways and chased her babies indoors whenever a tomcat dandy swaggered up the path.

We finally decided to give Boots away to a man with a house at the beach a few miles away, and early one morning I set out with her in a basket to walk to his house. It was just getting light. I became conscious that I was being followed, and I turned around. There, walking behind me in a silent single file, were a dozen of the most eligible cat bachelors in the neighborhood. And they kept following Boots—and me—all the way to the beach.

One eccentric cat I met—and let this be a lesson to cat-owners who keep their pets cooped up in city apartments—got real neurotic in the residential hotel where he lived and imagined himself a dog.

He showed this by becoming one of those retrieving pests you find so often among our canine friends. If you came visiting, this befuddled cat would bring a ball over to you as soon as you sat down and drop it appealingly at your feet. For a cat-lover like me, this was a pitiful sight, because normal cats are above learning such trite tricks.

A far more useful trick, for my money, is that of a tabby who can tell time. The owner who told me about it explained that this cat sleeps in his bedroom through the night. His alarm clock customarily went off at 8 A.M. But one night the electric power was interrupted in his house. When, at two minutes after eight, according to his watch, the alarm hadn't rung, the cat jumped on the bed and slapped him in the face! On the following nights he experimented, and discovered that he didn't need the alarm clock at all; he could depend on the cat. The only drawback was that on Saturday nights he had to put the cat in the cellar if he hoped to enjoy a late Sunday-morning snooze.

Two of the nuttiest cats I've ever run across were a father and daughter who lived in a New York bar and grill. The father's name was Blackie; his daughter's, Sheila. Now, there's nothing in the world cats need less than money, but Blackie and Sheila risked life and limb daily to steal it.

They stole the customers' change off the bar, and the instant the cash drawer opened, one or the other would leap on it swiftly and fish out bills—singles, fives, or tens—they didn't care which as long as it was folding money. When they snatched a bill, they'd all but fly with it to the cellar or some other nook and tear it to bits.

"At first," the bartender reported bitterly, "only Blackie stole. The daughter picked it up from him. I'd like to give them away, but who'd take them in with records like they got?"

Remind me to stay away from that bar and grill!

One question people frequently ask is: Why aren't licenses required for cats the same as for dogs? Not long ago I put the question to our local "dogcatcher." His answer, I think, confirms all I have said about the independent spirit, resourcefulness, and charming lunacy of my beloved furry friends. He said: "Why don't we license cats? Because, first, you've got to catch a cat. Did you ever try to catch a cat?"

THE FAT CAT

BY *Q. Patrick*

THE MARINES FOUND HER WHEN they finally captured the old mission house at Fufa. After two days of relentless pounding, they hadn't expected to find anything alive there—least of all a fat cat.

And she was a very fat cat, sandy as a Scotchman, with enormous agate eyes and a fat amiable face. She sat there on the mat—or rather what was left of the mat—in front of what had been the mission porch, licking her paws as placidly as if the shell-blasted jungle were a summer lawn in New Jersey.

One of the men, remembering his childhood primer, quoted: 'The fat cat sat on the mat."

The other men laughed; not that the remark was really funny, but laughter broke the tension and expressed their relief at having at last reached their objective, after two days of bitter fighting.

The fat cat, still sitting on the mat, smiled at them, as if to show she didn't mind the joke being on her. Then she saw Corporal Randy Jones, and for some reason known only to herself ran toward him as though he was her long-lost master. With a refrigerator purr, she weaved in and out of his muddy legs.

Everyone laughed again as Randy picked her up and pushed his ugly face against the sleek fur. It was funny to see any living thing show a preference for the dour, solitary Randy.

A sergeant flicked his fingers. 'Kitty. Come here. We'll make you B Company mascot."

But the cat, perched on Randy's shoulder like a queen on her throne, merely smiled down majestically as much as to say: "You can be my subjects if you like. But this is my man—my royal consort."

And never for a second did she swerve from her devotion. She lived with Randy, slept with him, ate only food provided by him.

C<small>AT AND</small> S<small>NAKE</small>. Katherine Schmidt. *Courtesy The Metropolitan Museum of Art*

Almost every man in Co. B tried to seduce her with caresses and morsels of canned ration, but all advances were met with a yawn of contempt.

For Randy this new love was ecstasy. He guarded her with the possessive tenderness of a mother. He combed her fur sleek; he almost starved himself to maintain her fatness. And all the time there was a strange wonder in him. The homeliest and ungainliest of ten in a West Virginia mining family, he had never before aroused affection in man or woman. No one had counted for him until the fat cat.

Randy's felicity, however, was short-lived. In a few days B Company was selected to carry out a flanking movement to surprise and possibly capture the enemy's headquarters, known to be twenty miles away through dense, sniper-infested jungle. The going would be rugged. Each man would carry his own supply of food and water, and sleep in foxholes with no support from the base.

The C.O. was definite about the fat cat: the stricken Randy was informed that the presence of a cat would seriously endanger the safety of the whole company. If it were seen following him, it would be shot on sight. Just before their scheduled departure, Randy carried the fat cat over to the mess of Co. H, where she was enthusiastically received by an equally fat cook. Randy could not bring himself to look back at the reproachful stare which he knew would be in the cat's agate eyes.

But all through that first day of perilous jungle travel, the thought of the cat's stare haunted him, and he was prey to all the heartache of parting; in leaving the cat, he had left behind wife, mother, and child.

Darkness, like an immense black parachute, had descended hours ago on the jungle, when Randy was awakened from exhausted sleep. Something soft and warm was brushing his cheek; and his foxhole resounded to a symphony of purring. He stretched out an incredulous hand, but this was no dream. Real and solid, the cat was curled in a contented ball at his shoulder.

His first rush of pleasure was chilled as he remembered his C.O.'s words. The cat, spurning the blandishments of H Co.'s cuisine, had followed him through miles of treacherous jungle, only to face death the moment daylight revealed her presence. Randy was in an agony of uncertainty. To carry her back to the base would be desertion. To beat and drive her away was beyond the power of his simple nature.

The cat nuzzled his face again and breathed a mournful meow. She was hungry, of course, after her desperate trek. Suddenly Randy saw what he must do. If he could bring himself not to feed her, hunger would surely drive her back to the sanctuary of the cook.

She meowed again. He shushed her and gave her a half-hearted slap. "Aint got nothing for you, honey. Scram. Go home. Scat."

To his mingled pleasure and disappointment, she leaped silently out of the foxhole. When morning came there was no sign of her.

As B Company inched its furtive advance through the dense undergrowth, Randy felt the visit from the cat must have been a dream. But on the third night it came again. It brushed against his cheek and daintily took his ear in its teeth. When it meowed, the sound was still soft and cautious, but held a pitiful quaver of beseechment which cut through Randy like a Jap bayonet.

On its first visit, Randy had not seen the cat, but tonight some impulse made him reach for his flashlight. Holding it carefully downward, he turned it on. What he saw was the ultimate ordeal. The fat cat was fat no longer. Her body sagged; her sleek fur was matted and mud-stained, her paws torn and bloody. But it was the eyes, blinking up at him, that were the worst. There was no hint of reproach in them, only an expression of infinite trust and pleading.

Forgetting everything but those eyes, Randy tugged out one of his few remaining cans of ration. At the sight of it, the cat weakly licked its lips. Randy moved to open the can. Then the realization that he would be signing the cat's death warrant surged over him. And, because the pent-up emotion of him had to have some outlet, it turned into unreasoning anger against this animal whose suffering had become more than he could bear. "Skat," he hissed. But the cat did not move.

He lashed out at her with the heavy flashlight. For a second she lay motionless under the blow. Then with a little moan she fled.

The next night she did not come back and Randy did not sleep.

On the fifth day they reached really dangerous territory. Randy and another marine, Joe, were sent forward to scout for the Jap command headquarters. Suddenly, weaving through the jungle, they came upon it.

A profound silence hung over the glade, with its two hastily erected shacks. Peering through dense foliage, they saw traces of recent evacuation—waste paper scattered on the grass, a pile of fresh garbage, a Jap army shirt flapping on a tree. Outside one of the shacks, under an awning, stretched a rough table strewn with the remains of a meal. "They must have got wind of us and scrammed," breathed Joe.

Randy edged forward—then froze as something stirred in the long grasses near the door of the first shack. As he watched, the once fat cat hobbled out into the sunlight.

A sense of heightened danger warred with Randy's pride that she had not abandoned him. Stiff with suspense, he watched it disappear into the shack. Soon it padded out.

"No Japs," said Joe. "That cat'd have raised 'em sure as shooting."

He started boldly into the glade. "Hey, Randy, there's a whole chicken on that table. Chicken's going to taste good after K ration."

He broke off, for the cat had seen the chicken too, and with pitiful clumsiness had leaped onto the table. With an angry yell Joe stooped for a rock and threw it.

Indignation blazed in Randy. He'd starved and spurned the cat, and yet she'd followed him with blind devotion. The chicken, surely, should be her reward. In his slow, simple mind it seemed the most important thing in the world for his beloved to have her fair share of the booty.

The cat, seeing the rock coming, lumbered off the table just in time, for the rock struck the chicken squarely, knocking it off its plate.

Randy leaped into the clearing. As he did so, a deafening explosion made him drop to the ground. A few seconds later, when he raised himself, there was no table, no shack, nothing but a blazing wreckage of wood.

❧

Dazedly he heard Joe's voice: "Booby trap under that chicken. Gee, if that cat hadn't jumped for it, I wouldn't have hurled the rock; we'd have grabbed it ourselves—and we'd be in heaven now." His voice dropped to an awed whisper. "That cat. I guess it's blown to hell . . . But it saved our lives." Randy couldn't speak. There was a constriction in his throat. He lay there, feeling more desolate than he'd ever felt in his life before.

Then from behind came a contented purr.

He spun round. Freakishly, the explosion had hurled a crude rush mat out of the shack. It had come to rest on the grass behind him.

And, seated serenely on the mat, the cat was smiling at him.

THE SONG OF MEHITABEL

BY *don marquis*

this is the song of mehitabel
of mehitabel the alley cat
as i wrote you before boss
mehitabel is a believer
in the pythagorean
theory of the transmigration
of the soul and she claims
that formerly her spirit
was incarnated in the body
of cleopatra

that was a long time ago
and one must not be
surprised if mehitabel
has forgotten some of her
more regal manners

i have had my ups and downs
but wotthehell wotthehell
yesterday sceptres and crowns
fried oysters and velvet gowns
and today i herd with bums
but wotthehell wotthehell

there's a dance in the old
dame yet. George Herri-
man. *From Archy and Me-
hitabel* by Don Marquis,
Copyright 1933 by Double-
day and Co., Inc.

i wake the world from sleep
as i caper and sing and leap
when i sing my wild free tune
wotthehell wotthehell
under the blear eyed moon
i am pelted with cast off shoon
but wotthehell wotthehell

do you think that i would change
my present freedom to range
for a castle or moated grange
wotthehell wotthehell
cage me and i d go frantic
my life is so romantic
capricious and corybantic
and i m toujours gai toujours gai

i know that i am bound
for a journey down the sound
in the midst of a refuse mound
but wotthehell wotthehell
oh i should worry and fret
death and i will coquette
there s a dance in the old dame yet
toujours gai toujours gai

i once was an innocent kit
wotthehell wotthehell
with a ribbon my neck to fit
and bells tied onto it
o wotthehell wotthehell
but a maltese cat came by
with a come hither look in his eye
and a song that soared to the sky
and wotthehell wotthehell
and i followed adown the street
the pad of his rhythmical feet
o permit me again to repeat
wotthehell wotthehell

my youth i shall never forget
but there s nothing i really regret
wotthehell wotthehell
there s a dance in the old dame yet
toujours gai toujours gai

the things that i had not ought to
i do because i ve gotto
wotthehell wotthehell
and i end with my favorite motto
toujours gai toujours gai

boss sometimes i think
that our friend mehitabel
is a trifle too gay

THE HAPPY CAT

LIVES OF TWO CATS

BY *Pierre Loti*

I HAVE OFTEN SEEN, with a questioning restlessness infinitely
sad, the soul of animals meet mine from the depths of their
eyes: the soul of a cat, the soul of a dog, the soul of a monkey, as
pathetically, for an instant, as a human soul, revealing itself suddenly in a glance and seeking my own soul with tenderness,
supplication, or terror; and I have felt perhaps more pity for these
souls of animals than for those of my own brethren, because they
are speechless, incapable of emerging from their semi-intelligence;
above all, because they are more humble and despised.

The two cats whose histories I am about to write are associated
in memory with comparatively happy years of my life,—years
scarce past by the dates they bear, but years already seeming in the

remote past, borne away by the frightfully accelerating speed of time, and which, placed beside the gray to-day, bear tints of early dawn or last rosy light of morning. So fast our days hasten to the twilight, so fast our fall to the night.

Pardon me that I call each of my cats Pussy. At first I had no idea of giving names to my pets. A cat was "Pussy," a kitten "Kitty;" and surely no names could be more expressive and tender than these. I shall call the poor little personages of my story by the names they bore in their real lives, Pussy White and Pussy Gray; the latter often known as Pussy Chinese.

As the oldest, allow me first to present the Angora, Pussy White. Her visiting card, by her desire, was thus inscribed—

MADAME MOUMOUTTE BLANCHE
PREMIÈRE CHATTE

Chez M. Pierre Loti.

On a memorable evening nearly twelve years ago, I saw her for the first time. It was a winter's evening, on one of my returns home at the close of some Eastern campaign. I had been in the house but a few moments, and was warming myself before a blazing wood fire, seated between my mother and my aunt Clara. Suddenly something appeared on the scene, bounding like a panther, and then rolling itself wildly on the hearth rug like a live snowball on its crimson ground. "Ah!" said aunt Clara, "you don't know her; I will introduce her; this is our new inmate, Pussy White! We thought we would have another cat, for a mouse had found our closet in the saloon below."

The house had been catless for a long time; succeeding the mourning for a certain African cat that I had brought home from my first voyage and worshiped for two years, but who one fine morning, after a short illness, breathed out her little foreign soul, giving me her last conscious glance, and whom I had afterward buried beneath a tree in the garden.

I lifted for a closer view the roll of fur which lay so white on the crimson mat. I held her carefully with both hands, in a position cats immediately comprehend, and say to themselves, "Here is a man who understands us; his caresses we can gratefully condescend to receive."

The face of the new cat was very prepossessing. The young, brilliant eyes, the tip of a pink nose, and all else lost in a mass of silken Angora fur; white, warm, clean, exquisite to fondle and caress. Besides, she was marked nearly like her predecessor from Senegal, which fact probably decided the selection of my mother and aunt Clara,—to the end that I might finally regard the two as one, in my somewhat fickle affections. Above the cat's eyes, a capote shaped spot, jet black in color, was set straight, forming a band over the bright eyes; another and larger spot, shaped like a cape, lay over her shoulders; a plumy black tail, moving like a superb train or an animated fly-brush, completed the costume. Her breast, belly, and paws were white as the down of a swan; her "total" gave me the impression of a ball of animated fur; light, soft, and moved by some capricious hidden spring. After making my acquaintance, Pussy White left my arms to recommence her play. And in these first moments of arrival, inevitably melancholy, because they marked another epoch in my life, the new black and white obliged me to busy my thoughts with her, jumping on my knee to reiterate my welcome, or stretching herself with feigned weariness on the floor, that I might better admire the silken whiteness of her belly and neck. So she gambolled, the new cat, while my eyes rested with tender remembrances on the two dear faces which smiled on me, somewhat aged and framed in grayer curls; upon the family portraits which preserved their expression and age in their frames upon the walls; upon the thousand objects seen in their accustomed places; upon the well known furniture of this hereditary dwelling immovably fixed there, while my unquiet, restless, changing being had roamed over a changing world.

And this is the persistent, distinct image of our Pussy White, with me still, long after her death: an embodied frolic in fur, snowy white and bounding or rolling on the crimson rug between the sombre black robes of my mother and aunt Clara, in the evening of one of my great returns.

Poor Pussy! During the first winter of her life she was usually the familiar demon, the hearthstone imp, who enlivened the loneliness of the blessed guardians of my home, my mother and aunt Clara. While I sailed over distant seas, when the house resumed its grand emptiness, in sombre twilights and interminable December nights, she was their constant attendant, though often their tormentor; leaving upon their immaculate black gowns, precisely alike, tufts of her white fur. With reckless indiscretion she took forcible possession of a place on their laps, their work table, or in the centre of their work baskets, tangling beyond rearrangement their skeins of wool, their reels of silk. Then they would say with great pretense of anger, meanwhile longing to laugh, "Oh! that cat, that bad cat, she will never learn how to behave herself! Get out, miss! Get out! Were there ever such actions as these!" They busied themselves inventing methods for her amusement, even to keeping a jumping-jack, a ludicrous wooden toy, for her special edification.

She loved them cattishly, with indocility, but added thereto a touching constancy, for which alone her little incomplete and fantastic existence merits my lasting remembrance.

In springtime, when the March sun began to brighten our courtyard, she experienced new and endless surprises in seeing, awake and crawling from his winter retreat, our tortoise Suleïma, her fellow resident and friend.

During the beautiful month of May she seemed seized by yearnings for space and freedom; then she made excursions on the walls, the roof, through the lanes, in the neighboring gardens, and even nocturnal absences, which I should here state were unacccountable in the austere circle where fate had placed her.

In summer she was languid as a creole. For entire days she lay lazily in the sunshine on the old wall top among the honeysuckles and roses, or, extended on the tiled walks, turned her white belly to the sun amidst the pots of red or golden cacti.

Extremely careful of her little person, always neat, correct, aristocratic, even to the ends of her toes, she was haughtily disdainful of other cats, and conducted herself as if ill bred if any neighbor cat called on her. In this courtyard, which she considered her own domain, she conceded no right of entry. If, above the adjoining garden wall, two ear tips, a cat's nose, rose timidly, or if something stirred in the vines or moss, she upsprang like a young fury, bristling angrily to the tip of her tail, impossible to restrain, quite beside herself! Cries in harsh tones and bad taste followed, struggles, blows, and savage clawings.

In fact, our pet was ferociously independent. She was also extremely affectionate when so inclined, caressing, cajoling, uttering so gentle a cry of joy, a tremulous "miaou" every time she returned from one of her vagabond tramps in the vicinity.

She was then five years old, in the mature beauty of an Angora, with superb attitudes of dignity and the graces of a queen. I had become much attached to her in the course of my absences and returns, considering her one of our home treasures, when there appeared on the scene—three thousand miles afar in the Gulf of Pekin, and of a far less distinguished family than the Angoras—the kitten destined to become her inseparable friend, the most unique little personage I have yet known, "Pussy Gray" or "Pussy Chinese."

MADAME MOUMOUTTE CHINOISE
DEUXIÈME CHATTE

Chez M. Pierre Loti.

Most singular was the destiny which united to me this cat of the yellow race, progeny of obscure parentage and destitute of all beauty.

It was at the close of our last foreign war, one of those evenings of revelry which often occurred at that time. I know not how the little distraught creature, driven from some wrecked junk or sampan, came on board our warship, in great terror, seeking a refuge in my cabin beneath my berth. She was young, not half grown, thin and melancholy, having doubtless, like her relatives and masters subsisted meanly on fishes' heads with a bit of cooked rice. I pitied her much and bade my servant give her food and drink.

With an unmistakable air of humility and gratitude she accepted my kindness,—and I can see her now, creeping slowly toward the unhoped-for repast, advancing first one foot, then another, her clear eyes fixed on mine to assure herself that she was not deceived, that it was really intended for her.

In the morning I wished to turn her away. After giving her a farewell breakfast, I clapped my hands loudly, and stamping both feet together by way of emphasis, I said in a harsh tone, "Get out, go away, little Kitty!"

But no, she did not go, the little pagan. Evidently she felt no fear of me, intuitively certain that all this angry noise was a pretense. With an air that seemed to say, "I know very well that you will not harm me," she crouched silently in the corner, lying close to the floor in a supplicating attitude, fixing upon me two dilated eyes, alight with a human look that I have never seen except in hers.

What could I do? Impossible to domicile a cat in the contracted cabin of a warship. Besides, she was such a distressingly homely little creature, what an encumbrance by and by!

Then I lifted her carefully to my neck, saying to her, "I am very sorry, Kitty;" but I carried her resolutely the length of the deck, to the further end of the battery, to the sailors' quarters, who usually are both fond of and kind to cats of whatever age or pedigree.

Flattened close to the deck, her head imploringly turned towards me, she gave me one beseeching look; then rose and fled with a queer and swift gait in the direction of my cabin, where she arrived first in the race between us; when I entered I found her crouched obstinately in the corner from which I had taken her, with an expression, a remonstrance in her golden eyes, that deprived me of all courage to again take her away. And this is the way by which Pussy Chinese chose me for her owner and protector.

My servant, evidently on her side from the début of the contest, completed immediate preparations for her installment in my cabin, by placing beneath my bed a lined basket for her bed, and one of my large Chinese bowls, very practically filled with sand; an arrangement which froze me with fright.

Day and night she lived for seven months in the dim light and unceasing movement of my cabin, and gradually an intimacy was established between us, simultaneously with a faculty of mutual comprehension very rare between man and animal.

I recall the first day when our relations became truly affectionate. We were far out in the Yellow Sea, in gloomy September weather. The first autumnal fogs had gathered over the suddenly cooled and restless waters. In these latitudes cold and cloud come suddenly, bringing to us European voyagers a sadness whose intensity is proportioned to our distance from home. We were steaming eastward against a long swell which had arisen, and rocked in dismal monotony to the plaintive groans and creakings of the ship. It had become necessary to close my port, and the cabin received its sole light through the thick bull's-eye, past which the crests of the waves swept in green translucency, making intermittent obscurity. I had seated myself to write at the little sliding table, the same in all our cabins on board,—during one of those rare moments, when our service allows a complete freedom and peace, and when the longing comes to be alone as in a cloister.

Pussy Gray had lived under my berth for nearly two weeks. She had behaved with great circumspection; melancholy, showing herself seldom, keeping in darkest corners as if suffering from homesickness and pining for the land to which there was no return.

Suddenly she came forth from the shadows, stretched herself leisurely, as if giving time for farther reflection, then moved towards me, still hesitating with abrupt stops; at times affecting a peculiarly Chinese gesture, she raised a fore paw, holding it in the air some seconds before deciding to make another advancing step; and all this time her eyes were fixed on mine with infinite solicitude.

What did she want of me? She was evidently not hungry: suitable food was given her by my servant twice daily. What then could it be?

When she was sufficiently near to touch my leg, she sat down, curled her tail about her, and uttered a very low mew; and still looked directly in my eyes, as if they could communicate with hers, which showed a world of intelligent conception in her little brain. She must first have learned, like other superior animals, that I was not a thing, but a thinking being, capable of pity and influenced by the mute appeal of a look; besides, she felt that my eyes were for her eyes, that they were mirrors, where her little soul sought anxiously to seize a reflection of mine. Truly they are startlingly near us, when we reflect upon it, animals capable of such inferences.

As to myself, I studied for the first time the little visitor who for two weeks had shared my lodging: she was fawn-colored like a wild rabbit, mottled with darker spots like a tiger, her nose and neck were white; homely in effect, mainly consequent on her extremely thin and sickly condition, and really more odd looking than homely to a man freed like myself from all conventional ideas of beauty. Besides, she was quite unlike our French cats: low on the legs, very long bodied, a tail of unusual length, large upright ears, and a triangular face; all her charm was in the eyes, raised at the outer corners like all eyes of the extreme Orient, of a fine golden yellow instead of green, and ever changing, astonishingly expressive.

While examining her, I laid my hand gently upon her queer little head, stroking the brown fur in a first caress.

Whatever she experienced was an emotion beyond mere physical pleasure; she felt the sentiment of a protection, a pity for her condition of an abandoned foundling. This, then, was why she came out of her retreat, poor Pussy Gray; this was why she resolved, after so much hesitation, to beg from me not food or drink, but, for the solace of her lonely cat soul, a little friendly company and interest.

Where had she learned to know that, this miserable outcast, never stroked by a kind hand, never loved by any one,—if not perhaps in the paternal junk, by some poor Chinese child without playthings, and without caresses, thrown by chance like a useless weed in the immense yellow swarm, miserable and hungry as herself, and whose incomplete soul in departing, left behind no more trace than her own?

Then a frail paw was laid timidly upon me—oh! with so much delicacy, so much discretion!—and after looking at me a long time beseechingly, she decided to venture upon my knee. Jumping there lightly she curled herself in a light, small mass, making herself small as possible and almost without weight, never taking her eyes from me. She lay a long time thus, much in my way, but I had not the heart to dislodge her, which I should doubtless have done had she been a gay pretty kitten in the bloom of kittenhood. As if in fear at my least movement, she watched me incessantly, not fearing that I should harm her—she was too intelligent to think me capable of that—but with an air that seemed to ask: "Is it true that I do not weary you, that I do not trouble you?" and then, her eyes growing still more tender and expressive, saying to mine very plainly: "On this dismal autumn day, so depressing to the soul of cats, since we two are here so lonely, in this abode so strange, so unquiet, shaken and lost amid I know not what dangerous and endless space, can we not give to each other a little of that sweet thing, immaterial and beyond the power of death, which is called affection and which sometimes shows itself in a caress?"

As soon as the treaty of friendship was signed between this cat and myself, anxieties arose within me concerning her future. What could I do with her? Carry her to France over so many thousand miles and difficulties innumerable? To be sure, my home would be for her the unhoped-for asylum where the short mysterious dream of her little life would pass with least suffering and most peace. But I could not see, without forebodings, this sickly, illy-robed foreigner the fellow resident of our superb Pussy White, so jealous, who would certainly drive her from the premises as soon as she appeared. No, that was impossible.

On the other side, to abandon her at our next port of call, among chance new friends—that was equally impossible; I could have done so had she been vigorous and beautiful, but this melancholy little creature, with her human eyes, held me to her by a profound pity.

Our intimacy, founded on mutual loneliness, constantly increased. Weeks and months passed, on the never resting seas, while all remained the same in the obscure corner of the ship where Pussy had chosen her abode. For us men who sail the seas there are

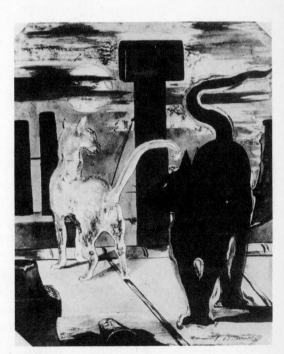

MEETING OF TWO
CATS. Edouard
Manet

always the strong winds that buffet us, the starry nights on deck, and the goings on shore in foreign ports—always some event to break the monotony of sea life. She, on the contrary, knew nothing of the vast world over which her prison moved, nothing of her kindred, or of the sun, or of verdure, or of shade. And, never going outside, she lived in the solitude of my narrow cabin; it was a glacial place at times when the door swung open to the fierce wind sweeping the decks; oftener it was a hot and stifling furnace, where Chinese incense burned before the expatriated idols as if in a Buddhist temple. For companions in her musings she had monsters in wood or bronze, fixed to the walls, and grinning with malicious laughter; in the midst of a mass of relics of things sacred in her country, pillaged from dwellings and temples, she wasted away, without air, among the silken hangings that she loved to tear with her restless little claws.

As soon as I entered my cabin she would come forward with her soft welcoming cry of joy, springing like a jack in the box from behind some curtain, desk, or chest. If by chance I seated myself to write, she very slyly, very tenderly, seeking protection and caresses, would softly take her place on my knees and follow the comings and goings of my pen,—sometimes effacing, with an unintentional stroke of her paw, lines of whose tenor she disapproved.

The shocks, the pitchings of the ship in rough weather, the noise of our cannon, gave her great terror: at these times, she threw herself against the walls, spun around like a mad creature, after which she would stop breathless, and hide herself in the darkest corner, with a terrified and sad expression.

Her cloistered youth resulted in an unnatural state of invalidism, becoming daily more and more pronounced. Her appetite continued normal, but she was emaciated, her face grew, if possible, more triangular, her ears pointed sharply and bat-like, her large golden eyes sought mine with an air of distress, uncomfortably humanlike, or with questionings on the problem of life, perhaps equally troubling and far more unanswerable to her little intelligence than to my own.

She was very curious about outside matters, despite her unaccountable determination never to cross the threshold of my door, and never failed to examine with extreme attention any new object brought to our common lodging, probably giving her confused impressions of the foreign ports where our ship called. In India, for example, I remember she was once deeply interested, even to the total neglect of her breakfast, in a bouquet of fragrant orchids,—so extraordinary for her who had never known garden or forest, never seen other than the withered or dead flowers in my bronze vases. As an offset to her rough and discolored fur, which at first sight gave her a gutter-cat air, she was finely formed, and the least movement of her delicate paws was of patrician grace. While watching her, I sometimes fancied her some little enchanted princess, condemned by wicked fairies to share my solitude in this lowly guise; and I called to mind a story of the mother of the great Tchengiz-Khan, which an old Armenian priest of Constantinople, my teacher of the Turkish language, had given me to translate:

"The young princess Ulemalik-Kurekli, doomed before her birth to die if she beheld the light of day, lived shut up in an obscure dungeon. And she asked her servants: 'Is this what they call the world? Tell me, is there anything else outside these walls? is this tower in something?'

" 'No, princess, this is not the world: that is outside and very much larger. And there are also things they call stars, that they call sun and they call moon.'

" 'Oh!' replied Ulemalik, 'let me die, but let me see them!' "

It was at the close of winter, one of the first warm days of March, that Pussy Chinese made her début at my home in France. Pussy White still wore at that season her royal winter robe, and I had never seen her more imposing. The contrast would be the more overwhelming for my poor favorite, lean, lank, with her faded fawn-colored fur looking as if moth-eaten. I felt myself much embarrassed when our man Sylvester, returning with my pet from the ship, lifted, with a half disdainful air, the cover of the basket where he had placed her, and I saw, in the midst of the assembled family, my little Chinese friend creep tremblingly forth.

Most deplorable was her first appearance. I felt the impression of the group in Aunt Clara's simple exclamation: "Oh! my friend, how homely she is!"

Homely indeed! And in what way, under what pretense could I present her to the magnificent Pussy White? In utter helplessness

I had her carried, for the time being, to an isolated granary,—that I might gain time to reflect on the situation.

Their first interview was certainly terrible. It was unpremeditated, a few days after, in the kichen (a locality of irresistible attractions, where the cats of the same household, do what one can to prevent, will some day meet). The servants summoned me hastily and I ran to the battlefield, where, uttering unearthly yells, a shapeless package of fur and claws formed of their closely clinched little bodies, rolled and bounded,—shattering glasses, plates, and dishes, while tufts of white fur, gray fur, black fur, and fawn fur flew and floated everywhere. It was necessary to interfere energetically and instantly: to separate them I threw upon them a whole carafe of water. I was at my wits' end.

Breathless, scratched, and bleeding, her heart beating as if it must break, Pussy Gray was gathered to my breast, where she clung closely, growing more quiet in the consciousness of sweet security; then she became less and less rigid and as limp and inert as if dying, which is a way cats have of showing entire confidence in one who holds them. Pussy White, seated thoughtful and gloomy in a corner, looked at us with surprised eyes, and a deduction from the view was formed in her little jealous brain; that she, who from one year's end to the other had driven from the neighboring walls all other cats, unwilling even to endure their presence, must acknowledge this ugly pagan as mine, since I held her so tenderly, so closely; then it became necessary that she, Pussy White, should tolerate her presence in the mansion and trouble her no more.

My surprise and admiration were great to see these two, an instant after, pass by each other, not merely with indifference but calmly, civilly,—and all was ended. During their lives they never quarreled again.

❦

The springtime of the following year! How pleasant my reminiscences of its sunny days.

Very short as all seasons now seem, it was the last which held a charm for me, like the mysterious enchantment of childhood's days, passed in the same environment of verdure and bloom, in the midst of flowers blooming anew in their annual ranks, the same jasmines, the same roses. After my campaigns I joyfully returned there, to forget other continents and the immense seas; again, as in my infancy, I limited the exterior world to the old walls hung with vines and mosses, which bounded my rambles; the distant lands where I have since lived seeming unreal as those of which I dreamed, having never seen. The far horizons fade; they vanish imperceptibly and nothing is real to me save our mossy stones, our trees, our trellises, and our beloved white roses!

At that time, I had built in a corner of my mansion a Buddhist pagoda, the collected débris of original temples. From the large cases opened daily in the courtyard in the warm sunshine there arose that indefinable and mingled odor of China, from pedestals of columns, bas-reliefs of ceilings, carved altars, and mouldy old idols and vases. It was interesting and unique, this unpacking; to watch these grotesque objects reappearing one by one, arranging themselves, as it were, on the grass or the mossy pavement,—all this assembly of monsters of far Asia, bearing on their faces the same frowns and grimaces they had borne for ages. Occasionally my mother and Aunt Clara would come out to look at them, astonished at their overwhelming ugliness. Pussy Gray was the most interested spectator of these unpackings; recognizing her ocean surroundings, she sniffed all with confused memories of her native land; afterward, habituated to dwelling so long in semi-darkness, she would crawl into the boxes and hide herself in the empty spaces, under the exotic straw still smelling of sandal-wood and musk.

It was an exhilarating and beautiful springtime, bird songs filling the air; and Pussy Gray thought it marvelous. Poor little recluse, grown up in the stifling obscurity of my rolling home! Bright sunlight, balmy air, the vicinity of feline friends alike astonished and charmed her. She now made long and exhaustive explorations of the courtyard and garden, smelling every blade of grass, every new plant; in fact everything that sprang fresh and odorous from the awakened earth. These forms, these colors, old as the world, which plants unconsciously produce every succeeding spring, these immutable laws, perfectly and silently obeyed by unfolding leaf and bursting bud, were phenomena for her who had never known springtime or verdure. And Pussy White, formerly absolute and intolerant queen of the place, had deigned to share her domain with the forlorn stranger, allowing her to roam at will among the evergreens, the potted flowers, or along the promenade on the gray wall-top under the pendent boughs. Pussy Chinese was especially impressed by a minature lake, so closely interwoven with my infantile memories, which fascinated her for a long time. There, in the grass each day higher and more luxuriant, she crouched close to the earth, like a panther intent on his prey (doubtless inheriting this movement from her ancestors, Mongolian cats with uncultivated manners). She hid behind the lilliputian rocks, buried herself beneath the vines like a little tiger in a miniature virgin forest.

I found great pleasure in watching her goings and comings, her sudden haltings, her surprises; when she realized that I was watching her, she in turn watched me, posing in an attitude peculiarly her own;—very graceful, but very like a Chinese belle, with a paw extended as if holding a fan, just as I have seen one holding an article raise coquettishly the little finger; and her droll golden eyes grew infinitely expressive, "speaking" to mine. "Please permit me to amuse myself? Does it incommode you in the least? Look! I walk with lightness, I play with extreme carefulness, I go about with discretion among these beautiful green things that smell so sweetly, and this good air is so refreshing in this wide, free space! And these other strange objects that I see in turn high over us, 'Things they call stars, that they call sun, and they call moon!' Oh! how different from our trembling lodging on the ship and how delightful to be here together in this happy place!"

This home, so new to her, was equally for me the oldest, the most familiar of all places on the earth; whose least details, whose feeblest blade of grass were known to me since the earliest and most impressible days of my existence. So dear to me that I am bound to it with all my being, so dear that I love with a love akin to idolatry the old vines and shrubs which are there, the jasmine, the honeysuckles, and a certain dielytra rose, which every returning March unfolds its precocious leaves, gives the same April roses, fades in the June sun, then burns in August heat and seems to perish.

And while Pussy Gray abandons herself to the joy of youth and springtime, I, on the contrary, knowing that all this will pass away, feel for the first time in my life, shadows like those of evening stealing over my own life,—presages of the inexorable night, the morningless night of the final autumn,—never to be succeeded by spring.

And with profound sadness in this courtyard bright with sunshine, I gaze upon the two dear ones, their silvery hair, their mourning robes—my mother and Aunt Clara, going and coming, stooping down as has been their wont for many springs, to discover what flower seeds had come up, or raising their heads to see the buds of honeysuckles and rose trees. And when their sombre robes vanished from my view, at the end of the green avenue, which is the vestibule of our family residence, I am forced to notice that their steps are slower and less firm. Oh, time, perhaps near, when in the unchanging green avenue I shall behold them no more. Can it be possible that time may arrive? If ever they shall be gone I have the illusion that it will not be an entire departure, so long as I remain there recalling their presence;—that in the quiet summer evenings I shall sometimes see their spirits glide beneath the jasmine; that something of their existence will still live in the plants they have tended, and breathe from the falling honeysuckle, the old dielytra rose.

Since her life in open air, my favorite flourished visibly. The bare and unsightly spots in her rabbit-colored coat were covered with new glossy fur; she was less thin, more careful of her little person, and bore no longer the appearance of a witch's cat. My mother and Aunt Clara often stopped to speak to her, interested in her odd ways, her expressive eyes, and her soft responsive "Trr! trr! trr!" that she never failed to utter when addressed.

"Certainly," they said, "this Chinese pussy seems very happy with us; no cat's face could show greater content."

A happy look, in fact; even a look of gratitude to me, who had brought her to her new home. And the happiness of young animals is perfect, perhaps because they have not, like us, forebodings of the inevitable future.

She passed deliciously dreamy days in most luxuriant idleness, extended on the warm tiles or the soft moss, enjoying the silence—somewhat depressing to me—of this abode where neither the contention of wind and wave or the terrible shock of cannon troubled her repose. She had reached the distant peaceful haven, the last port in her short life's voyage, and rested happily unconscious of the end.

One fine day, without intervention, seized by some sudden whim, the indifference of Pussy White changed to a tender friendship. She came deliberately to Pussy Gray and rubbed her nose against her own affectionately, which is with her race the equivalent of a kiss. Sylvester, who was present at the performance, showed himself skeptical regarding its good intent. "Did you see," said I, "the kiss of peace?" "Oh no, sir!" he replied, in that tone of accomplished connoisseur, assumed whenever any question arises concerning my cats, dogs, horses, or any other animals; "Oh no, sir! it is simply that Pussy White wishes to ascertain if Pussy Gray has been stealing her meat."

He was mistaken for once nevertheless,—and from that hour they were fast friends. They could be seen sitting in the same chair, eating the same food, even from the same plate, and every morning running to exchange salutations, rubbing together the tips of their soft noses, one yellow, the other pink.

After this we said, "The cats did this or that." They were an intimate and inseparable pair, taking counsel together, following each other in the least and most trivial actions of their lives; and making their toilets together, licking each other with mutual interest.

Pussy White maintained her position as the special cat of Aunt Clara, while the Chinese continued my faithful little friend, holding fast to her old habits of following me with her speaking eyes, and replying in her expressive "Trr-trr-trr," whenever I spoke to her. Scarcely would I be seated before a light paw rested on me, as in the old evenings on the ship; two questioning eyes sought mine, then a bound and she was on my knees,—slowly making her preparations for a nap; plying her fore paws alternately, turning herself round to the right, then to the left, and usually finding the right position by the time I was ready to depart.

What a mystery! A soul's mystery perhaps, this constant affection of an animal and its unchanging gratitude.

They were much spoiled, the two cats; admitted to the dining-room at meal times; often seated one on my right and the other on my left; recalling to me, ocasionally, their presence by a light stroke of the paw on my napkin, and watching for tit-bits that I fed them surreptitiously, like a guilty schoolboy, from the tip of my fork.

In recording this, I still farther darken my reputation, which, it seems, is already reputed incorrect and eccentric. I can however criticise a certain member of the Academy, who, having done me the honor of dining at my table, did not refrain from offering to our pussies, even in his own spoon, a little Chantilly cream.

The following summer was for Pussy Gray a period of absolutely delicious life. With her originality and her foreign air, she had grown almost beautiful, so finely reclad in glossy fawn color. All around, in the cat world, in the gardens and on the roofs, the news had circulated of the presence of this piquant stranger; and candidates for her smiles were numerous; they smirked and serenaded beneath her windows in the balmy nights filled with perfume of honeysuckle and rose.

During September, the two cats experienced, at almost the same time, the joy of motherhood.

Pussy White, it is needless to relate, was already a well known matron. As to Pussy Gray, when her first moments of surprise had passed, she tenderly licked the precious tiny gray kitten, spotted and mottled like a tiger,—her only son.

The reciprocal attachment of the two families was touching; the comical little Chinese and the little Angora, round as a powder puff, frolicking together, and nourished, washed, and watched by one or the other mother with an almost equal solicitude.

☙

In the winter season pussy becomes peculiarly the hearthstone guest, constant companion of the fireside, sharing with us, before the flickering flames, vague melancholies and endless reveries of the long twilights.

Since the first frost Pussy Gray had lost all roughness of her mottled coat, and Pussy White had donned a most imposing cravat, a boa of snowy whiteness that framed her face like a

Medici ruff. It is well known that in winter the cat attains its fullest perfection of flesh and fur. Their attachment grew as they warmed themselves together by the fireside; they slept entire days in each other's arms, on the cushions in the armchairs, rolled in a single ball where heads and tails were alike indistinguishable.

Pussy Gray could never get sufficiently close to her friend. Returning from some scamper in open air, if she perceived the Angora sleeping before the fire, she softly, very softly approached her, as if about to spring upon a mouse; the other, always nervous, whimsical, irritated at being disturbed, sometimes gave her a light cuff of disapproval. She never retaliated, the Chinese, but merely raising her little paw, as if quite ready to laugh, then saying to me from a corner of her eyes, "You must allow that she is rather cross! But I don't mind it at all, you may be sure!" Then, with redoubled precaution, she always attained her desired purpose, which was to lay herself completely upon the other, her head sunk in the silky snow,—and before sleeping she said to me, from half-closed eyes: "This is all I wanted! Here I am!"

Oh! our winter's evenings of that time! In the most sheltered corner of the mansion, elsewhere closed and left silent and dark, was a small and warm parlor facing the sun, the courtyard, and the gardens, where my mother and Aunt Clara sat beneath their hanging lamp, in their usual places where so many past and similar winters had found them. And, usually, I was there also, that I might not lose an hour of their presence on earth and of my days at home near them. On the other side of the mansion, far from us, I abandoned my study, leaving it dark and fireless that I might simply pass my evenings in their dear company, within the cosy room, innermost sanctuary of our family life, the home dearest to us all. (No other spot has given me a fuller, a sweeter impression of a nest; nowhere have I warmed myself with more tranquil melancholy than before the blaze in its small fireplace.) The windows, whose blinds were never closed, so confident were we in our security, the glass door, almost too summer-like, opened upon the desolation of naked trees and vines, brown leaves, and despoiled trellises often silvered by pale moonlight. Not a sound reached us from the street, which was some rods distant,—and besides a very quiet one, its silence rarely broken save by the songs of sailors celebrating, at long intervals, their safe returns. No, we had rather the sounds of the country, whose nearness was felt beyond the gardens and old ramparts of the city;—in summer, immense concerts of frogs in the marshes which surrounded us smooth as steppes, and the intermittent flutelike note of the owl; in the winter evenings of which I write, the shrill cry of the marsh bird, and above all, the long wail of the west wind coming from the sea.

Upon the round table, covered with a gayly flowered cloth, which I have known all my life, my mother and aunt Clara placed their workbaskets, containing articles that I would fain designate "fondamentales," if I dared employ that word which, in the present instance, will signify nothing save to myself; those trifles, now sacred relics, which hold in my eyes, in my memory, in my life, a supreme importance: embroidery scissors, heirlooms in the family, lent me rarely when a child, with manifold charges to carefulness, that I might amuse myself with paper cutting; winders for thread, in rare colonial woods, brought long years ago from over the oceans by sailors, and giving material for deep reveries; needlecases, thimbles, spectacles, and pocketbooks. How well I know and love every one of them, the trifles so precious, spread out every evening for so many years on the gay old tablecloth, by the hands of my mother and Aunt Clara; after each distant voyage with what tenderness I see them again and bid them my good-day of return! In writing of them I have used the word "fondamentale," so inappropriate I confess, but can only explain it thus: if they were destroyed, if they ceased to appear in their unchanged positions, I should feel as if I had taken a long step nearer the annihilation of my being, towards dust and oblivion.

And when they shall be gone, my mother and Aunt Clara, it seems to me that these precious little objects, religiously treasured after their departure, will recall their presence, will perhaps prolong their stay in our midst.

The cats, naturally, remained usually in our common room,— sleeping together, a warm, soft ball, upon some taboret or cushioned chair, the nearest to the fire. And their sudden awakenings, their musings, their droll ways, cheered our somewhat monotonous evenings.

Once it was Pussy White who, seized by a desire to be in our closer company, leaped upon the table and sat gravely down upon the sewing work of Aunt Clara, turning her back upon her mistress, after unceremoniously sweeping her plumy tail over her face; afterwards remaining there, obstinately indiscreet, and gazing abstractedly at the flame of the lamp. Once in a night of tingling frost, so excitable to a cat's nerves, we heard, in a near garden, an animated discussion: "Miaou! Miaraouraou!" Then from the mute fur ball, which slumbered so soundly, upsprang two heads, two pair of shining eyes. Again: "Miaraou! Miaraou!" The quarrel goes on! The Angora rose up resolutely, her fur bristling in anger, and ran from door to door, seeking an exit as if called outside by some imperative duty of great importance: "No, no, Pussy," said Aunt Clara, "believe me, there is no necessity for your interference; they will settle their quarrel without your help!" And the Chinese, on the contrary, always calm and averse to perilous adventure, contented herself by glancing at me with a knowing air, evidently regarding her friend's movements as ridiculous, and asking me, "Am I not right in keeping away from this fracas?"

A certain beatitude, profound and almost infantile, pervaded the silent little parlor where my mother and Aunt Clara sat at work. And if by turns I remembered, with a dull heart throb, having possessed an oriental soul, an African soul, and a number of other souls, of having indulged, under divers suns, in numberless fantasies and dreams, all that appeared to me as far distant and forever finished. And this roving past let me more thoroughly to enjoy the present hour, the side-scene in this interlude of my life, which is so unknown, so unsuspected, which would astonish many people, and perhaps make them smile. In all sincerity of purpose, I said to myself that nothing could again take me from my home, that nothing could be so precious as the peace of dwelling there, and finding again part of my first soul; to feel around me, in this nest of my infancy, I know not what benignant protection against worthlessness and death; to picture to myself through the window, in all the obscurity of dying foliage, beneath the winter moon, this court-yard which once held my entire world, which has remained the same all these years past, with its vines, its mimic rocks, its old walls, and which may perhaps resume its importance in my eyes, its former greatness, and repeople itself with the same dreams. Above all, I resolved that nothing in the wide world was worth the gentle bliss of watching mother and Aunt Clara sewing at the round table, bending toward the bright flowered cloth their caps of black lace, their coils of silvery hair.

Oh! one evening I will recall. There was a scene, a drama among the cats! Even now I cannot recall it without laughter.

It was a frosty night about Christmas time. In the deep silence we had heard passing above the roofs, through cold and cloudless skies, a flock of wild geese, emigrating to other climates: a sound of harsh voices, very numerous, wailing not too harmoniously together and soon lost in the infinite regions of the sky. "Do you hear? Do you hear?" said Aunt Clara with a slight smile and an anxious look to banter me; recalling the fact that in my childhood I was greatly alarmed by these nocturnal flights of birds. To hear their voices one should have a keen ear and listen in an otherwise silent place.

Our room then resumed its calm,—a calm so profound that I heard the complaint of the blazing wood on the hearth, and the regular breathing of our cats seated in the chimney corner.

Suddenly, a certain large yellow gentleman cat, held in horror by Pussy White, but persistently pursuing her with his declarations, appeared behind a window pane, showing in full relief against the background of dark foliage, looking at her with an impertinent and excited air and uttering a formidable "Miaou" of provocation. Then she sprang up at the window like a panther, or a ball deftly thrown, and there, nose to nose, on each side of the pane, there was a useless battle, a volley of unpardonable insults poured out in shrill, coarse tones; blows of unsheathed claws given with emphasis, vain scratchings across the glass, which made great noise and did nothing. Oh! the fright of my mother and Aunt Clara, starting from their chairs at the first alarm,—then their hearty laugh afterward, the ridiculousness of all this impetuous racket breaking in upon the intense silence,—and above all the visage of the visitor, the yellow cat, discomfited and breathless, whose eyes blazed so drolly behind the glass!

"Putting the pussies to bed" was in those evenings, one of the important events,—"primordiales" shall I call it?—of our daily existence. They were never allowed, as are many other cats, to roam all night among the vines and flowers, beneath the stars, or contemplating the moon; we held opinions upon that subject from which we never departed and made no compromises.

The going to bed was merely shutting them up in an old granary at the end of the courtyard, almost hidden under a growth of vines and honeysuckles; it was really in Sylvester's quarters, beside his chamber; so that every evening they said good-night together, the cats and he. When each one of these days—these unappreciated days now wept for—was ended, fallen in the abyss of time, Sylvester was called and my mother would say in a half solemn tone, as if fulfilling a religious duty, "Sylvester, it is time for the cats to go to bed."

At the first words of this phrase, uttered in ever so low a voice, Pussy White pricked up her ears; then knowing there was no mistake about it, jumped down from her cushion with an important though disturbed air, and ran to the door, that she might make her exit first, and on her own feet, unwilling to be carried, and determined to go of her own free will or not at all. The Chinese, on the contrary, endeavored to delay the inevitable change; reluctant to quit the warm room, she got down slyly, crouching very low on the carpet to be less in view, and glancing around to ascertain if any one had seen her, would hide under some article of furniture. The big Sylvester, accustomed to these subterfuges, called with his childlike tone and smile: "Where are you, Pussy Gray? I know you are not far off." Tenderly she responded "Trr! Trr! Trr!" knowing further pretense useless, and allowing herself to be lifted to the broad shoulder of her friend. The procession finally took up the line of march: at the head, Pussy White, independent and superb; behind followed Sylvester who said "Good-night," and who in one hand carried his lantern, and with the other grasped the long tail of Pussy Gray which hung pendent on his breast. The Angora usually proceeded resignedly to her proper sleeping place. Sometimes it happened, at certain phases of the moon, that vagabond fancies seized her, aspirations to play the truant and sleep at the angle of some roof, or at the summit of a solitary pear tree, in the bracing air of December, after having passed the entire day in an armchair by the fireside. On these occasions Sylvester soon reappeared with a drolly despondent face, still holding the tail of Pussy Gray who clung close to his neck: saying "Again that Pussy White will not go to bed!"—"Again! Ah! what actions!" replied Aunt Clara indignantly. And she stepped outside, herself, to try the effect of her authority, calling "Pussy, Pussy" in her dear, feeble voice which I can hear now, as it echoed then in the courtyard through the sonorous depth of the winter night. But no, Pussy obeyed not; from the height of a tree, from the top of a wall she gazed about her with a nonchalant air, seated at her ease on her chosen throne, her furry robe making a white spot in the darkness and her eyes emitting tiny phosphorescent gleams. "Pussy, Pussy! Oh you naughty creature! It is shameful, miss, such conduct, shameful!"

Then out in her turn came my mother, shivering in the cold, and trying to make Aunt Clara come in. An instant after, I follow to bring both indoors. And then to see ourselves gathered in the courtyard, in a freezing night, Sylvester also of the group and still holding his cat by the tail, and all this united authority set at defiance by a little cat perched high above us, gave an irresistible desire to laugh at ourselves, beginning with Aunt Clara, and in which we all joined. I have never believed there existed in the entire world two such blessed old ladies,—Oh, how old, alas!— capable of such hearty laughter with the young; knowing so well how to be amiable, how to be gay. Truly I have been happier with them than with any or all others; they always discovered in seemingly insignificant trifles an amusing or comical aspect. Pussy White decidedly had the best of the discussion! We reëntered, crestfallen and chilled, the little room too much cooled by the opened door, to gain our respective chambers by a series of stairways and sombre passages. And Aunt Clara, with a relapse of anger, when reaching her threshold, said to me, "Good-night; but, on the whole, what is your opinion of that cat?"

The life of a cat may extend over a period of twelve to fifteen years, if no accident occurs.

Our two pets lived to enjoy together the light and warmth of another delicious summer; they found again their days of blissful idleness, in company of the everlasting tortoise, Suleïma, whom the years forgot, between the blooming cacti, on the sun-heated pavements,—or stretched on the old wall amidst the profusion of jasmines and roses. They had many kittens, raised with tender care and afterward advantageously domiciled in the neighborhood; those of the Chinese were in great demand, being of a peculiar color and bearing distinctive race marks.

They lived another winter and recommenced their long naps

in the chimney corner, their meditations before the changing aspect of the flame or embers of our wood fire.

But this was their last season of health and joy, and soon after, their decline began. In the succeeding spring some mysterious malady attacked their little bodies, which should have endured vigorous and sound for still some years.

Pussy Chinese, first attacked, seemed stricken by some mental trouble, a sombre melancholy,—regrets perhaps for her native Mongolia. Refusing both food and drink, she made long retreats to the wall top, lying there motionless for entire days; replying only to our appeals by a sorrowful glance and plaintive "Meaou."

The Angora also, from the first warm days, began to languish, and by April both were really ill.

Doctors, called in consultation, gravely prescribed absurd medicines and impossible treatments. For one, pills morning and evening and poultices applied to the belly! For the other, a hydropathic course, close shaving of the body, and a cold plunge bath twice daily! Sylvester himself, who adored the pussies, who obeyed him as they would no one else, declared all this impossible. We then tried the efficacy of domestic remedies; the mothers Michel were summoned, but their simple prescriptions were of no avail.

They were going from us, our beloved and cherished pets, filling our hearts with great compassion,—and neither the loveliness of spring nor its glory of returning sunshine could rouse them from the torpor of approaching death.

One morning as I arrived from a trip to Paris, Sylvester, while receiving my valise, said to me sadly, "Sir, the Chinese is dead."

She had disappeared for three days, she so orderly, so domestic, who never left our premises. Doubtless, feeling her end near, she had fled, obedient to an impulse or sentiment of extreme modesty which leads some animals to hide themselves to die. "She remained all the week," said Sylvester, "up on the high wall lying on the red jasmine vine, and would not come down to eat or drink; but she always answered when we spoke to her, in such a little feeble voice!"

Where then had she gone, poor Pussy Gray, to meet the terrible hour? Perhaps, in her ignorance of the world, to some strange house, where she was not allowed to die in peace, but was tormented, driven out,—and afterwards cast on the dunghill. Truly, I would have chosen that she might die at her home; my heart swelled a little at the remembrance of her strange human glances, so beseeching, so indicative of that need of affection which she could not otherwise express, seeking my own eyes with mute interrogation forever unutterable.—Who knows what mysterious agonies rend the little, disturbed souls of the lower animals in their dying hours?

As if a fatal spell had been cast upon our cats, Pussy White, also, seemed near her end.

By fantasy of the dying, she had selected her last lodging in my dressing-room,—upon a certain lounge whose rose color doubtless pleased her.

There we carried to her a little food, a little milk, which were alike untasted; she looked at us whenever we entered, with kind eyes, glad to see us, and still purred feebly when caressed.

Then, one pleasant morning, she also disappeared, and we thought she would return no more.

She did return, however, and I recall nothing more sad than her reappearance. It was about three days after, in one of those delightful periods at the commencement of June, which shine and glow in the unclouded heavens,—deceivers with promises of eternal duration, woeful to beings born to die. Our courtyard displayed all its leaves, all its flowers, all its roses upon its walls, as in so many past Junes; the martinets, the swallows, exhilarated with light and life, darted about with songs of joy in the blue above us; there was a universal festival of things without Soul and gay animals unconscious of death.

Aunt Clara, walking there, watching the opening blossoms, called to me suddenly, and her voice showed that something unusual had occurred.

"Oh! come! look here.—Our poor Pussy has returned."

She was there indeed, reappearing as a wretched little phantom, emaciated, weak, her fur already discolored with earth;—she was half dead. Who knows what emotion led her home: an afterthought, a lack of courage at the last hour, a longing to see us once more!

With extreme exertion she had surmounted the lower wall, so familiar, which she was wont to cross in two bounds, when she returned from her beat of police guard, to cuff some acquaintance, to correct some neighbor. Breathless from her supreme effort, she lay extended on the new grass at the margin of the mimic lake, bending her poor head to lap a mouthful of fresh water. And her imploring eyes called for aid. "Do you not see that I am dying? Can you do nothing to help me live a little longer?"

Presages of death everywhere, this fair June morning, beneath its resplendent sky: Aunt Clara, leaning over her suffering favorite, seemed to me suddenly, so old, feebler than ever before, ready also to go from us.

We decided to carry Pussy White back to the dressing-room, and place her on the rose-colored lounge she herself had chosen the preceding week, and which had seemed to please her. I resolved to watch carefully that she should not depart again, that at least her bones might rest in the earth of our courtyard, that she should not be thrown on some dunghill,—like that of my poor Chinese companion, whose anxious eyes still haunted me. I held her to my breast with careful tenderness, and, contrary to her habitude, she allowed herself to be carried, this time, in complete confidence, her drooping head leaning on my arm.

Upon the rose-colored lounge she struggled against death for three days, so great is a cat's vitality. The sun shone on the mansion and the gardens around us. We continued to visit her often, and she always endeavored to rise to greet us with a grateful and pathetic air, her eyes telling as plainly as those of a human being the presence and the distress of what we call the soul.

One morning I found her dead, rigid, her open eyes glassy, expressionless,—a corpse, a thing to be hidden from view. Then I bade Sylvester make a grave in a terrace of the courtyard, at the foot of a tree. Whither had fled that which I had seen shine forth from her dying eyes; the restless Spark within, whither had it gone?

The burial of Pussy White, in the quiet courtyard, under the blue sky of June, in the full sunlight of two o'clock!

At the chosen place Sylvester dug the grave,—then stopped, looking at the bottom of the excavation, and stooping to pick up something that surprised him. "What is this," said he, stirring the small white bones which he had discovered,—"a rabbit?"

The bones of an animal, indeed; those of my cat from Senegal, an old pussy, my companion in Africa, very much beloved long ago, that I had buried there a dozen years before, and then forgotten, in the abyss where beings and things that disappear forever accumulate. And while looking at these bones mingled with the earth, these tiny legs like white sticks, this collection still suggesting what was once the back and tail of an animal,—there arose before me, with an inclination to smile and a heavy heart-throb, a scene well-nigh forgotten, a certain occasion when I had seen this same posterior of a cat, clothed in agile muscles and in silky fur, fly before me comically, tail in air, in the very height of terror.

It was one day when, with the obstinacy natural to her race, she had climbed again on a piece of furniture twenty times forbidden, and had there broken a vase which I prized very highly. I had at first given her a cuff; then my temper rising, I followed it by a rather brutal kick. She, surprised only by the blow, realized by the succeeding kick that war was declared; it was then that she swiftly fled, her plumy tail in the air, and from her refuge beneath the sofa she turned to give me a reproachful and distressed look, believing herself lost, betrayed, assassinated by him she loved, and to whose hands she had confided her fate; and as my eyes still were angry she uttered finally her cry of surrender, of hopeless despair, that peculiar and sinister cry of animals that realize themselves on the verge of death. All my anger vanished; I called her, caressed her, still trembling and panting, upon my knees. Oh! the last agonized cry of an animal, be it that of the ox, drawn down to the abattoir, even that of the miserable rat held between the teeth of a bulldog; that hopeless appeal, addressed to no one, which seems a protest addressed to nature itself,—an appeal to an unknown, impersonal mercy, pervading all space.

Two or three bones sunken at the foot of a tree is all now remaining of the once cherished creature that I recall so living and so droll. And her flesh, her little person, her attachment to me, her intense terror on a certain occasion, her precipitate flight, her plaintive reproach, all finally that encompassed these bones,—has become a little earth. When the hole was sufficiently deep, I went upstairs where all that remained of our beautiful Angora lay rigid on the rose-colored lounge. And in descending with my light burden, I found, in the courtyard, my mother and Aunt Clara seated on a bench in the shade, assuming to be there by chance, and pretending to converse unconcernedly: that we should thus assemble expressly for this burial would seem rather ridiculous, and we perhaps should have smiled despite our grief.

There never glowed a brighter day; never was balmier silence, unbroken save by the hum of insects; the garden was in full bloom, the rose-trees white with their blossoms; the peace of the country brooded over the neighborhood, the martinets and swallows slept, the everlasting tortoise, most lively when the sun shone hotly, trotted aimlessly to and fro on the pavement. Everything was imbued with the melancholy of too tranquil skies, of a season too monotonous, of the oppression of noonday. Against the fresh green verdure, the dazzling brightness of color, the two similar robes of my mother and Aunt Clara formed two intensely black spots. Their silvery heads were bowed down as if somewhat weary of having seen and reseen so many times, almost eighty times, the deceitful renewal. Everything around them, trees, birds, insects, and flowers, seemed chanting the triumph of their perpetual resurrection, regardless of the fragile beings who listened, already agonized by the presage of their inevitable end.

I laid Pussy White in her grave, and the black and white fur disappeared under a falling mass of earth. I was glad that I had succeeded in keeping her in her last days with us, that she had not died elsewhere like the other; at least her body would decay in our courtyard, where for so long a period she had laid down the law for all cats of the neighborhood, where she had idled away the summer hours on the vine-covered wall, and where on winter nights, at her capricious hour for retiring, her name had resounded so many times in the silence, called by the failing voice of Aunt Clara.

It seemed to me that her death was the beginning of the end of the dwellers in our home; in my consciousness, this cat was bound like a long cherished plaything to the two well-beloved guardians of my hearthstone, seated there upon the bench, and to whom she had been a faithful companion in my absences afar. My sorrow was less for herself, inexplicable and uncertain little soul, than for her existence which had just finished. It was like ten years of our own life that we had buried there in the earth.

THE KITTEN

BY *Joanna Baillie*

Wanton droll, whose harmless play
Beguiles the rustic's closing day,
When drawn the evening fire about,
Sit aged Crone and thoughtless Lout,
And child upon his three-foot stool,
Waiting till his supper cool;
And maid, whose cheek outblooms the rose,
As bright the blazing fagot glows,
Who, bending to the friendly light,
Plies her task with busy sleight;
Come, show thy tricks and sportive graces,
Thus circled round with merry faces.

Backward coiled, and crouching low,
With glaring eyeballs watch thy foe,
The housewife's spindle whirling round,
Or thread, or straw, that on the ground
Its shadow throws, by urchin sly
Held out to lure thy roving eye;
Then, onward stealing, fiercely spring
Upon the futile, faithless thing.
Now, wheeling round, with bootless skill,
Thy bo-peep tail provokes thee still,
As oft beyond thy curving side
Its jetty tip is seen to glide;
Till, from thy centre starting fair,
Thou sidelong rearest, with rump in air,
Erected stiff, and gait awry,
Like madam in her tantrums high:
Though ne'er a madam of them all,
Whose silken kirtle sweeps the hall,

More varied trick and whim displays,
To catch the admiring stranger's gaze.

The featest tumbler, stage-bedight,
To thee is but a clumsy wight,
Who every limb and sinew strains
To do what costs thee little pains;
For which, I trow, the gaping crowd
Requites him oft with plaudits loud.
But, stopped the while thy wanton play,
Applauses, too, thy feats repay:
For then beneath some urchin's hand,
With modest pride thou tak'st thy stand,
While many a stroke of fondness glides
Along thy back and tabby sides.
Dilated swells thy glossy fur,
And loudly sings thy busy purr.
As, timing well the equal sound,
Thy clutching feet bepat the ground,
And all their harmless claws disclose,
Like prickles of an early rose;
While softly from thy whiskered cheek
Thy half-closed eyes peer mild and meek.

But not alone by cottage-fire
Do rustics rude thy feats admire;
The learned sage, whose thoughts explore
The widest range of human lore,
Or, with unfettered fancy, fly
Through airy heights of poesy,
Pausing, smiles with altered air
To see thee climb his elbow-chair,
Or, struggling on the mat below,
Hold warfare with his slippered toe,
The widowed dame, or lonely maid,
Who in the still but cheerless shade
Of home unsocial spends her age,
And rarely turns a lettered page;
Upon her hearth for thee lets fall
The rounded cork, or paper-ball,
Nor chides thee on thy wicked watch

THE BUTTERFLY. Eugene Lambert

The ends of ravelled skein to catch,
But lets thee have thy wayward will,
Perplexing oft her sober skill.
Even he, whose mind of gloomy bent,
In lonely tower or prison pent,
Reviews the coil of former days,
And loathes the world and all its ways;
What time the lamp's unsteady gleam
Doth rouse him from his moody dream,
Feels, as thou gambol'st round his seat,
His heart with pride less fiercely beat,
And smiles, a link in thee to find
That joins him still to living kind.

Whence hast thou, then, thou witless Puss,
The magic power to charm us thus?
Is it that in thy glaring eye
And rapid movements we descry,
While we at ease, secure from ill,
The chimney-corner snugly fill,
A lion, darting on the prey,
A tiger, at his ruthless play?
Or is it that in thee we trace,
With all thy varied wanton grace,
An emblem viewed with kindred eye,

Of tricksy, restless infancy?
Ah! many a lightly sportive child,
Who hath, like thee, our wits beguiled,
To dull and sober manhood grown,
With strange recoil our hearts disown.
Even so, poor Kit! must thou endure,
When thou becomest a cat demure,
Full many a cuff and angry word,
Chid roughly from the tempting board.
And yet, for that thou hast, I ween,
So oft our favored playmate been,
Soft be the change which thou shalt prove,
When time hath spoiled thee of our love;
Still be thou deemed, by housewife fat,
A comely, careful, mousing cat,
Whose dish is, for the public good,
Replenished oft with savoury food.
Nor, when thy span of life is past,
Be thou to pond or dunghill cast,
But gently borne on good man's spade,
Beneath the decent sod be laid,
And children show, with glistening eyes,
The place where poor old Pussy lies.

THE INDEPENDENT CAT

THE CAT THAT WALKED
BY HIMSELF

BY *Rudyard Kipling*

THIS BEFEL AND BEHAPPENED and became and was, O, my
Best Beloved, when the tame animals were wild. The Dog was
wild, and the Horse was wild, and the Cow was wild, and the Sheep
was wild, and the Pig was wild—as wild as could be—and they

walked in the wet wild woods by their wild lones, but the wildest of all the wild animals was the Cat. He walked by himself, and all places were alike to him.

Of course the Man was wild too. He was dreadfully wild. He didn't even begin to be tame till he met the Woman and she did not like living in his wild ways. She picked out a nice dry cave, instead of a heap of wet leaves, to lie down in, and she strewed clean sand on the floor, and she lit a nice fire of wood at the back of the cave, and she hung a dried Wild Horse skin, tail down, across the opening of the cave, and she said: "Wipe your feet when you come in, and now we'll keep house."

That night, Best Beloved, they ate Wild Sheep roasted on the hot stones and flavored with wild garlic and wild pepper, and Wild Duck stuffed with wild rice, and wild fenugreek and wild coriander, and marrow-bones of Wild Oxen, and wild cherries and wild granadillas. Then the Man went to sleep in front of the fire ever so happy, but the Woman sat up, combing. She took the bone of the shoulder of mutton, the big flat blade-bone and she looked at the wonderful marks on it, and she threw more wood on the fire and she made a magic. She made the first Singing Magic in the world.

Out in the wet wild woods all the wild animals gathered together where they could see the light of the fire a long way off, and they wondered what it meant.

Then Wild Horse stamped with his foot and said: "O, my friends and my enemies, why have the Man and the Woman made that great light in that great cave, and what harm will it do us?"

Wild Dog lifted up his nose and smelled the smell of the roast mutton and said: "I will go up and see and look and stay: for I think it is good. Cat, come with me."

"Nenni," said the Cat. "I am the Cat who walks by himself, and all places are alike to me. I will not come."

"Then we will never be friends again," said Wild Dog, and he trotted off to the cave.

But when he had gone a little way the Cat said to himself: "All places are alike to me. Why should I not go too and see and look and come away?" So he slipped after Wild Dog softly, very softly, and hid himself where he could hear everything.

When Wild Dog reached the mouth of the cave he lifted up the dried Horse skin with his nose a little bit and sniffed the beautiful smell of the roast mutton, and the Woman heard him and laughed and said: "Here comes the First wild thing out of the wild woods. What do you want?"

Wild Dog said: "O, my enemy and wife of my enemy, what is this that smells so good in the wild woods?"

Then the Woman picked up a roasted mutton bone and threw it to Wild Dog and said: "Wild thing out of the wild woods, taste and try." Wild Dog gnawed the bone and it was more delicious than anything he had ever tasted, and he said: "O, my enemy and wife of my enemy, give me another."

The Woman said: "Wild thing out of the wild woods, help my Man to hunt through the day and guard this cave at night and I will give you as many roast bones as you need."

"Ah!" said the Cat listening, "this is a very wise Woman, but she is not so wise as I am."

Wild Dog crawled into the cave and laid his head on the Woman's lap and said: "O, my friend and wife of my friend, I will help your Man to hunt through the day, and at night I will guard your cave."

"Ah!" said the Cat listening, "that is a very foolish Dog." And he went back through the wet wild woods waving his tail and walking by his wild lone. But he never told anybody.

When the Man waked up he said: "What is Wild Dog doing here?" And the Woman said: "His name is not Wild Dog any more, but the First Friend because he will be our friend for always and always and always. Take him with you when you go hunting."

Next night the Woman cut great green armfuls of fresh grass from the water-meadows and dried it before the fire so that it smelt like new-mown hay, and she sat at the mouth of the cave and plaited a halter out of Horse-hide, and she looked at the shoulder of mutton bone—at the big broad blade-bone—and she made a magic. She made the second Singing Magic in the world.

Out in the wild woods all the wild animals wondered what had happened to Wild Dog, and at last Wild Horse stamped with his foot and said: "I will go and see why Wild Dog has not returned. Cat, come with me."

CAT ON PAPYRUS. *Painting after a detail from Egyptian wall design XII dynasty*

"Nenni," said the Cat. "I am the Cat who walks by himself, and all places are alike to me. I will not come." But all the same he followed Wild Horse softly, very softly, and hid himself where he could hear everything.

When the Woman heard Wild Horse tripping and stumbling on his long mane she laughed and said: "Here comes the Second wild thing out of the wild woods. What do you want?"

Wild Horse said: "O, my enemy and wife of my enemy, where is Wild Dog?"

The Woman laughed and picked up the blade-bone and looked at it and said: "Wild thing out of the wild woods, you did not come here for Wild Dog, but for the sake of this good grass."

And Wild Horse, tripping and stumbling on his long mane, said: "That is true, give it me to eat."

The Woman said: "Wild thing out of the wild woods, bend your wild head and wear what I give you and you shall eat the wonderful grass three times a day."

"Ah," said the Cat listening, "this is a clever Woman, but she is not so clever as I am."

Wild Horse bent his wild head and the Woman slipped the plaited hide halter over it, and Wild Horse breathed on the woman's feet and said: "O, my mistress and wife of my master, I will be your servant for the sake of the wonderful grass."

"Ah," said the Cat listening, "'that is a very foolish Horse." And he went back through the wet wild woods, waving his wild tail and walking by his wild lone.

When the Man and the Dog came back from hunting the Man said: "What is Wild Horse doing here?" And the Woman said: "His name is not Wild Horse any more, but the First Servant because he will carry us from place to place for always and always and always. Take him with you when you go hunting."

Next day, holding her wild head high that her wild horns should not catch in the wild trees, Wild Cow came up to the cave, and the Cat followed and hid himself just the same as before; and everything happened just the same as before; and the Cat said the same things as before, and when Wild Cow had promised to give her milk to the Woman every day in exchange for the wonderful grass, the Cat went back through the wet wild woods walking by his lone just the same as before.

And when the Man and the Horse and the Dog came home from hunting and asked the same questions, same as before, the Woman said: "Her name is not Wild Cow any more, but the Giver of Good Things. She will give us the warm white milk for always and always and always, and I will take care of her while you three go hunting."

Next day the Cat waited to see if any other wild thing would go up to the cave, but no one moved, so the Cat walked there by himself, and he saw the Woman milking the Cow, and he saw the light of the fire in the cave, and he smelt the smell of the warm white milk.

Cat said: "O, my enemy and wife of my enemy, where did Wild Cow go?"

The Woman laughed and said: "Wild thing out of the wild woods, go back to the woods again for I have braided up my hair and I have put away the blade-bone, and we have no more need of either friends or servants in our cave."

Cat said: "I am not a friend and I am not a servant. I am the Cat who walks by himself and I want to come into your cave."

The Woman said: "Then why did you not come with First Friend on the first night?"

Cat grew very angry and said: "Has Wild Dog told tales of me?"

Then the Woman laughed and said: "You are the Cat who walks by himself and all places are alike to you. You are neither a friend nor a servant. You have said it yourself. Go away and walk by yourself in all places alike."

Then the Cat pretended to be sorry and said: "Must I never come into the cave? Must I never sit by the warm fire? Must I never drink the warm white milk? You are very wise and very beautiful. You should not be cruel even to a Cat."

Then the Woman said: "I knew I was wise but I did not know I was beautiful. So I will make a bargain with you. If ever I say one word in your praise you may come into the cave."

"And if you say two words in my praise?" said the Cat.

"I never shall," said the Woman, "but if I say two words you may sit by the fire in the cave."

"And if you say three words?" said the Cat.

"I never shall," said the Woman, "but if I do you may drink the warm white milk three times a day for always and always and always."

Then the Cat arched his back and said: "Now let the curtain at the mouth of the cave, and the fire at the back of the cave, and the milk-pots that stand beside the fire remember what my enemy and the wife of my enemy has said." And he went away through the wet wild woods waving his wild tail and walking by his wild lone.

That night when the Man and the Horse and the Dog came home from hunting, the Woman did not tell them of the bargain that she had made because she was afraid that they might not like it.

Cat went far and far away and hid himself in the wet wild woods by his wild lone for a long time till the Woman forgot all about him. Only the Bat—the little upside-down Bat—that hung inside the cave knew where Cat hid, and every evening he would fly to Cat with the news.

One evening the Bat said: "There is a Baby in the cave. He is new and pink and fat and small, and the Woman is very fond of him."

"Ah," said the Cat listening, "but what is the Baby fond of?"

"He is fond of things that are soft and tickle," said the Bat. "He is fond of warm things to hold in his arms when he goes to sleep.

He is fond of being played with. He is fond of all those things."

"Ah," said the Cat, "then my time has come."

Next night Cat walked through the wet wild woods and hid very near the cave till morning-time. The woman was very busy cooking, and the Baby cried and interrupted; so she carried him outside the cave and gave him a handful of pebbles to play with. But still the Baby cried.

Then the Cat put out his paddy-paw and patted the Baby on the cheek, and it cooed; and the Cat rubbed against its fat knees and tickled it under its fat chin with his tail. And the Baby laughed; and the Woman heard him and smiled.

Then the Bat—the little upside-down Bat—that hung in the mouth of the cave said: "O, my hostess and wife of my host and mother of my host, a wild thing from the wild woods is most beautifully playing with your Baby."

"A blessing on that wild thing whoever he may be," said the Woman straightening her back, "for I was a busy Woman this morning and he has done me a service."

That very minute and second, Best Beloved, the dried Horseskin curtain that was stretched tail-down at the mouth of the cave fell down—So!—because it remembered the bargain, and when the Woman went to pick it up—lo and behold!—the Cat was sitting quite comfy inside the cave.

"O, my enemy and wife of my enemy and mother of my enemy," said the Cat, "it is I, for you have spoken a word in my praise, and now I can sit within the cave for always and always and always. But still I am the Cat who walks by himself and all places are alike to me."

The Woman was very angry and shut her lips tight and took up her spinning-wheel and began to spin.

But the Baby cried because the Cat had gone away, and the Woman could not hush him for he struggled and kicked and grew black in the face.

"O, my enemy and wife of my enemy and mother of my enemy," said the Cat, "take a strand of the thread that you are spinning and tie it to your spindle-wheel and drag it on the floor and I will show you a magic that shall make your Baby laugh as loudly as he is now crying."

"I will do so," said the Woman, "because I am at my wits' end, but I will not thank you for it."

She tied the thread to the little pot spindle-wheel and drew it across the floor and the Cat ran after it and patted it with his paws, and rolled head over heels, and tossed it backward over his shoulder, and chased it between his hindlegs, and pretended to lose it, and pounced down upon it again till the Baby laughed as loudly as he had been crying, and scrambled after the Cat and frolicked all over the cave till he grew tired and settled down to sleep with the Cat in his arms.

"Now," said the Cat, "I will sing the Baby a song that shall keep him asleep for an hour." And he began to purr loud and low, low and loud, till the Baby fell fast asleep. The Woman smiled as she looked down upon the two of them and said: "That was wonderfully done. Surely you are very clever, O, Cat."

That very minute and second, Best Beloved, the smoke of the fire at the back of the cave came down in clouds from the roof because it remembered the bargain, and when it had cleared away—lo and behold!—the Cat was sitting, quite comfy, close to the fire.

"O, my enemy and wife of my enemy and mother of my enemy," said the Cat, "it is I, for you have spoken a second word in my praise, and now I can sit by the warm fire at the back of the cave for always and always and always. But still I am the Cat who walks by himself and all places are alike to me."

Then the Woman was very, very angry and let down her hair and put more wood on the fire and brought out the broad blade-bone of the shoulder of mutton and began to make a magic that should prevent her from saying a third word in praise of the Cat. It was not a Singing Magic, Best Beloved, it was a Still Magic; and by and by the cave grew so still that a little we-wee Mouse crept out of a corner and ran across the floor.

"O, my enemy and wife of my enemy and mother of my enemy," said the Cat, "is that little Mouse part of your magic?"

"No," said the Woman, and she dropped the blade-bone and jumped upon a footstool in front of the fire and braided up her hair very quick for fear that the Mouse should run up it.

"Ah," said the Cat listening, "then the Mouse will do me no harm if I eat it?"

"No," said the Woman, braiding up her hair; "eat it quick and I will always be grateful to you."

Cat made one jump and caught the little Mouse, and the Woman said: "A hundred thanks to you, O, Cat. Even the First Friend is not quick enough to catch little Mice as you have done. You must be very wise."

That very moment and second, O, Best Beloved, the milkpot that stood by the fire cracked in two pieces—So!—because it remembered the bargain, and when the Woman jumped down from the foot-stool—lo and behold!—the Cat was lapping up the warm white milk that lay in one of the broken pieces.

"O, my enemy and wife of my enemy and mother of my enemy," said the Cat, "it is I, for you have spoken three words in my praise, and now I can drink the warm white milk three times a day for always and always and always. But *still* I am the Cat who walks by himself and all places are alike to me."

Then the Woman laughed and set him a bowl of the warm white milk and said: "O, Cat, you are as clever as a Man, but remember that the bargain was not made with the Man or the Dog, and I do not know what they will do when they come home."

"What is that to me?" said the Cat. "If I have my place by the fire and my milk three times a day I do not care what the Man or the Dog can do."

That evening when the Man and the Dog came into the cave the Woman told them all the story of the bargain, and the Man said: "Yes, but he has not made a bargain with me or with all proper Men after me." And he took off his two leather boots and he took up his little stone axe (that makes three) and he fetched a piece of wood and a hatchet (that is five altogether), and he set them out in a row, and he said: "Now we will make a bargain. If you do not catch Mice when you are in the cave, for always and always and always, I will throw these five things at you whenever I see you, and so shall all proper Men do after me."

"Ah," said the Woman listening. "This is a very clever Cat, but he is not so clever as my Man."

The Cat counted the five things (and they looked very knobby) and he said: "I will catch Mice when I am in the cave for always and always and always: but still I am the Cat that walks by himself and all places are alike to me."

"Not when I am near," said the Man. "If you had not said that I would have put all these things away (for always and always and always), but now I am going to throw my two boots and my little stone axe (that makes three) at you whenever I meet you, and so shall all proper Men do after me."

Then the Dog said: "Wait a minute. He has not made a bargain with me." And he sat down and growled dreadfully and showed all his teeth and said: "If you are not kind to the Baby while I am in the cave for always and always and always I will chase you till I catch you, and when I catch you I will bite you, and so shall all proper Dogs do after me."

"Ah," said the Woman listening. "This is a very clever Cat, but he is not so clever as the Dog."

Cat counted the Dog's teeth (and they looked very pointed) and he said: "I will be kind to the Baby while I am in the cave as long as he does not pull my tail too hard for always and always and always. But still I am the Cat that walks by himself and all places are alike to me."

"Not when I am near," said the Dog. "If you had not said that I would have shut my mouth for always and always and always, but now I am going to chase you up a tree whenever I meet you, and so shall all proper Dogs do after me."

Then the Man threw his two boots and his little stone axe (that makes three) at the Cat, and the Cat ran out of the cave and the Dog chased him up a tree, and from that day to this, Best Beloved, three proper Men out of five will always throw things at a Cat whenever they meet him, and all proper Dogs will chase him up a tree. But the Cat keeps his side of the bargain too. He will kill Mice and he will be kind to Babies when he is in the house, as long as they do not pull his tail too hard. But when he has done that, and between times, he is the Cat that walks by himself and all places are alike to him, and if you look out at nights you can see him waving his wild tail and walking by his wild lone—just the same as before.

THE CAT'S BEHAVIOR
IN TWO WORLDS

BY *Frances and Richard Lockridge*

IT MAY BE that the cat lives emotionally in two worlds, the human and his own, and that this is more true of him than of the other animals who associate with man, although it is to some degree true of all of them. Even chickens, creatures of exceptional stupidity and little emotional warmth, seem dimly to adjust to man's habits. Dogs, although always knocking hopefully at the door of man's world, have also a world of their own and it is conceivable that cows, gathering at the pasture gate toward the hour of going home, think mistily bovine thoughts while waiting for the herdsman. But it may be that no other animal makes the distinction so sharply as it is made in the logical mind of the cat.

As he moves between the two worlds, the cat speaks languages suitable to the comprehension of the other denizens—speaks in one fashion to men and women and in quite another to his fellow cats, and to the mice and birds and, lamentably, dogs who share or intrude upon the feline world. To show affection for another cat, a cat licks it and the greatest affection is shown by licking the other cat's face. When a cat wishes to join another, or several others, in a preempted place—a box, a warm ledge, a cushion—the newcomer must first lick, if only in token, the cat or cats who got there first. Failure to do this is bad manners and may lead to ejection by the resident. Now and then, the cat who has been moved in on may comment audibly, giving permission or expressing disapproval, but this is unusual, even among quite talkative cats. Except in anger or other passion, and as between mother cats and kittens, audible conversation is the exception between cat and cat. Beyond hissing, which is done by curling the tongue up at the sides, making it into a kind of trough, cats have little to say to dogs, and a minor growl will do for a rat or mouse.

But with humans who, as the cat has noticed, communicate with one another by making sounds, almost all cats talk audibly and some talk a good deal. (Siamese are traditionally, and in our experience actually, the most frequent talkers.) They speak abruptly when they want out or want dinner; some of them talk uninterruptedly while their meals are being prepared; they purr when stroked (as, although more rarely, they purr when licked by one another); many of them respond, usually in a monosyllable or two, when spoken to in greeting; Martini has a special quick ejaculation used only when she wishes to jump to human shoulders—it is at once request and warning, although more the latter than the former. If offended by a human, a cat will growl briefly in admonition—as it will with another cat; if sufficiently alarmed by human, as by dog or other cat, a cat will hiss.

The cat has discovered, however, that humans are slow of understanding and so adds pantomime to words, as humans do when seeking to explain something to other humans of imperfect understanding—as, for example, foreigners. Thus a cat wanting dinner may add to his vocal announcement the pantomimic explanation of going to the place in which food is prepared; Gin, when the ordeal of waiting for food to be warmed becomes unbearable, when her most audible instructions to hurry up—can't you see I'm starving?—do not produce the speed she wishes, goes to a pile of paper plates and paws at the topmost, knowing that it is the one on which food will eventually—but how long, oh God?—be served.

All cats go to the door and speak there when they want to go out, many reach toward the knob or latch, not a few learn to manipulate the lock and go out by themselves if the door opens away from them. Gin used to climb into a chair which stood near an outer door and do her talking from there because then, since the door opened inward, she was out of the path of its swing and could go out faster. All cats know that people speak cat imperfectly and that the simplest things have to be acted out, as in a charade. Some of these performances become so familiar, and so stylized, that cats probably hardly know they are engaged in them and people take them for granted. Thus even Dr. Shaler no doubt took for granted that when a cat said he was hungry, and then acted as if he was hungry, he *was* hungry. Almost without knowing what he did, he took the cat's word for it—the cat's words and actions.

SIAMESE

BURMESE

OF CATS.

Walter Chandoha

Tabby
(Domestic Shorthair)

Abyssinian

PERSIAN
(Longhair)

RUSSIAN BLUE

Maine Coon Cat

Manx
(Tailless)

But often, in any cat's life in the human world, situations arise which require greater thought on the part of both feline and human if communication is to be established. If the thing to be expressed has to do with an objective matter, this need not long baffle an intelligent or a reasonably attentive human. Thus Martini once communicated to one of us an emergency which had arisen in connection with her toilet pan, and did it with an explicitness which no one could fail to understand.

Martini was, when living in town, "broken" to torn-up newspaper. The quotation marks are used because, as is usually true of cats, we did not "break" her to this sanitary arrangement. We provided pan and torn-up papers and, although the result is by no means a cat's idea of toilet facilities, it was better than anything else available. Being a reasonable person, no holder-out for unobtainable perfection, Martini promptly used pan and paper and, when it became necessary, pointed out the pan to her kittens. Thereafter, all three used the same pan.

The flaw in this, from the cats' point of view and ours, was that we and our maid had always to be thinking of whether the pan was clean and dry and that our minds too often wandered from this, to the cats, essential, preoccupation. On the day when Martini explained things to one of us, we had apparently been thinking for some hours of lesser matters. Martini probably spoke about it several times and got no answer, which gave her a low view of our intelligence and also annoyed her considerably, since she is uncommonly fastidious and insists on a dry pan.

So she came to the room where one of us was working and gave that one a final chance. She got onto a couch and spoke so loudly, so insistently, that no concentration could withstand her voice. The human turned and said, "What's the matter, Teeney?"

Martini spoke again, more briefly. Then she assumed a characteristic and unmistakable position on the couch.

"Teeney!" the human said, very loudly, in surprise and shock. "Teeney!" The human also got up. "You bad—" the human began.

But then Teeney left the couch. She left hurriedly, and resumed her vocal instructions. She also went toward the kitchen, in which the pan was kept. She went hurriedly. The one of us summoned went after her and found her standing in front of the pan, looking at it, her upper lip slightly curled back, as cats curl back their lip when they encounter something unpleasant. She let the human see this attitude of hers. Then she looked up. Then she said, "Yah!"

The human changed the pan. Martini used it.

Now this, while requiring some ingenuity on Martini's part, was not too complicated for a bright cat and it does not, one would think, admit of more than one explanation. Martini wanted something done and saw it was done. Presumably a person who knows little of cat's habits might argue that she had really intended to use the couch, so that her actions were not pantomimic but real. There are several things against this. Healthy cats, except females in season, almost never break habit; Martini, locked up in the Brewster cabin for hours together—the cats reasonably enough decline to use the pan in the country and Martini, for reasons of her own, for a time abandoned the fireplace—waits until she is let out, no matter how long the waiting is. (Cats have unhuman control in such matters.) And, if she had been going to break habit on the couch, she would certainly not have announced it to one of us, nor have used a cushioned surface in an occupied room.

But often cats must talk with humans on subjects more abstract— must communicate such emotions as jealousy, hurt feelings and, most frequently of all, affection. Some of them seem to feel these emotions more keenly than do others; some are more adept at communicating them. But neither of us ever knew a cat who could not, in one way or another, express himself on these matters and who did not do so when the need arose. It seems to us, as it does to most people who have spent any appreciable time around cats, that a cat's expression of, for example, love for a human is often quite as clear as a cat's expression of a desire to go out doors.

There was, for example, the case of the cat called Pammy who, like Martini later, was a very special cat—a cat about whom one would like to write a book, as Michael Joseph did about Charles; or such an essay as Charles Dudley Warner wrote about the incomparable Calvin, who used to turn on a furnace register "in a retired room, where he used to go when he wished to be alone" and when he required more heat. (Any writer would like to have done either of these perceptive pieces, as a craftsman even if not as a cat lover.)

Pammy, who as we have said is dead now, was a longish gray cat, with a white collar; her mother was Siamese and her father anybody, and she came to us years ago with her brother Jerry. Of

these two, and of other cats of ours, we may tell more on later
pages; what is significant here is that, from the time she was a small
kitten, Pammy formed a special attachment for one of us—the one,
as it happened, the more aggressive Jerry did not prefer. He would
slap her down if she approached Frances. All the affection of a very
gentle cat was thus channeled toward one human, and it was shown
in soft sounds, in purring, in a desire always to be close—in all the
little ways which are convincing to those less adamant than the Dr.
Shalers.

But then the war came and for a couple of months it became
necessary for the one to whom Pammy was devoted to be away. The
room in which he worked, and in which Pammy tried, with soft
paws, with endearments, to keep him from working, was tem-
porarily otherwise occupied. And Pammy was brokenhearted—one
does not like to use terms so extreme, but other terms are inade-
quate. The bottom dropped out of Pammy's life.

She would go to the door of the small room in which the man
should have been, had always been. She did not need to enter to
know that he was not there; there was another smell there, even
when the room was empty. She would look into the room and raise
her head and give a small, hopeless cry. Then she would turn away
and wander the apartment restlessly, and return to the room and
again find it empty—find it worse than empty, because someone else
was occupying it. She would turn away again and then, perhaps,
she would hear the front door opening a flight below. Then, instantly, she was all a listening animal, but only for an instant. The
sound of footsteps was as wrong as the scent had been and again
she would cry, and begin to wander.

For the first few weeks she would have nothing to do with the
one who remained. She displayed the detached courtesy she always
showed; she was never a rude cat. But the affection freely offered
by one who was lonely too, in a human fashion, was accepted only
absent-mindedly, did not touch the cat. Pammy continued to eat;
there was no change there, except that she seemed to eat with no
great pleasure. (The one who was gone had almost never fed her.)
But she did not play with her brother; she merely drifted through
the apartment, searching; merely listened at the door, hoping.

Finally, she appeared more or less to give up, but that was after
weeks. She began to look up into the human face which remained

and, although she still expressed her loneliness with a little cry, it was clear that she also sought friendship and reassurance. Finally, after about six weeks, she appeared to accept her loss and to make the new adjustment. When the wanderer returned she was clearly very glad to see him and sat as much as possible on his lap. But she was never again a one-man cat; she had learned, as humans most often have to, that there is danger in channeling love so narrowly; she had widened her emotional field.

But if, during those weeks, she did not feel deeply the loss of someone she loved, then the actions of cats and men make no sense at all, and the words we use have no meaning. We may guess that emotions were inchoate in her mind; that she did not form an "idea" of her loss, although in this we may well be wrong. But she did all a sentient being could to reveal that underlying disappointment, that feeling of depression, which, for some time after an affectional trauma, also underlies the human consciousness, is never quite absent even when the surface mind is busiest.

Martini, in all respects a more violent person and not a cat to take anything sitting down, showed a similar response when it was necessary for both of us to leave her at a crucial time in her life. We had to go away for ten days or so when the kittens were very small and she was their only source of sustenance. Martini merely quit eating and, since she continued to provide food, she faded alarmingly. The person who was, very generously, acting as cat sitter became alarmed and summoned the veterinarian. Martini retired to an inaccessible position, prepared in advance, and growled and hissed. She would not allow herself to be touched; she met coaxing with angry warnings. And, since she had never been a cat to fool with, she was allowed her way, which was to continue to refuse food. When we returned, she swore at us for a couple of days, and would not let us touch her or the kittens, but she ate.

Obviously, if one of the things so many people "know" about cats had been true of Martini, none of this would have happened. She was in a familiar place, and places, many people tell one another, are all cats care about. She was not even with a strange person; her sitter was one she had known and liked since she was a kitten. She had been deserted by people she loved and, being the kind of person she is, this made her furious; Martini is of a temperament to kill the things she loves; she is very proud and one rejects her at his peril. Her love is violent.

It is more violent than that of most cats we have known even when nothing in particular has happened to upset her, even in its day-to-day expression. When she chooses to express affection—usually toward Frances, whom she owns—there is nothing half way about it. Lap sitting, quiet purring, is not enough. She lies up a chest, with her whiskers tickling a cheek; she puts paw to face, and arms about neck. When she is in this position she expects to be talked to, touched gently, to hear her name often spoken in a soft voice. During this period, the occupied person must sit quietly, must not try to read, must not answer the telephone if it rings. A movement, any wavering in concentration on cat, and Martini is down with an oath, is on the floor, sitting with back to the offender, not answering if spoken to. She is not to be lightly wooed, our major cat; she has no patience with casual affection.

She and her daughters always greet us when we return after an absence; they are always sitting at the door before we reach it. Martini usually moves a little away from the others and rolls over on her back. She expects to be greeted first; it is wise not to notice the others until her emotional needs are gratified. Then one may speak to Gin and Sherry, who are rubbing against legs, purring furiously. (Martini herself has a very small purr; often it is almost soundless, and merely a matter of vibrating cat.)

If we have been gone for some hours, the cats—after being greeted—usually run excitedly through the house, wrestling with one another, leaping onto things and off of them, emitting sharp cries of excitement. Martini at such times, and often at other times, forgets the dignity of a matron and romps furiously, leaping half across a room, her tail bushy, to land almost upon another cat, to lock with it and roll it on the floor, pretending to tear it apart with tooth and claw. Both of them are larger cats than she, and stronger; both have been under her paw since they were kittens.

Not all of our cats have been so demonstrative in the world they share with humans. Pammy was, in her fashion. She, also, met us at doors. Jerry did sometimes, when he happened to think of it, but perhaps only because Pammy did, and he wondered—in his rather vague fashion—what she was up to. Jerry liked attention well enough, but he did not seem to be a deeply affectionate cat. Pete was wont merely to look up when we entered, smile faintly, and go back to sleep again. Sometimes he would roll over to be rubbed, but not always. But he was a great cat to follow us around, as Martini also is. Pete kept an eye on us and did not let us wander far afield. One night, when we stayed too long with friends at a near-by cabin, Pete came across the fields after us, looked in the window, opened the screen door, and entered to tug at our clothing and to tell us it was high time we came home with him.

Pete lived longer than the others a semi-migratory existence between town and country, since during the earlier of the ten years or so he lived with us we stayed most of our time in New York and got to the country only for weekends and for vacations. Pete traveled, usually by car but now and then by train, always in a carrying case which he hated thoroughly. But he never showed any signs of a place fixation; if he was in the apartment, that was all right; if he was in the country, that was fine. After his first visit to the country it never seemed to surprise him, although for some time, of course, it required investigation. There was never any thought in our minds, or apparently in his, that he might try to walk back to New York. Home was where we were; he might have been contented in the traveling box if it had been convenient for one of us to ride in it with him.

The more recent cats have all shared his indifference to places and addiction to people; we have, indeed, never known a cat who felt otherwise, nor have we ever heard of one at firsthand. (If cat stories have any value—which many dispute—they have it only at firsthand; what somebody has heard about somebody else's cat is seldom instructive and never evidence.) But the cats we have known, and know most about, were cats who, in their homes, were treated as persons, not as furniture. Presumably a cat treated like a piece of furniture would begin to act like one, at least to human eyes. He would not feel like one, but he might come to feel like part of the house.

Cats appear to recognize their people by sight and sound, rather than by scent, although they do a great deal of smelling of their friends and more—sometimes embarrassingly more—of strangers. Apparently they tell a good deal about people by the way their fingers smell, and a good deal of where people have been by the way their shoes smell. Probably their sense of smell is highly selective rather than keen, but of course it is infinitely more acute in all respects than that of a human. We have seen a cat who had had, during his absence, a dog visitor, trace the every movement the dog had made over the floor of a room half an hour after the dog had left. The cat's lip was curled throughout, perhaps in contempt for so smelly an animal.

A cat will, normally, recognize a friend as far as he can see him, which is a good distance. Now and then, for reasons not entirely clear, recognition may be uncertain until the cat is spoken to. Then the cat is usually very chagrined—an anthropomorphic word; they cannot be avoided by anthropoids—at having been caught out. They are also chagrined when, as sometimes happens, they stalk cautiously a familiar object which happens to be in an unfamiliar place; Martini once with the utmost gingerliness stalked half across a lawn a cushion which was drying in the sun and was six feet from it before she found out what it was. She stopped in her tracks, then, and looked off to one side, as if the whole approach had been an elaborate feint, and the real object of her interest had all the time been elsewhere. She rather spoiled this pantomime, however, by looking back over her shoulder to see how we were taking it. We were amused; she recognized this instantly and went off with slow and rather contemptuous dignity. And familiar persons in unexpected postures—such as standing on the head—may frighten a cat.

Cats go by shapes and positions, and show little interest in color, probably because they are largely color blind. That they are completely color blind is something which everyone "knows" about cats; the cat's-eye view of color—shades of intensity in a primarily monotone world—is frequently pictured in books on color blindness although, so far as we know, none of these pictures was ever painted by a cat. Investigators constantly remind one another, and their readers, that no one can get inside the mind of a cat, or see with a cat's eyes—and many of them are as constantly doing what amounts to precisely that. The degree of color blindness in the cat can only be guessed at by those who are not cats, and that rather haphazardly. Of the two best planned investigations of the cat's color vision, one proved conclusively that it did not exist, the second that it was very acute. Anecdotal evidence from lay cat owners does little to resolve this scientific confusion; some people are sure cats are sensitive to colors; some that they are not. Our own experience has been that color, at the best, means little to a cat; they are attracted to flowers, as most of them are, by the scent, not the color. Most cats evidently enjoy smelling flowers; some of them like to eat flowers. Almost all, incidentally, like to drink water in which flowers have stood, and this when much fresher water is available.

Dr. Georgina Ida Stickland Gates, a psychologist who has gone into the matter—but evidently with a volume of Thorndike propped between her and the cat—is confident not only that cats do not see color but that they do not see much of anything else, and hear very little. Her cat, she writes, "probably sees me as a vague form. Just as she does not distinguish the color of my dress, so it is improbable that she perceives slight variations of facial expression or that she notes changes in costume. She probably feels me in gross, as a large total thing, the parts of which are but vaguely apprehended."

One man's probability is another's unlikelihood; to us it does not seem at all probable that the cat does not notice changes of costume, chiefly because our cats so evidently do. Pete knew in town when we changed to clothing we wore to the country, and hid at once to avoid the carrier, which we never touched until the last possible moment. But when we packed suitcases to go somewhere in city clothes, he paid little attention, being well able to tell the difference. And all cats examine the costumes of people they propose to occupy; when either of us is wearing shorts or other tennis clothes, the cats, after a quick examination, decide we are not dressed to be sat upon.

It was also Dr. Gates's conviction, based on heaven knows what evidence, that cats have little or no tonal perception, although all the cats we have known seemed to show a good deal—very evidently responded favorably to soft tones of the human voice and unfavorably to harsh or high-pitched voices. There is a considerable body of evidence, largely anecdotal to be sure, that some cats enjoy music, although none of ours has ever seemed to pay much attention to it. Martini did, on one occasion, respond angrily to the sound of an Egyptian flute which emerged, rather unexpectedly to us also, from the radio, but otherwise she can take music or leave it, even when she happens to be sitting on the radio. But she hates whistling, as has every cat with whom we have been associated.

Dr. Gates also questioned whether cats know their own names, which is merely arrant nonsense. Cats who are always called "kitty" presumably think "kitty" is their name. Other cats know their names about as well as people know theirs; many will answer when spoken to by name and all will come when called by name if, at the moment, coming seems like a good idea to the cat. It was perhaps Dr. Gates's careless observation in this particular which led Nelson Antrim Crawford to characterize her cat book as "a dull and dubious study of feline psychology."

It is difficult for the human not to assume that obedience is synonymous with comprehension or should be so in the case of small and admittedly dependent animals. It may be that Dr. Gates, and others who have questioned whether a cat ever learns his name, subconsciously assume, although they may consciously know better, that if a cat recognizes his name he will come running when it is called. A dog does; why should a cat differ from a dog?

And, quite often, cats do come, often at breakneck speed. They will do this most often, of course, when it is near mealtime, since then it is almost always worth the trouble. But they are quite likely to do the same thing at other times, if it seems a good idea. What makes it seem a good idea no human knows, or is likely to know. We have no idea at all why, one day, Sherry will come across a lawn as if blown by a high wind, her hind legs clearly moving faster than her front, to her evident confusion, when we call her name; why, the next day, with conditions apparently almost identical, she will merely look around languidly and go back to eating grass, which we have never been able to convince her is bad for cats. It is not true that she knows her name one day and not the next, but beyond that the human can only vaguely speculate.

It is this exercise of judgment, this apparent consideration of and response to only the specific circumstances of a certain time, which gives the cat its rather exaggerated reputation for independence—that and, of course, the fact that a cat will not be bullied by anything, on two legs or four, or on multiple legs or no legs at all. The cat will come or not come as suits the cat, the cat will withdraw if it grows bored; no cat will ever suffer politely at a cocktail party. Because of this attitude, the cat is "independent"; he may be termed "anti-social" or even, by some, "stupid." Perhaps it would be more accurate to say that, instead of being primarily any of these things, the cat is selective and that the bases of his selection are not always clear to the human mind.

All, or almost all, cats who have humans to depend upon become dependent on them—for affection, for an emotional center, as well as for their obvious needs of food and warmth and shelter. They are to a considerable, although as we have seen seldom to a complete, degree capable of fending for themselves, but they much prefer not to. With humans most of them are anything but antisocial, although among humans many of them make sharp selection, and again without always making their reasons clear. As people move from room to room of a house, staying now in one room and now in another, most cats will follow them; all our cats habitually, when we lived in the city, stayed in the living room with us while we remained there; moved with us into the bedroom when we went there, as we often did, to read in bed. They did not do this for any discernible reason, except that they preferred our company to our absence. They did not always do it at all. They did it if they felt like it; they felt like it, at a guess, two times out of three. All of them would show attention when spoken to by name, sometimes they would come and sometimes not, and they varied in this from cat to cat; Martini almost always answers whether she moves or not, but she will not continue to answer if spoken to repeatedly, declining to labor the point.

Their choices among people are often entirely inexplicable. For many years in New York we had a maid of whom we, and all our cats but one, were fond—she was as gentle with the cats as she was expert and faithful in meeting our needs; she often fed them as she for years fed us. Pete openly adored her and used to play games with her; Pam and Jerry seemed fond of her; Sherry liked her from the first and Gin, who makes friends slowly, came to approve her and to sit watching her by the hour. Gin was particularly entertained when she mopped the kitchen floor, and would lie across the threshold, one paw in the kitchen, and raise the paw to be mopped under.

But Martini, who knew Elizabeth almost as early in her young cathood as she knew us, could never abide her. She would run from her sometimes; other times, she would stand in a doorway and, hissing, refuse permission to cross. During several years of acquaintance, Martini never altered her views about Elizabeth, although in many ways, because of a change in her life, Martini did alter her views on other matters. Neither we nor Elizabeth ever understood why this was, and we all regretted it. Since she had kittens, and then was spayed, Martini has not been particularly bad-tempered with other people, although it would be absurd to contend that she is an especially amiable cat. But she never liked Elizabeth.

Sherry likes everybody and, although afraid of mice, was only mildly alarmed when she first met children and soon came to be fond of them, although most cats who grow up with adults are greatly disturbed by small humans who must, to a cat, seem an unnatural compromise. Gin likes almost nobody the first time, but relents to a degree later, although without ever approaching Sherry's cordiality. But even Sherry likes some people better than others, and not always merely because she knows them better. Nor does she always show herself most friendly to those who most readily offer her friendship. Like most cats, she picks and chooses.

Cats so much insist on this prerogative of selection that all experienced people in meeting unfamiliar cats wait to be chosen, usually with fingers dangled, as if by chance, near a cat's nose. The hand of a wise human is, at such times, held near the floor, or near whatever the cat happens to be on, and not above the cat's head. Cats do not like to have things come down on them from above; their invariable habit, in environments not tested and found safe, is to get under something and look around. For all the cat knows, any strange object descending from above may be a great horned owl, and a nervous cat may act accordingly. A cat wants to see the proffered fingers as well as smell them; he will then make up his own mind as to the human's acceptability. He will not necessarily like a person because other cats like that person and this is sometimes confusing to people who are sure they "have a way with cats." Martini, in the pre-operation days when she was not well and very nervous and irritable, once rather thoroughly scratched a visitor who, in spite of warnings—not from us; we probably could have controlled the cat, if not the person—chose to prove that there wasn't a cat in the world he couldn't handle. Perhaps Martini resented being placed in a category, knowing indignantly well that she was a person.

Unaltered cats are, generally, more insistent on making their own choices, as they are, again generally, more insistent about most things. Martini's attitude toward life has not, to be sure, appreciably altered, but she is less violent in her means of expression. And we once met a large and beautiful tom who, in spite of living with an extremely nervous collie pup and another dog who talked a good deal, was calm and placid and would lie relaxed on almost any lap offered, beaming up at the lap owner and purring loudly. But a human can never tell about a cat he doesn't know, and can tell rather less if the animals are fully sexed. Cats one knows well, cats one lives with, are generally as predictable as most individualistic creatures, and rather more predictable than people. Cats also, of course, seem sometimes to have got up on the wrong side of the bed, as it is said of people; some cats, like many people, appear to be mildly manic-depressive.

When they are feeling a little grumpy, cats will reject attentions they at other times enjoy and may even warn a human off, either in pantomime or vocally. None of our cats has ever offered to do more than this to us—except, of course, when being held for examination by a veterinarian or, as has now and then been necessary, while hypodermic injections were administered. Cats are not tolerant of pain and, if being tormented, will bite the tormenter if he is within reach, and more or less without regard for his identity. Now and then, a male may grow entirely disenchanted with life and people as he grows old; we knew one, Deuces Wild, a delightful fellow in his prime, who became too difficult for anyone to handle in old age and had finally to be killed. Humans also sometimes become personality problems as they approach senility, but human ethics do not permit their destruction. Also, of course, aged humans have neither such dangerous claws nor such sharp teeth.

But cats in health, when treated with consideration and rudimentary courtesy, are almost never entirely unpredictable in their dealings with humans, and only an occasional cat is at all difficult. Now and then, of course, one encounters an apparently psychotic cat; we have heard of, but not met, one who is clearly a homicidal maniac, seeking only to kill all living things—with the single exception of a pet human he keeps as an attendant. Our own Jerry, although quite harmless, was clearly a neurotic, probably suffering from a manic-depressive psychosis. But most cats probably are saner than most people, which is possibly not high praise. Although they live in two worlds, they are infrequently schizophrenic.

It is, of course, difficult for a human to examine with any exactitude the cat's life in his own world of other cats and other non-moral creatures. If the human is present to observe, the human becomes a condition of the problem and so modifies it. Now and then one may eavesdrop, but may not end up the wiser. When one cat sits on a stone wall and another on the ground near by, and when they converse lengthily in wails, yet without apparently meaning either to fight or to love, the human is apt to remain baffled. It is fairly evident that the cats understand each other, that they are abiding by certain feline conventions. If one cat is a resident and the other an intruder, the home cat may be warning the other off. (Such encounters do, indeed, seem frequently to have this purpose, since the visiting cat often turns away toward the end, although clearly not in fear, and permits the occupying cat the satisfaction of a token chase.) These discussions may, incidentally, take place between neuters and spays, neuters or spays and un-altered cats of either sex, and it is reasonably certain that there is no question of mistaken gender. In such matters, cats do not fall into error.

Cats are not, by nature, gregarious with others of their kind; stray cats meeting do not romp and play together. One who has cats already may add to them and many people do constantly, but rather careful introductions usually are necessary. But to this rule, as to all rules about cats, there are many exceptions. Now and then cats do meet and make friends with other cats; there are many stories of well-cared-for cats who brought home strays to share their good fortune. Now and then, without human intervention, cats and dogs similarly make friends; we were once acquainted with a fine German shepherd bitch who more or less adopted, apparently from a Baltimore sidewalk, a large black tomcat and brought him home to live. The cat, although not accepting entirely the sanctuary offered—the cat was a wanderer and had been for years—nevertheless used the dog's home for some time as a base of operations, and was clearly devoted to the big shepherd. The dog used to walk slowly across a room, and the cat would walk, more rapidly, in and out between the large canine legs. Both seemed to enjoy this pastime, which was engaging but rather meaningless to human observers.

With human intervention, on human insistence, cats and dogs

often live happily, and even affectionately, together; almost any animal "family" can be artificially created by those who find it worth the trouble. The chief reward, presumably, is that such odd assortments may be pictured in the newspapers, or even in *Life*. But no cat would choose to live in friendship with a bird and most would rather have nothing to do with dogs. Now and then a cat may enjoy teasing a dog; one of us watched such an intentional badgering a few years ago from the windows of a second floor apartment in downtown New York.

Across the street, there was a row of houses with old-fashioned "stoops"—stair flights running up to entrance doors some feet above street level. A large black cat was sitting in front of one of these stoops, washing himself. He looked up the street and saw an approaching dog, running illegally free with a master sauntering at some distance behind. The dog was inquisitive; as he came along he looked around each stoop to see what might be there. The cat watched this for a time with interest. Then, thoughtfully, the cat withdrew out of sight behind his own stoop.

Dramatic comedy then built to climax with almost classical inevitability. The dog came to the fourth stoop up the street and looked behind it and found nothing and bounced out; the dog looked behind the third stoop and then behind the second. He went into the matter of the stoop beyond the cat's, and found nothing and bounced out. The cat, now, could hear the scratch of canine nails on the cement. The cat gave a final casual lick to one shoulder, as if he had been adding a touch of makeup in a dressing room, and crouched. The dog reached the stair flight and the cat waited; the dog turned around the stoop.

The cat did not really try to harm the dog; the cat did not even leap at him, but merely started up, black and threatening, and jabbed once at the dog's nose. It was almost make-believe, but that the dog could not know—he knew only that death confronted him, he could only brake frantically with all four paws, could only yelp his terror and anguish. And get out of there. He got.

The cat watched the dog, scampering with screams back to his master, and then came out and sat again on his sidewalk. It seemed to the human onlooker that he then looked up toward the window— as toward a balcony seat—and took a bow.

Certainly, even if this last is not precisely true, the cat had been engaged in play; had been producing, with some care and a fine sense of timing, what was essentially a practical joke. He had not been afraid of the dog, he had not even particularly disliked the dog. He had merely enjoyed scaring the dog and making it ridiculous, the butt of a jest. He would have liked applause, of which cats are fond. But if, as was probably true, he was unaware of the onlooker, the knowledge that he deserved applause was sufficient— that and the game itself.

It is because of this feline consciousness of the human onlooker that one can never be sure how much, in the play of friendly cats with one another, the cat's two worlds may overlap. Cats may not play together, indeed, when no humans are present; it would be hard for a human to say. Their play with one another may be always partly play to an audience.

This cat play—the big game of the cat—is a spectacle of which the owner of a single cat is, of course, deprived. Basically it is mimic warfare; it might be thought of as a feline encounter in a prize ring, except that cats do not hurt one another or intend to. It is also a wrestling match and often includes, at one or more stages, an obstacle race. Apparently it is played according to certain established rules; one cat watcher, a reformed sports writer, thought he had worked out a point-count which determined a winner, but he was either more observant or more imaginative than we have ever been. The game is, certainly, played to a more or less fixed conclusion; it may be called off at any time by the defensive cat. Recently, in a manner not apparent to us, Sherry violated one of the rules—apparently an important one—in playing the game with Gin, and thereafter Gin would not play it at all with her, although continuing to play it with Martini. When Sherry suggested the game, Gin jabbed at her, not intending to land but in warning, and hissed. Sherry did not appear to know what she had done, and it may be that, since she has grown heavier than her sister, it is her weight rather than her methods to which Gin objects. But the game has never been a great favorite of Gin's, who would rather be out hunting. Often, after a day in the fields, she regards the other two with weary forbearance as they romp, a business girl home from a long day at the office, too tired for the frivolity of those who do not know what it is to work for a living. When she plays at all, Gin is usually in the defensive position.

The cat on the offensive gives the preliminary signal for the game. That much is clear. If Martini wants to play, she crouches to leap, makes stalking movements and bushes her tail in excitement. The bushed tail, the rising fur along the backbone, are her idiosyncrasies; the others bush only when dealing with dogs. Sherry observes these preparatory motions and crouches in her turn. There is then, often, considerable stalking, usually ending in a chase. The chase may take both cats over chairs and sofas and, not infrequently, over the people sitting in them. Martini, as the instigator, is most often the pursuer, but at a certain stage she may permit herself to be pursued.

In the early stages, these activities may be interrupted, apparently on the choice of either cat, by brief rest periods, during which the cats will sit, paying little attention to each other, and wash up. One might think the game over, and now and then—for reasons never apparent to us—it actually is. Usually, however, it is merely that they are taking a break between rounds, changing courts after odd games. Usually, one of them—Martini most frequently—starts it up again.

Eventually, the contact stage is reached. At this stage, the defending cat lies on her side, feet extended, claws exposed, mouth open and teeth ready, and the offensive cat circles for an opening. The attacker also has claws exposed, ears laid back and mouth open, the incredibly sharp canines in readiness. There is, at this stage, considerable maneuvering for position, and if Sherry is the defender, not a little cat talk indicative of fear and pain. (This is no more to be taken seriously than a professional wrestler's groans and cries of anguish.)

At a certain stage, the attacking cat leaps in. If the defender can hold her off with stiffly extended legs and avoid being otherwise touched, it may be assumed the defender scores a point. If the attacker can break through the guard, she may pretend to tear at the unprotected belly, as in an actual fight she would seek to rip it with the claws of her hind feet; she may bite at the other's ear, she may merely circle the defender's neck with both front legs and apparently try to choke her to death. The distinction between defender and attacker is obscure at this point, the cats roll furiously in combat.

Either cat may break this off, but it is usually broken off by the original defender. There may then, apparently at the decision of the defending cat, be another chase and another tussle or an end of the game. The game is ended when either cat merely walks away, or sits and looks at something else, or goes for a drink of water. If the game is resumed it is, almost always, with the roles as they were before; seldom in any given series of contacts do the cats reverse position.

This much can be observed and certain of the rules may be guessed at. It is, for example, not considered good form to jump another cat who is seriously washing up. It is not cricket to attack a cat who has no room to maneuver; if a cat runs under something, as a sofa, the other cat seldom follows; if a cat indicates that he is actually hurt, the game ends at once. No cat ever is hurt, although the breath may be knocked out of him.

This is the way it is played. One must watch it to discover how exciting, how essentially gay, how amazingly dextrous it really is.

Cats in movement are always delightful, and during the game cats are constantly in movement—the game is an amazing spectacle of lithe grace, of dazzling acrobatics. The human, with his spine stiffened, his muscles unbalanced to make erect stature possible, cannot at his most flexible achieve a fraction of the agility of the least graceful cat. Martini is a little chunky for her breed, and slightly overweight. But it is nothing for her to leap into the air sideways during the game, to land on a sofa tiptoe with back at once arched and longitudinally curved, to dance thus for several steps while looking back over her shoulder at another cat, to take off then through the air, twisting in flight and landing not upon, but within grazing inches of, her adversary, to roll in a single motion as she lands, over and to her feet again—and then, perhaps, in what seems the same instant, become a sitting cat again, reflectively washing her right shoulderblade. When this is multiplied by Sherry, is on occasion multiplied still further by Gin, when all three cats at once are leaping and twisting in the air, each in her own fashion but each incomparably feline, there is no other pattern of animal movement approaching the game in grace and essential excitement. The human ballet, the best of ice skating, the most perfect of human play with balls, whether on court or diamond— all these activities, in which man most nearly shows grace, are heavy and contorted by comparison.

SIAMESE INTERLUDE. Gladys Emerson Cook

Man, slowly, effortfully, learns to do such things as these, achieving a partial triumph of imagination over rigidity. But he learns them arbitrarily, not from inner necessity; it is not required of man that he contort to live. Not even a Nijinsky can outjump a bullet; DiMaggio cannot hit an atom bomb out of the lot; pretty Miss Henie cannot skate her way out of danger.

But the game is part of the cat's life; in a sense it is practice for his life, as kitten chasing of a string is practice for hunting. Martini's life may at any moment depend on her ability to leap sidewise to a wall, land there in perfect balance on her toes, ready instantly to continue in another direction. No doubt it often has so depended. Cats play the big cat game for fun; there can be no doubt they enjoy it. But they play it also to keep their muscles supple and their reflexes almost instantaneous. Instinct—a human word for a complex of stimuli about which the human knows practically nothing—instructs the cat to keep his paw in, not to forget his tricks. If he ever goes out of a city apartment he may need them all.

It is when he goes out the front door that the cat most truly enters the non-human of his two worlds, and his every movement shows his knowledge of the risks involved. He shows it on the doorstep; not only Mr. Warner's inimitable Calvin, but all cats, stand on the sill, as Calvin always did, looking about the sky as if "thinking whether it were worth while to take an umbrella." Little as cats like being caught out in the rain, it is not likely that they hesitate to observe the weather. Danger may come from the sky on wings; it is wise to be sure before venturing farther. (Cats are most concerned about danger from above, since it is from above they are most vulnerable.) With the sky established as free from menace, the cat surveys the land about, checking for dogs and other dangers. This whole survey may take from seconds to several minutes; only when it is completed does the cat go about whatever his business of the moment is.

Unquestionably, the wandering dog is the most common danger to the cat, and this is particularly true of the suburban cat. A good farm dog expects cats to be around and expects to leave them alone; even when he is out hunting on his own, he recognizes cats as out of season. We have seen good farm dogs stick to this rule under the greatest provocation; one, whose ancestry had been lightly brushed by collie, allowed himself to be chivvied out of our yard one day by Martini, whose simple purpose it was to kill him. He made no move in self-defense, although he could—if luck had been with him—have killed her with one snap. He merely looked around at us, beseechingly, as if begging that we remove this annoying creature who was getting very much on his nerves, but still was sacrosanct.

But by no means all dogs are so trained; many dogs are cat killers. And almost no cat of any spirit recognizes at the start that he is outmatched. Against a medium-sized dog with no training against cats, the cat is quite right, of course. Either Martini or Gin would probably fare excellently against any but a large, tough dog; the dog might well be blinded. But neither seems able to tell a large tough dog from any other and Gin has had several bad experiences with dogs she thought she was going to chase off the premises. Too many cats—Gin is one of them, and Pete was another—willingly attack almost any recognizable dog. Pete once took on three, all of them large, and leaped for the eyes of the largest, but that time he was trapped and needed to create a diversion in order to reach a tree. Even he, who had a great contempt for dogs, probably would not voluntarily have taken on so many. (He had been spoiled by long association with an incompetent fox terrier, whose life he made miserable. It was an association Pete thoroughly enjoyed, but not one which taught him the facts of life.)

The facts of life are that dogs are very dangerous to cats and that the greater the cat's courage the greater the danger. Every cat who runs at large has many moments of peril when to escape with his life he needs all there is of feline skill at acrobatics, all that cats are provided with in reflex response. The cat cannot afford to grow rusty in a world of dogs and owls, of motor cars and, of course, other cats. He must practice constantly, and much of his play is practice.

Yet much of it also is clearly fun and some of it plain puckishness. When a cat lies crouched, tail moving slowly from side to side, ambushing a favorite human on a country path, leaps out at the human, touches a human shoe lightly—for all the world as if playing tag—it is hard to believe that his primary purpose is to keep in training. When a cat comes when called, and when wanted in, and then crouches until fingers brush him before leaping away, and when he continues to do this time after time, never really leaving, not trying seriously to avoid eventual capture, the cat is surely merely teasing, since this procedure has no apparent utility in the non-human world.

It is when the cat invents such games as these last—and any cat watcher has seen many such inventions—that the barrier between the feline and human mind seems thinnest. In such games there seems to be, on the cat's part, a kind of humor which, although physically expressed, is essentially not physical and certainly is not a practical joke. (A cat is quite capable of practical jokes, however, as the story of the cat on the stoop indicates.) One might almost think the cat capable of a concept of the ridiculous, which is certainly exemplified in the effort of human fingers to close upon a cat who, by perhaps no more than a foot or so, is no longer there.

Much of the cat's behavior, indeed, would seem to show something which approaches, if it does not reach, abstract intelligence—an ability to put two and two together; to perceive, if only dimly, causal relationships; even to form "ideas." One could almost swear, watching it, that in Martini's comic elusiveness there is not only a game, but the *idea* of a game. It is something to which she is not, at least in any obvious way, conditioned, as all cats are, of course, conditioned to certain actions which appear to bring them food; as they are conditioned by trial and error, and an accumulation of successes, to opening doors through which they want to go. (In the less obvious sense, it can be, and has been, argued that humans as well as cats are but aggregations of conditioned reflexes.)

It would seem, watching cats—and in this chapter, as all cat observers will agree, the vagaries of feline behavior are hardly more than suggested—that much of what they do results from the working of intelligence. Since no human has ever been a cat, no human knows. But, in their inquisitive simian fashion, humans have tried very hard to find out. This human study of feline intelligence is one of the most fascinating, and sometimes one of the oddest, episodes in the ancient association of cats and people.

THE UNFORTUNATE CAT

ON THE DEATH OF A FAVORITE CAT, DROWNED IN A TUB OF GOLD FISHES

BY *Thomas Gray*

'Twas on a lofty vase's side,
Where China's gayest art had dyed
   The azure flowers that blow;
Demurest of the tabby kind,
The pensive Selima, reclined,
   Gazed on the lake below.

Her conscious tail her joy declared;
The fair round face, the snowy beard,
   The velvet of her paws,
Her coat, that with the tortoise vies,
Her ears of jet, and emerald eyes,
   She saw; and purred applause.

Still had she gazed, but 'midst the tide
Two angel forms were seen to glide,
   The Genii of the stream:
Their scaly armor's Tyrian hue
Through richest purple to the view
   Betrayed a golden gleam.

The hapless Nymph with wonder saw:
A whisker first and then a claw,
   With many an ardent wish,
She stretched, in vain, to reach the prize.
What female heart can gold despise?
   What Cat's averse to fish?

Presumptuous Maid! with looks intent
Again she stretched, again she bent,
   Nor knew the gulf between.
(Malignant Fate sat by and smiled.)
The slippery verge her feet beguiled,
   She tumbled headlong in.

Eight times emerging from the flood
She mewed to every watery god,
   Some speedy aid to send.
No Dolphin came, no Nereid stirred:
Nor cruel Tom nor Susan heard,—
   A Favorite has no friend!

From hence, ye Beauties, undeceived,
Know, one false step is ne'er retrieved,
   And be with caution bold.
Not all that tempts your wandering eyes
And heedless hearts, is lawful prize;
   Nor all that glisters, gold.

CAT. Pablo Picasso. Illustration for Buffon: "Histoire Naturelle." 1936. Aquatint. *The Museum of Modern Art, New York. Gift of Mrs. John D. Rockefeller, Jr.*

THE PIEBALD DEVIL

BY *Svend Fleuron*

O NE AFTERNOON very early in spring a small, snow-white he-cat came strolling carelessly along the road. His ears were thrust forward, betraying his interest in something ahead: he meant to take a walk round the farm, whither the road led . . . there was a grey puss there who attracted him!

He ought to have been more cautious, the little white dwarf! A giant cat, a coloured rival, with the demon of passion seething in his blood and hate flaming from his eyes, caught sight of the hare-brained fellow from afar off and straight-way guessed his errand.

With rigid legs, lowered head, and loins held high, he comes rushing from behind . . . runs noiselessly over the soft grass at the side of the road and overhauls the other unperceived.

With one spring he plants all his foreclaws deep in the flesh of the smaller cat, who utters a loud wail and collapses on the ground.

The big one maintains his grip on his defeated foe's shoulder, crushing him ruthlessly in the dust. Then he presses back his torn ears, giving an even more hateful expression to the evil eyes, and lowering his muzzle, gloatingly he howls his song of victory straight into his fallen rival's face.

For a good quarter of an hour he continues to martyr his victim, who is too terrified to move a muscle; he tears the last shred of self-respect and honour from the coward—then releases him and stalks before him to the farm, without deigning to throw him another glance. He was too despicable a rival, the little white mongrel! The big, spotted he-cat considered it beneath his dignity even to thrash him.

But the little grey puss had other suitors still. . . . There was the squire's ginger cat and the bailiff's wicked old black one; so that both daring and cunning were necessary if one's courtship was to

191

be a success. At sunset they invaded the farm from every direction, stealing silently through corn or kitchen garden until they reached the garden path by the hedge.

The black ruffian, who considered himself the favourite suitor, arrived, as he imagined, first at the rendezvous. But simultaneously his ginger rival stuck his head through the hedge bordering the path. At sight of each other both halted abruptly, thrusting up their backs and blowing out their scarred, battle-torn cheeks.

For many minutes the two ugly fellows stood glaring silently at one another. . . . Then their whiskers bristled, their tattered ears disappeared, and their eyes became mere slits in their heads; hymns of hate wailed from their throats, and their tails writhed and squirmed like newly-flayed eels.

Suddenly the big, spotted cat appears in the garden. Tiger-like, with body almost brushing the ground, he glides silently past them.

They hate him, the low brute! . . . He is their common enemy! The sight of him caught in the act makes them allies in a flash. . . . They tear after him and surround him. Then they go for him tooth and nail.

All thoughts of the fair one have gone from their minds. War-cries cease; gasps and grunts of exertion punctuate the struggle; chests heave and ribs dilate with compressed air; whilst naked claws are plunged into skin and flesh. They are one to look at, one circular mass, as they whirl round inextricably interlocked, puffing their reeking breath into one another's faces.

The spotted devil's powerful hind legs are wedged in under the red cat's body. With his forepaws he grips him as if in a vice—and now thrusting the needle-pointed, razor-edged horn daggers from their sheaths, he straightens his hind legs simultaneously to a ter-rible, resistless, lacerating lunge. . . .

With a stifled hiss of fury the squire's cat falls back. It limps moaning from the battlefield, with blood pouring from its stomach.

Now comes the old black thief's turn! First the hair flies . . . it literally *steams* from the two rivals as they rush at each other. Their incredible activity is expressed in every movement. . . . After lying interlocked for some time on the ground they suddenly break away, and, as if by witchcraft, stand on all fours again.

The piebald is winning!

His claws comb like steel rakes. They tear the hair from the

CAT-FIGHT IN A LARDER. Paulos de Vos. *Courtesy The Prado, Madrid*

bailiff-cat's flanks, leaving them bare and shining. The latter often succeeds in parrying, and returns kick for kick, but his hind legs lack strength, and he cannot complete a full thrust.

Madness gleams in their eyes; they are beside themselves with frenzy; fear flies from their minds; they are exalted . . . for now they are *fighting!*

Until a sudden scuffle advertises that the bailiff-cat has had enough. He tears himself loose and bolts for his life.

The big piebald has won. He shakes himself and rolls over, gives a couple of energetic licks to his paws, and carefully brushes his whiskers; then he hastens through the garden up to the farmyard, where a little later he is to be seen promenading the pigsty roof.

With alert expression and nervously vibrating tail he looks inquiringly at all trap-doors and open windows. Suddenly he gives a start; there is Grey Puss on the manure heap beneath him.

Without a moment's hesitation he leaps down. . . . It was the decisive meeting!

She had always been true to this one lover. . . . And yet there had been times when all the gentlemen of the neighbourhood had paid court to her. Often she had reclined on the planking with one in front of her, one behind, and three or four in the elder tree above her head. . . . She had been literally besieged.

But however many suitors might appear—even though they came right up from the seacoast and the fishing village—she still loved him and him alone, the great piebald hero!

He was an exceptional cat; the ears, far apart and noticeably short, were set far back on the broad head; the neck was thick and powerful, the body long and heavy. When he ran, he moved with such swiftness that he seemed to glide, and he could leap two yards without effort.

He was all possible colours—black, red, yellow, and white. A tinge of green shone in the wicked golden eyes; they sat deep in his head, so that his cheeks stuck out each side like dumplings. . . . And in the middle of his bristly moustache protruded a small lacerated nose, which was always bright red and covered with half-healed wounds. He was always at war. . . .

Once he received a deep, horrid bite just under the throat, where he could not lick it. So he went to his sweetheart; she helped him. . . .

She was faithful and true to him . . . but she did not trust *him* beyond the threshold.

Had she reason to doubt him? He was chock-full of lust and vice, and great in merit as in fault; nevertheless—had she actual proof for doubting him?

One night her eyes were opened in the most sinister manner. The last rays of the setting sun had departed from the fields, leaving them wrapped in the summer evening's mist and obscurity. Only some horses greeted the solitary nocturnal marauder with warm, friendly neighing.

They knew him well, although he was only a cat, whose many-coloured body seemed grey, like all other cats, in the twilight. In doorway, at the pump, in yard, and in stable he was their daily companion. How nice to see him here on the meadow too! "Ehe-hehe," they neighed . . . welcome to the tethering-ground!

He ignored them completely, neither breaking his stride, nor wagging his tail, nor giving a single miauw. Past nuisances like foals which greeted him boisterously he went unresponsive and bored. He was out hunting now—nothing else mattered!

With gliding step he passes from clover field to seed ground, jumping with noiseless, tense spring over brook and ditch. His progress roused the lark from heavy slumber.

He reaches a copse—and soon afterward is heard the death-shriek of a captured blackbird. With covetous grasp he seizes his victim, buries his sharp teeth in its breast, and sucks with long sniffs the warm, odorous bird-smell. . . .

It was not hunger which drove him to the crime: he has just made a full meal off a couple of fat mice. But when coming unexpectedly upon the bird in the copse, he could not control his murderous impulse.

He sits with the booty in his jaws, purring contentedly, and ponders frowningly where he shall conceal his capture.

The summer moon shines big and round from the pale blue, starless sky—and white, pink-underlined layers of cloud hover like feathers far out on the horizon. Warm puffs of wind come and go, enveloping him in the meadow's silver mist, making the dim shelter of the hedge seem hot and oppressive.

His eyes fall on the three ancient willow stumps at the far end of the field! He, too, knows how rotten and hollow they are, and how well adapted for a hiding-place. True, it is rather a long way there . . . through the soaking wet rye—but that can't be helped!

The night is absolutely silent, broken only by the rasping song of the little reed-warbler from a swampy hole among the rye. The din of the farm has long since died down; not even the bark of a dog is heard, and neither water-pump nor wind-motor can summon up another note. How splendid to have ears, to be able to listen! Now he hears only the play of the grasshoppers, the love-song of the cockchafer, and the high-pitched music of the anthills.

Here, behind a knotted root at the base of the largest of the old willow trees, he conceals the blackbird, afterwards covering it carefully with earth and moss. Then he reaches his forepaws up to the trunk to stretch his limbs and sharpen his claws.

He gives a violent start! The scarred, rugged skin on his head wrinkles thoughtfully, as it always does when something attracts his attention. His multicoloured tail jerks uneasily, as he peers about him with uplifted ears.

The subdued rustling and squeaking noises from inside the tree trunk continue. . . .

Now there is no longer room for doubt. . . .

With a giant leap he springs up the tree, and next moment he is down in the bole.

Grey Puss is not at home. . . .

The little kittens swarm up to him. Tiny seeks to drink, while Black and Big make a joyful assault on his swiftly wagging tail. He lowers his nose to each of the little fellows in turn as if tasting their smell. Then, as if suddenly gone mad, he begins clawing about in all directions at the defenceless kittens. Mewing and squealing, they roll away to all sides like lumps of earth—but the he-cat's frenzy increases.

He seizes Tiny by the mouth, fixes an eye-tooth in his scruff and hurtles out of the willow with him. The little tot hangs limp and apparently lifeless in the jaw of his brutal sire; but, fortunately for him, the old cat is not hungry, and so is content with burying the kitten at the foot of the willow, by the side of the dead blackbird.

In justice to the criminal it must be stated that he has no conception of the enormity of his crime; only when he is on his way up the willow for the second time is he enlightened—and that in a most ruthless manner. Two rows of gimlet-pointed claws descend from nowhere and almost nail him to the bark. . . . Furious, he turns his visage . . . and the next second all his old half-healed wounds are torn open again!

Grey Puss has surprised him—and recognizes him instantly. So it is he who comes wrecking her maternal happiness; yes, she thought as much! And like a vice she clings to his back, biting and scratching and tearing as he flees panic-stricken along the hedge.

Away, away, home, anywhere!

He is more afraid of Grey Puss' mother-claws than of the raven's beak or the blade of the reaping-machine; he has learnt to his cost that a she-cat knows not the word mercy when her swollen udders are carrying milk for her young.

He lacked a conscience, this big, piebald he-cat—and he respected nothing except his own skin! The egg of the lark, the chick of the partridge, the young of the hare, were each and all grist to his mill; he took everything he could find, catch, or steal.

On the rafter at home in the farmyard, where Grey Puss used to lie, he had been allowed free passage, until the very moment when some small bundles lay shivering on the hay in the corner. Then the fascination of his black face and shining coat seemed to

vanish; she would not allow him to approach; he was not even admitted to the barn. If he just showed himself at the trap-door he
would become seized with frenzy, spring up, and fly at him as if he
were a dog! He had always to beat a hurried retreat!

Did she read his character; did she know that the feeling of
paternal love was foreign to his nature? In any case, she took no
risks; she never trusted him over the threshold. . . .

Grey Puss' milk tasted sour for a whole day following the adventure; she was frightfully restless and upset. Several of the young
ones had wounds and had to be licked. Time after time she ran her
glance over the small, rolled-up patches of colour; greedily her eyes
devoured each little furry coat; but it was with no trace of the sweetness of recollection or the joy of recognition.

Were they all there . . . all? Their villain of a father she had
already forgotten; not until she was giving suck did she become
suddenly nervous. She felt that one of the swollen udders remained swollen, and now she nuzzled with her nose along the row.
Big, Red, White, Grey . . . yes, she found them all! But where
was the little piebald one? . . .

The kittens buried their noses deep in her fur to get a good hold
of the small, sprouting milk-springs. All was quiet inside the willow
trunk; only now and again was heard the sucking of the eager little
lips. . . .

Yes, to be sure, she missed a colour . . . missed just that one
which—in spite of all—she unconsciously preferred to all the rest;
that seemed made up of bits of colour from all the other colours.
. . . Then suddenly a thin, feeble crying reached her ever-listening
ears. It seemed to her to come from under the willow bole. Perhaps
there was a crevice in the nursery?

Cautiously getting up, she begins to scratch a little with her forepaws in the floor; but finds no hole.

She dismisses the thought that one of the young ones is really
missing, and lies down again and resumes her maternal duties. For
a time all is peace, and she abandons herself completely to the
pleasure of being at the mercy of her kitten-flock, but again comes
the faint cry for help. This time it is so heart-rending that she
springs up, and then, half crouching, listens breathlessly.

"Mew, mew!" it tinkles to her from the distant depths. And now she begins to answer in anxious, encouraging tones, meanwhile pushing her snout among the young ones to count them. The tinkling from below upsets and worries her; but presently she stifles her anxiety by rolling right under the heap of kittens and congratulating herself that she has so many dear children safe and sound.

Meanwhile from his living tomb by the side of the blackbird, Tiny continues foghornlike, to emit at regular intervals his ceaseless signals for assistance. He has lain for a long time buried alive; but, accustomed as he is to having his brothers and sisters on top of him, the thin layer of moss and earth over him does not embarrass him particularly. Now he has recovered so much that he can not only squeal but wriggle also—a fact which serves to increase the air supply in his lungs, so that his weak cries gain momentarily in strength and resonance.

Suddenly the heap of earth is swept from him, and he hears his mother's soft voice right in his ear. Oh, what a stream of happiness flows through him! He stretches his tiny body towards the strong, comforting miauw, and like a freezing man making for the fire, he puts his wet, earth-cold head against the mother-cat's soft neck and feels her warm breath ripple over him.

Grey Puss' eyes shine green and evil; they speak plainly of surprise and emotion. She begins purring angrily, so that the young ones inside the tree lift their ears anxiously and wonder, "What's happening down there at the foot of the tree?"

Tiny's wound is licked, and the mother prepares to return. He must be carried, of course . . . and the problem is to find a hold which will not destroy the creature. She tries to grasp him by the scruff, but here he is so sore that time after time the attempt fails. Cautiously she presses her teeth into his back and shoulder; but cannot find a hold, although he seeks instinctively to help her by stiffening his body as she lifts.

However, it *must* be done somehow; there is not the slightest doubt that he is to be carried up! So she opens her mouth wide and puts her jaws round his neck. Then, disregarding his lively protests, she cautiously closes her mouth.

He becomes suddenly quite quiet. She needs all her presence of mind to judge how tightly she may grip him without making it his last journey.

He hangs there in his mother's jaws and closes his earth-clogged eyes, clutching her body tightly with his little legs. But he surrenders himself to her without complaint and without movement, bearing the pain in blind faith in her omnipotence.

In two jumps she reaches the top, slides down into the bole, and a moment later deposits him carefully on the ground among the others. A healing warmth envelops him—and, as the kittens are already satisfied, he secures an unusually large share of milk.

THE WORLDLY-WISE CAT

SONGS OF THE TOM-CAT HIDDIGEIGEI

BY *Joseph Victor Von Scheffel*

i

ART is grown a common treasure,
　Far and wide her votaries roam;
Every man can make at pleasure
　All the songs he needs, at home.

So my skill I fain would try it,
　Spread the poet's wings of flame:
Who so bold as dare deny it,
　Or despise the Tom-Cat's claim?

It is cheaper, poet-brothers,
　Than 'midst book-shops forth to fare,
Buying feeble songs by others,
　Bound in gilt and vellum there.

ii

When the storm o'er hill and valley
　Howls, at midnight's darkest hour,

Clamb'ring over ridge and chimney,
  Hiddigeigei seeks the tower.

Mounts in triumph, like a spirit,
  Stands in all his beauty there,
Sparks from out his eyes are flashing,
  Flashing from his bristling hair.

And he sings in wildest measure,
  His old feline battle-song,
That like distant peals of thunder,
  Through the night is borne along.

Human creatures cannot hear him,
  Each asleep within his house;
But far down in deepest cellar,
  Hears and straight turns pale the mouse.

Well she knew his awful singing,
  Sore she trembled as she sat:
Fearful in his wrath and grimness
  Is the ancient Hero-Cat.

iii

Here I sit, with clearest vision
  Gazing on the world and life,
Gazing from my proud position
  On that scene of party strife.

Smiling from the tower or steeple,
  Lo, the Cat all scornful stares
At the foolish pigmy people,
  Busied with their trifling cares.

Vain my thoughts—I cannot give them
  Access to my point of sight;
To their ignorance I leave them—
  Verily my loss is slight!

SEATED CAT (Swedish Granite). William
Zorach. *Courtesy The Metropolitan Museum
of Art, New York*

Warped and poor the human spirit,
　Human deeds of small behoof:
Calm, in consciousness of merit,
　Sits the Cat upon the roof.

iv

O, men do us vast injustice,
　And we look for thanks in vain;
They misunderstand completely
　All our nature's finer strain.

Waking from a drunken slumber,
　　Hark, the mortal, lying flat,
Mutters, with a throbbing forehead,
　　"I'm as nervous as a cat!"

Nervous as a cat—O insult!
　　Gentle are our tones and soft;
Human cries are harsh and boist'rous,
　　In the streets I've heard them oft.

Ay, they do us sore injustice;
　　Little do their rude hearts know
All that cats can bear of anguish,
　　Fierce and deep, and bitter woe!

v

O Hiddigeigei hath longed and yearned
　　For the True and the Good and the Fair;
O Hiddigeigei hath wept and mourned,
　　With tears and passionate prayer!

O Hiddigeigei with love hath glowed
　　For the fairest of feline race;
And his midnight mewings in melody flowed,
　　With all a troubadour's grace.

O Hiddigeigei his deeds of might
　　Hath wrought, like Roland in wrath!
But mortals put him with blows to flight,
　　And misfortune dogged his path.

O Hiddigeigei discovered too late
　　How false his love could be,
With a pitiful fellow she linked her fate,
　　In contemptible misery.

Thus Hiddigeigei is woefully wise,
    And his languishing dreams are o'er;
Reserved, defiant, with scornful eyes,
    He values the world no more.

vi

To the Cat thine hours are hateful,
    Month of May, so fair and green;
For the torments of thy singing
    Never hath he known so keen.

From the twigs and from the bushes
    All the birds are twittering;
Far and wide, as for a wager,
    Human throats with music ring.

Hark, the cook sings in the kitchen!
    Is she, too, by love befooled?
And her strains, in high falsetto,
    Stir my wrath that else had cooled.

Upward still I flee;—in safety
    On the balcony rejoice:
Woe is me! from out the garden,
    Pierces my blond neighbour's voice.

E'en the roof affords no refuge,
    Even there my rest's betrayed;
In the garret dwells a poet,
    Sings the songs himself hath made.

In despair I seek the cellar,
    Surely there the air is mute!
Hark! above me they are dancing
    To the bagpipe and the flute.

Senseless race! in self-delusion
　　Even thus ye'd sing and feast,
Though ye heard destroying thunders
　　Rolling, tragic, from the East!

vii

It is May; nor doth he marvel,
　　He, the Thinker, who can fathom
The Phenomena of Being.
　　In the Centre of Creation
Stand two Cats, snow-white and agèd,
　　Turn the Earth's enormous axis;
And the System of the Seasons
　　Is the outcome of their turning.

Ah, but wherefore in the May-time
　　Are my eyes so often moistened,
Are my heart-strings stirred so quickly
　　Wherefore must I, with no respite,
All the sixteen hours of daylight,
　　Toward the balcony be gazing;
Toward the golden Apollonia,
　　Toward the jet-black Jewess, Rachel?

viii

By the storms of fierce temptation
　　Undisturbed I long have dwelt;
Yet e'en pattern stars of virtue
　　Unexpected pangs have felt.

Hotter than in youth's hot furnace
　　Dreams of yore steal in apace,
And the Cat's winged yearnings journey,
　　Unrestrained, o'er Time and Space.

Naples, land of light and wonder,
　　Cup of nectar never dry!
To Sorrento I would hasten,
　　On its topmost roof to lie.

Greets me dark Vesuvius, greets me
    The white sail upon the sea;
Birds of spring make sweetest concert
    In the budding olive-tree.

Toward the loggia steals Carmela,
    Fairest of the feline race,
And she softly pulls my whiskers,
    And she gazes in my face,—

And my paw she gently presses:
    Hark! I hear a growling noise;
Can it be the Bay's hoarse murmur,
    Or Vesuvius' distant voice?

Nay, Vesuvius' voice is silent,
    For to-day he takes his rest,
In the yard, destruction breathing,
    Bays the dog of fiendish breast,—

Bays Francesco the Betrayer,
    Worst of all his evil race;
And I see my dream dissolving,
    Melting in the sky's embrace.

ix

Clear is Hiddigeigei's conscience,
    Strict his walk, his conduct wise;
Yet when neighbour cats are flirting,
    He, indulgent, shuts his eyes.

Lo, he lives for his vocation,
    For the slaughter of the mouse:
Yet he is not wroth though others
    Live for singing and carouse.

Hiddigeigei speaks, the Ancient:—
    "Pluck the fruits before they fall;
Should the years of famine follow
    Memory's joys will never pall."

x

E'en an earned life and godly
    Cannot shield us from old age,
And my coat is turning silver,
    As I see with fruitless rage.

Time destroys, relentless, steady,
    All that effort brave hath wrought,
And against that sharp-toothed foeman
    Weapons fail us—bitter thought!

All unhonoured and forgotten
    Fall we victims to his power:—
O, in wrath I'd fain devour them,
    Both the clock-hands on the tower!

xi

Earth once was untroubled by man, they say,
    Those days are over and fled,
When the forest primeval crackling lay
    'Neath the mammoth's mighty tread.

Ye may search throughout all the land in vain
    For the lion, the desert's own;
In sooth we are settled now, 'tis plain,
    In a truly temperate zone.

The palm is borne, in life and in verse,
    By neither the Great nor the Few;
The world grows weaker and ever worse,
    'Tis the day of the Small and the New.

When we Cats are silenced ariseth the Mouse,
    But she, too, must pack and begone,
And the Infusoria's Royal House
    Shall triumph, at last, alone.

xii

Near the close of his existence
  Hiddigeigei stands and sighs;
Death draws nigh with fell insistence,
  Ruthlessly to close his eyes.

Fain from out his wisdom's treasure,
  Counsels for his race he'd draw,
That amid life's changeful measure
  They might find some settled law.

Fain their path through life he'd soften,
  Rough it lies and strewn with stones;
E'en the old and wise may often
  Stumble there, and break their bones.

Life with many brawls is cumbered,
  Useless wounds and useless pain;
Cats both black and brave unnumbered
  Have for nought been foully slain.

Ah, in vain our tales of sorrow!
  Hark! I hear the laugh of youth.
Fools to-day and fools to-morrow,
  Woe alone will teach them truth.

All in vain is history's teaching;
  Listen how they laugh again!
Hiddigeigei's lore and preaching
  Locked in silence must remain.

xiii

Soon life's thread must break and ravel,
  Weak this arm, once strong and brave:—
In the scene of all my travail,
  In the granary, dig my grave.

Warlike glory there I won me,
   All the fight's fierce joy was mine;
Lay my shield and lance upon me,
   As the last of all my line.

Ay, the last! The children's merit
   Like their sires' can never grow;
Nought they know of strife of spirit;
   Upright are they, dull and slow.

Dull and meagre; stiffly, slowly,
   Move their minds, of force bereft;
Few indeed will keep as holy
   The bequest their sires have left.

Yet once more, in days far distant,
   When at rest I long have lain,
One fierce caterwaul insistent
   Through your ranks shall ring again:—

"Flee, ye fools, from worse than ruin!"
   Hark to Hiddigeigei's cry;
Hark, his wrathful ghostly mewing:—
   "Flee from mediocrity!"

THE OUTSPOKEN CAT

TOBERMORY

BY *Saki* (*H. H. Munro*)

IT WAS A CHILL, rain-washed afternoon of a late August day, that indefinite season when partridges are still in the security of cold storage, and there is nothing to hunt—unless one is bounded on the north by the Bristol Channel, in which case one may lawfully gallop after fat red stags. Lady Blemley's house-party was not bounded on the north by the Bristol Channel, hence there was a full gathering of her guests round the tea-table on this particular afternoon. And, in spite of the blankness of the season and the triteness of the occasion, there was no trace in the company of that fatigued restlessness which means a dread of the pianola and a subdued hankering for auction bridge. The undisguised, open-mouthed attention of the entire party was fixed on the homely, negative personality of Mr. Cornelius Appin. Of all her guests, he was the one who had come to Lady Blemley with the vaguest reputation. Someone had said he was "clever," and he had got his invitation in the moderate expectation, on the part of his hostess, that some portion at least of his cleverness would be contributed to the general entertainment. Until tea-time that day she had been unable to discover in what direction, if any, his cleverness lay. He was neither a wit nor a croquet champion, a hypnotic force nor a begetter of amateur theatricals. Neither did his exterior suggest the sort of man in whom women are willing to pardon a generous measure of mental deficiency. He had subsided into mere Mr. Appin, and the Cornelius seemed a piece of transparent baptismal bluff. And now he was claiming to have launched on the world a discovery beside which the invention of gun powder, of the printing-press, and of steam locomotion were inconsiderable trifles. Science had made bewildering strides in many directions during recent decades, but this thing seemed to belong to the domain of miracle rather than to scientific achievement.

"And do you really ask us to believe," Sir Wilfrid was saying, "that you have discovered a means for instructing animals in the art of human speech, and that dear old Tobermory has proved your first successful pupil?"

"It is a problem at which I have worked for the last seventeen years," said Mr. Appin, "but only during the last eight or nine months have I been rewarded with glimmerings of success. Of course I have experimented with thousands of animals, but latterly only with cats, those wonderful creatures which have assimilated themselves so marvelously with our civilization while retaining all their highly developed feral instincts. Here and there among cats one comes across an outstanding superior intellect, just as one does among the ruck of human beings, and when I made the acquaintance of Tobermory a week ago I saw at once that I was in contact with a 'Beyond-cat' of extraordinary intelligence. I had gone far along the road to success in recent experiments; with Tobermory, as you call him, I have reached the goal."

Mr. Appin concluded his remarkable statement in a voice which he strove to divest of a triumphant inflexion. No one said "Rats," though Clovis's lips moved in a monosyllabic contortion which probably invoked those rodents of disbelief.

"And do you mean to say," asked Miss Resker, after a slight pause, "that you have taught Tobermory to say and understand easy sentences of one syllable?"

"My dear Miss Resker," said the wonder-worker patiently, "one teaches little children and savages and backward adults in that piece-meal fashion; when one has once solved the problem of making a beginning with an animal of highly developed intelligence one has no need for those halting methods. Tobermory can speak our language with perfect correctness."

This time Clovis very distinctly said, "Beyond-rats!" Sir Wilfrid was more polite, but equally sceptical.

"Hadn't we better have the cat in and judge for ourselves?" suggested Lady Blemley.

Sir Wilfrid went in search of the animal, and the company settled themselves down to the languid expectation of witnessing some more or less adroit drawing-room ventriloquism.

In a minute Sir Wilfrid was back in the room, his face white beneath its tan and his eyes dilated with excitement.

"By Gad, it's true!"

His agitation was unmistakably genuine, and his hearers started forward in a thrill of awakened interest.

Collapsing into an armchair he continued breathlessly: "I found him dozing in the smoking-room, and called after him to come for his tea. He blinked at me in his usual way, and I said, 'Come on, Toby; don't keep us waiting'; and, by Gad! he drawled out in a most horribly natural voice, that he'd come when he dashed well pleased! I nearly jumped out of my skin!"

Appin had preached to absolutely incredulous hearers; Sir Wilfrid's statement carried instant conviction. A Babel-like chorus of startled exclamation arose, amid which the scientist sat mutely enjoying the first fruit of his stupendous discovery.

In the midst of the clamour Tobermory entered the room and

made his way with velvet tread and studied unconcern across to the group seated round the tea-table.

A sudden hush of awkwardness and constraint fell on the company. Somehow there seemed an element of embarrassment in addressing on equal terms a domestic cat of acknowledged mental ability.

"Will you have some milk, Tobermory?" asked Lady Blemley in a rather strained voice.

"I don't mind if I do," was the response, couched in a tone of even indifference. A shiver of suppressed excitement went through the listeners, and Lady Blemley might be excused for pouring out the saucerful of milk rather unsteadily.

"I am afraid I have spilt a good deal of it," she said apologetically.

"After all, it's not my Axminster," was Tobermory's rejoinder.

Another silence fell on the group, and then Miss Resker, in her best district-visitor manner, asked if the human language had been difficult to learn. Tobermory looked squarely at her for a moment and then fixed his gaze serenely on the middle distance. It was obvious that boring questions lay outside his scheme of life.

"What do you think of human intelligence?" asked Mavis Pellington lamely.

"Of whose intelligence in particular?" asked Tobermory coldly.

"Oh, well, mine for instance," said Mavis, with a feeble laugh.

"You put me in an embarrassing position," said Tobermory, whose tone and attitude certainly did not suggest a shred of embarrassment. "When your inclusion in this house party was suggested, Sir Wilfrid protested that you were the most brainless woman of his acquaintance, and that there was a wide distinction between hospitality and the care of the feeble-minded. Lady Blemley replied that your lack of brain-power was the precise quality which had earned you your invitation, as you were the only person she could think of who might be idiotic enough to buy their old car. You know, the one they call 'The Envy of Sisyphus,' because it goes quite nicely up-hill if you push it."

Lady Blemley's protestations would have had greater effect if she had not casually suggested to Mavis only that morning that the car in question would be just the thing for her down at her Devonshire home.

Major Barfield plunged in heavily to effect a diversion.

"How about your carryings-on with the tortoise-shell puss up at the stables, eh?"

The moment he had said it every one realized the blunder.

"One does not usually discuss these matters in public," said Tobermory frigidly. "From a slight observation of your ways since you've been in the house I should imagine you'd find it inconvenient if I were to shift the conversation on to your own little affairs."

The panic which ensued was not confined to the Major.

"Would you like to go and see if cook has got your dinner ready?" suggested Lady Blemley hurriedly, affecting to ignore the fact that it wanted at least two hours to Tobermory's dinner-time.

"Thanks," said Tobermory, "not quite so soon after my tea. I don't want to die of indigestion."

"Cats have nine lives, you know," said Sir Wilfrid heartily.

"Possibly," answered Tobermory; "but only one liver."

"Adelaide!" said Mrs. Cornett, "do you mean to encourage that cat to go out and gossip about us in the servants' hall?"

The panic had indeed become general. A narrow ornamental balustrade ran in front of most of the bedroom windows at the Towers, and it was recalled with dismay that this had formed a favourite promenade for Tobermory at all hours, whence he could watch the pigeons—and heaven knew what else besides. If he intended to become reminiscent in his present outspoken strain the effect would be something more than disconcerting. Mrs. Cornett, who spent much time at her toilet table, and whose complexion was reputed to be of a nomadic though punctual disposition, looked as ill at ease as the Major. Miss Scrawen, who wrote fiercely sensuous poetry and led a blameless life, merely displayed irritation; if you are methodical and virtuous in private you don't necessarily want every one to know it. Bertie van Tahn, who was so depraved at seventeen that he had long ago given up trying to be any worse, turned a dull shade of gardenia white, but he did not commit the error of dashing out of the room like Odo Finsberry, a young gentleman who was understood to be reading for the Church and who was possibly disturbed at the thought of scandals he might hear concerning other people. Clovis had the presence of mind to maintain a composed exterior; privately he was calculating how long it would take to procure a box of fancy mice through the agency of the *Exchange and Mart* as a species of hush-money.

Even in a delicate situation like the present, Agnes Resker could not endure to remain too long in the background.

"Why did I ever come down here?" she asked dramatically. Tobermory immediately accepted the opening.

"Judging by what you said to Mrs. Cornett on the croquet-lawn yesterday, you were out for food. You described the Blemleys as the dullest people to stay with that you knew, but said they were clever enough to employ a first-rate cook; otherwise they'd find it difficult to get any one to come down a second time."

"There's not a word of truth in it! I appeal to Mrs. Cornett—" exclaimed the discomfited Agnes.

"Mrs. Cornett repeated your remark afterwards to Bertie van Tahn," continued Tobermory, "and said, 'That woman is a regular Hunger Marcher; she'd go anywhere for four square meals a day,' and Bertie van Tahn said—"

At this point the chronicle mercifully ceased. Tobermory had caught a glimpse of the big yellow Tom from the Rectory working his way through the shrubbery towards the stable wing. In a flash he had vanished through the open French window.

With the disappearance of his too brilliant pupil Cornelius Appin found himself beset by a hurricane of bitter upbraiding, anxious inquiry, and frightened entreaty. The responsibility for the situation lay with him, and he must prevent matters from becoming worse. Could Tobermory impart his dangerous gift to other cats? was the first question he had to answer. It was possible, he replied, that he might have initiated his intimate friend the stable puss into his new accomplishment, but it was unlikely that his teaching could have taken a wider range as yet.

"Then," said Mrs. Cornett, "Tobermory may be a valuable cat and a great pet; but I'm sure you'll agree, Adelaide, that both he and the stable cat must be done away with without delay."

"You don't suppose I've enjoyed the last quarter of an hour, do you?" said Lady Blemley bitterly. "My husband and I are very fond of Tobermory—at least, we were before this horrible accomplishment was infused into him; but now, of course, the only thing is to have him destroyed as soon as possible."

"We can put some strychnine in the scraps he always gets at

dinner-time," said Sir Wilfrid, "and I will go and drown the stable cat myself. The coachman will be very sore at losing his pet, but I'll say a very catching form of mange has broken out in both cats and we're afraid of it spreading to the kennels."

"But my great discovery!" expostulated Mr. Appin; "after all my years of research and experiment—"

"You can go and experiment on the short-horns at the farm, who are under proper control," said Mrs. Cornett, "or the elephants at the Zoological Gardens. They're said to be highly intelligent, and they have this recommendation, that they don't come creeping about our bedrooms and under chairs, and so forth."

An archangel ecstatically proclaiming the Millennium, and then finding that it clashed unpardonably with Henley and would have to be indefinitely postponed, could hardly have felt more crestfallen than Cornelius Appin at the reception of his wonderful achievement. Public opinion, however, was against him—in fact, had the general voice been consulted on the subject it is probable that a strong minority vote would have been in favour of including him in the strychnine diet.

Defective train arrangements and a nervous desire to see matters brought to a finish prevented an immediate dispersal of the party, but dinner that evening was not a social success. Sir Wilfrid had had rather a trying time with the stable cat and subsequently with the coachman. Agnes Resker ostentatiously limited her repast to a morsel of dry toast, which she bit as though it were a personal enemy; while Mavis Pellington maintained a vindictive silence throughout the meal. Lady Blemley kept up a flow of what she hoped was conversation, but her attention was fixed on the doorway. A plateful of carefully dosed fish scraps was in readiness on the sideboard, but sweets and savoury and dessert went their way, and no Tobermory appeared either in the dining-room or kitchen.

The sepulchral dinner was cheerful compared with the subsequent vigil in the smoking-room. Eating and drinking had at least supplied a distraction and cloak to the prevailing embarrassment. Bridge was out of the question in the general tension of nerves and tempers, and after Odo Finsberry had given a lugubrious rendering of "Melisande in the Wood" to a frigid audience, music was tacitly avoided. At eleven the servants went to bed, announcing that the small window in the pantry had been left open as usual for Tobermory's private use. The guests read steadily through the current batch of magazines, and fell back gradually on the "Badminton Library" and bound volumes of *Punch*. Lady Blemley made periodic visits to the pantry, returning each time with an expression of listless depression which forestalled questioning.

At two o'clock Clovis broke the dominating silence.

"He won't turn up tonight. He's probably in the local newspaper office at the present moment, dictating the first instalment of his reminiscences. Lady What's-her-name's book won't be in it. It will be the event of the day."

Having made this contribution to the general cheerfulness, Clovis went to bed. At long intervals the various members of the house followed his example.

The servants taking round the early tea made a uniform announcement in reply to a uniform question. Tobermory had not returned.

Breakfast was, if anything, a more unpleasant function than dinner had been, but before its conclusion the situation was relieved. Tobermory's corpse was brought in from the shrubbery, where a gardener had just discovered it. From the bites on his throat and the yellow fur which coated his claws it was evident that he had fallen in unequal combat with the big Tom from the Rectory.

By midday most of the guests had quitted the Towers, and after lunch Lady Blemley had sufficiently recovered her spirits to write an extremely nasty letter to the Rectory about the loss of her valuable pet.

Tobermory had been Appin's one successful pupil, and he was destined to have no successor. A few weeks later an elephant in the Dresden Zoological Garden, which had shown no previous signs of irritability, broke loose and killed an Englishman who had apparently been teasing it. The victim's name was variously reported in the papers as Oppin and Eppelin, but his front name was faithfully rendered Cornelius.

"If he was trying German irregular verbs on the poor beast," said Clovis, "he deserved all he got."

THE RETIRED CAT

BY *William Cowper*

A Poet's Cat, sedate and grave
As poet well could wish to have,
Was much addicted to inquire
For nooks to which she might retire,
And where, secure as mouse in chink,
She might repose, or sit and think.
I know not where she caught the trick;
Nature perhaps herself had cast her
In such a mold PHILOSOPHIC,
Or else she learned it of her master.
Sometimes ascending, debonair,
An apple tree or lofty pear,
Lodged with convenience in the fork,
She watched the gardener at his work;
Sometimes her ease and solace sought
In an old empty watering-pot,
There wanting nothing save a fan
To seem some nymph in her sadan,
Appareled in exactest sort,
And ready to be borne to court.

But love of change it seems has place
Not only in our wiser race;
Cats also feel as well as we
That passion's force, and so did she.
Her climbing, she began to find,
Exposed her too much to the wind,
And the old utensil of tin
Was cold and comfortless within;
She therefore wished, instead of those,

Some place of more serene repose,
Where neither cold might come, nor air
Too rudely wanton in her hair,
And sought it in the likeliest mode
Within her master's snug abode.

A drawer, it chanced, at bottom lined,
With linen of the softest kind,
With such as merchants introduce
From India, for the ladies' use;
A drawer, impending o'er the rest,
Half open, in the topmost chest,
Of depth enough and none to spare,
Invited her to slumber there;
Puss with delight beyond expression,
Surveyed the scene and took possession.
Recumbent at her ease, ere long,
And lulled by her own humdrum song,
She left the cares of life behind,
And slept as she would sleep her last,
When in came, housewifely inclined,
The chambermaid, and shut it fast,
By no malignity impelled,
But all unconscious whom it held.
Awakened by the shock (cried Puss),
"Was ever cat attended thus!
The open drawer was left, I see,
Merely to prove a nest for me,
For soon as I was well composed,
Then came the maid, and it was closed.
How smooth those 'kerchiefs and how sweet,
Oh, what a delicate retreat!
I will resign myself to rest
Till Sol declining in the West,
Shall call to supper, when no doubt,
Susan will come and let me out."

The evening came, the sun descended,
And Puss remained, still unattended.

The night rolled tardily away
(With her, indeed, 'twas never day),
The sprightly morn her course renewed,
The evening gray again ensued,
And Puss came into mind no more
Than if entombed the day before;
With hunger pinched and pinched for room,
She now presaged approaching doom.
Nor slept a single wink, nor purred,
Conscious of jeopardy incurred.

That night, by chance, the poet, watching,
Heard an inexplicable scratching;
His noble heart went pit-a-pat,
And to himself he said, "What's that?"
He drew the curtain at his side,
And forth he peeped, but nothing spied.
Yet by his ear directed, guessed
Something imprisoned in the chest;
And doubtful what, with prudent care
Resolved it should continue there.
At length a voice, which well he knew
A long and melancholy mew,
Saluting his poetic ears,
Consoled him and dispelled his fears;
He left his bed, he trod the floor,
He 'gan in haste the drawers explore,
The lowest first, and without stop
The next in order to the top.
For 'tis a truth well known to most,
That whatsoever thing is lost,
We seek it, ere it come to light,
In every cranny but the right.
Forth skipped the cat, not now replete
As erst with airy self-conceit,
Nor in her own fond comprehension,
A theme for all the world's attention,
But modest, sober, cured of all
Her notions hyperbolical

And wishing for a place of rest,
Anything rather than a chest.
Then stepped the poet into bed
With this reflection in his head:

Moral.

Beware of too sublime a sense
Of your own worth and consequence.
The man who dreams himself so great,
And his importance of such weight,
That all around in all that's done,
Must move and act for him alone,
Will learn in school of tribulation
The folly of his expectation.

❦

THE CONTEMPTUOUS CAT

AGRIPPINA

BY *Agnes Repplier*

SHE IS SITTING ON MY DESK, as I write, and I glance at her with deference, mutely begging permission to begin. But her back is turned to me, and expresses in every curve such fine and delicate disdain that I falter and lose courage at the very threshold of my task. I have long known that cats are the most contemptuous of creatures, and that Agrippina is the most contemptuous of cats. The spirit of Bouhaki, the proud Theban beast that sat erect, with gold earrings in his ears, at the feet of his master, King Hana; the spirit of Muezza, whose slumbers Mahomet himself was not bold enough to disturb; the spirit of Micetto, Châteaubriand's ecclesiastical pet, dignified as a cardinal, and conscious ever that he was the gift of a sovereign pontiff,—the spirits of all arrogant cats that have played scornful parts in the world's great comedy look out from

Agrippina's yellow eyes and hold me in subjection. I should like to explain to her, if I dared, that my desk is small, littered with many papers, and sadly overcrowded with the useful inutilities which affectionate friends delight in giving me at Christmas time. Sainte-Beuve's cat, I am aware, sat on his desk, and roamed at will among those precious manuscripts which no intrusive hand was ever permitted to touch; but Sainte-Beuve probably had sufficient space reserved for his own comfort and convenience. I have not; and Agrippina's beautifully ringed tail flapping across my copy distracts my attention and imperils the neatness of my penmanship. Even when she is disposed to be affable, turns the light of her countenance upon me, watches with attentive curiosity every stroke I make, and softly, with curved paw, pats my pen as it travels over the paper,—even in these halcyon moments, though my self-love is flattered by her condescension, I am aware that I should work better and more rapidly if I denied myself this charming companionship.

But in truth it is impossible for a lover of cats to banish these alert, gentle, and discriminating little friends, who give us just enough of their regard and complaisance to make us hunger for more. M. Fée, the naturalist, who has written so admirably about animals, and who understands, as only a Frenchman can understand, the delicate and subtle organization of a cat, frankly admits that the keynote of its character is independence. It dwells under our roof, sleeps by our fire, endures our blandishments, and apparently enjoys our society, without for one moment forfeiting its sense of absolute freedom, without acknowledging any servile relation to the human creature who shelters it. "The cat," says M. Fée, "will never part with its liberty; it will neither be our servant, like the horse, nor our friend, like the dog. It consents to live as our guest; it accepts the home we offer and the food we give; it even goes so far as to solicit our caresses, but capriciously, and when it suits its humor to receive them."

Rude and masterful souls resent this fine self-sufficiency in a domestic animal, and require that it should have no will but theirs, no pleasure that does not emanate from them. They are forever prating of the love and fidelity of the dog, of the beast that obeys their slightest word, crouches contentedly for hours at their feet,

CAT IN A MUFF.
H. Claudius

is exuberantly grateful for the smallest attention, and so affectionate that its demonstrations require to be curbed rather than encouraged. All this homage is pleasing to their vanity; yet there are people, less magisterial perhaps, or less exacting, who believe that true friendship, even with an animal, may be built up on mutual esteem and independence; that to demand gratitude is to be unworthy of it; and that obedience is not essential to agreeable and healthy intercourse. A man who owns a dog is, in every sense of the word, its master; the term expresses accurately their mutual relations. But it is ridiculous when applied to the limited possession of a cat. I am certainly not Agrippina's mistress, and the assumption of authority on my part would be a mere empty dignity, like those swelling titles which afford such innocent delight to the Freemasons of our severe republic. If I call Agrippina, she does not come; if I tell her to go away, she remains where she is; if I try to persuade her to show off her one or two little accomplishments, she refuses, with courteous but unswerving decision. She has frolicsome moods, in which a thimble, a shoe-buttoner, a scrap of paper, or a piece of string will drive her wild with delight; she has moods of inflexible gravity, in which she stares solemnly at her favorite ball rolling over the carpet, without stirring one lazy limb to reach it. "Have I seen this foolish toy before?" she seems to be asking herself with musing austerity; "and can it be possible that there are cats who run after such frivolous trifles? Vanity of vanities, and all is vanity, save only to lie upon the hearth-rug, and be warm, and 'think grave thoughts to feed a serious soul.'" In such moments of rejection and humiliation, I comfort myself by recalling the words of one too wise for arrogance. "When I play with my cat," says Montaigne, "how do I know whether she does not make a jest of me? We entertain each other with mutual antics; and if I have my own time for beginning or refusing, she, too, has hers."

This is the spirit in which we should approach a creature so reserved and so utterly self-sufficing; this is the only key we have to that natural distinction of character which repels careless and unobservant natures. When I am told Agrippina is disobedient, ungrateful, cold-hearted, perverse, stupid, treacherous, and cruel, I no longer strive to check the torrent of abuse. I know that Buffon said all this, and much more, about cats, and that people have gone on repeating it ever since, principally because these spirited little beasts have remained just what it pleased Providence to make them, have preserved their primitive freedom through centuries of effete and demoralizing civilization. Why, I wonder, should a great many good men and women cherish an unreasonable grudge against one animal because it does not chance to possess the precise qualities of another? "My dog fetches my slippers for me every night," said a friend triumphantly, not long ago. "He puts them first to warm by the fire, and then brings them over to my chair, wagging his tail, and as proud as Punch. Would your cat do as much for you, I'd like to know?" Assuredly not! If I waited for Agrippina to fetch me shoes or slippers, I should have no other resource save to join as speedily as possible one of the bare-footed religious orders of Italy. But, after all, fetching slippers is not the whole duty of domestic pets. As La Fontaine gently reminds us,

"*Tout animal n'a pas toutes propriétés.*"

We pick no quarrel with a canary because it does not talk like a parrot, nor with a parrot because it does not sing like a canary. We find no fault with a King Charles spaniel for not flying at the throat of a burglar, nor with a St. Bernard because we cannot put it in our pocket. Agrippina will never make herself serviceable, yet nevertheless is she of inestimable service. How many times have I rested tired eyes on her graceful little body, curled up in a ball and wrapped round with her tail like a parcel; or stretched out luxuriously on my bed, one paw coyly covering her face, the other curved gently inwards, as though clasping an invisible treasure! Asleep or awake, in rest or in motion, grave or gay, Agrippina is always beautiful; and it is better to be beautiful than to fetch and carry from the rising to the setting of the sun. She is droll, too, with an unconscious humor even in her most serious and sentimental moods. She has quite the longest ears that ever were seen on so small a cat, eyes more solemn than Athene's owl blinking in the sunlight, and an air of supercilious disdain that would have made Diogenes seem young and ardent by her side. Sitting on the library table, under the evening lamp, with her head held high in air, her tall ears as erect as chimneys, and her inscrutable gaze fixed on the darkest corner of the room, Agrippina inspires in the family sentiments of mingled mirthfulness and awe. To laugh at her in such moments, however, is to incur her supreme displeasure. I have known her to jump down from the table and walk haughtily out of the room, because of a single half-suppressed but wholly indecorous giggle.

Schopenhauer has said that the reason domestic pets are so lovable and so helpful to us is because they enjoy, quietly and placidly, the present moment. Life holds no future for them, and consequently no care; if they are content, their contentment is absolute; and our jaded and wearied spirits find a natural relief in the sight of creatures whose little cups of happiness can so easily be filled to the brim. Walt Whitman expresses the same thought more coarsely when he acknowledges that he loves the society of animals because they do not sweat and whine over their condition, nor lie awake in the dark and weep for their sins, nor sicken him with discussions of their duty. In truth, that admirable counsel of Sydney Smith's, "Take short views of life," can be obeyed only by the brutes; for the thought that travels even to the morrow is long enough to destroy our peace of mind, inasmuch as we know not what the morrow may bring forth. But when Agrippina has breakfasted, and washed, and sits in the sunlight blinking at me with affectionate contempt, I feel soothed by her absolute and unqualified enjoyment. I know how full my day will be of things that I don't want particularly to do, and that are not particularly worth doing; but for her time and the world hold only this brief moment of contentment. Slowly the eyes close, gently the little body is relaxed. Oh, you who strive to relieve your overwrought nerves, and cultivate power through repose, watch the exquisite languor of a drowsy cat, and despair of imitating such perfect and restful grace! There is a gradual yielding of every muscle to the soft persuasiveness of slumber; the flexible frame is curved into tender lines, the head nestles lower, the paws are tucked out of sight; no convulsive throb or start betrays a rebellious alertness; only a faint quiver of unconscious satisfaction, a faint heaving of the tawny sides, a faint gleam of the half-shut yellow eyes, and Agrippina is asleep. I look at her for one wistful moment, and then turn resolutely to my work. It were ignoble to wish myself in her place, and yet how charming to be able to settle down to a nap, *sans peur et sans reproche*, at ten o'clock in the morning!

These, then, are a few of the pleasures to be derived from the society of an amiable cat; and by an amiable cat I mean one that, while maintaining its own dignity and delicate reserve, is nevertheless affable and condescending in the company of human beings. There is nothing I dislike more than newspaper and magazine stories about priggish pussies—like the children in Sunday-school books—that share their food with hungry beasts from the back alleys, and show touching fidelity to old blind masters, and hunt partridges in a spirit of noble self-sacrifice for consumptive mistresses, and scorn to help themselves to delicacies from the kitchen tables, and arouse their households so often in cases of fire that I should suspect them of starting the conflagrations in order to win applause by giving the alarm. Whatever a real cat may or may not be, it is never a prig, and all true lovers of the race have been quick to recognize and appreciate this fact.

"I value in the cat," says Châteaubriand, "that independent and almost ungrateful temper which prevents it from attaching itself to any one; the indifference with which it passes from the salon to the housetop. When you caress it, it stretches itself out and arches its back, indeed; but that is caused by physical pleasure, and not, as in the case of the dog, by a silly satisfaction in loving and being faithful to a master who returns thanks in kicks. The cat lives alone, has no need of society, does not obey except when it likes, pretends to sleep that it may see the more clearly, and scratches everything that it can scratch."

Here is a sketch spirited enough and of good outline, but hardly correct in every detail. A cat seldom manifests affection, yet is often distinctly social, and likes to see itself the petted minion of a family group. Agrippina, in fact, so far from living alone, will not, if she can help it, remain for a moment in a room by herself. She is content to have me as a companion, perhaps in default of better;

but if I go upstairs or downstairs in search of a book, or my eye-glasses, or any one of the countless things that are never where they ought to be, Agrippina follows closely at my heels. Sometimes, when she is fast asleep, I steal softly out of the door, thinking to escape her vigilance; but before I have taken a dozen steps she is under my feet, mewing a gentle reproach, and putting on all the injured airs of a deserted Ariadne. I should like to think such behavior prompted by affection rather than curiosity; but in my candid moments I find this "pathetic fallacy" a difficult sentiment to cherish. There are people, I am aware, who trustfully assert that their pets love them; and one such sanguine creature has recently assured the world that "no man who boasts the real intimacy and confidence of a cat would dream of calling his four-footed friend 'puss.'" But is not such a boast rather ill-timed at best? How dare any man venture to assert that he possesses the intimacy and confi-dence of an animal so exclusive and so reserved? I doubt if Cardinal Wolsey, in the zenith of his pride and power, claimed the intimacy and confidence of the superb cat that sat in a cushioned armchair by his side, and reflected with mimic dignity the full-blown honors of the Lord High Chancellor of England. Agrippina, I am humbly aware, grants me neither her intimacy nor her confidence, but only her companionship, which I endeavor to receive modestly, and without flaunting my favors to the world. She is displeased and even downcast when I go out, and she greets my return with de-light, thrusting her little gray head between the banisters the instant I open the house door, and waving a welcome in mid-air with one ridiculously small paw. Being but mortal, I am naturally pleased with these tokens of esteem, but I do not, on that account, go about with arrogant brow and boast of my intimacy with Agrippina. I should be laughed at, if I did, by everybody who is privileged to possess and appreciate a cat.

As for curiosity, that vice which the Abbé Galiani held to be unknown to animals, but which the more astute Voltaire detected in every little dog that he saw peering out of the window of its master's coach, it is the ruling passion of the feline breast. A closet door left ajar, a box with half-closed lid, an open bureau drawer,— these are the objects that fill a cat with the liveliest interest and delight. Agrippina watches breathlessly the unfastening of a parcel, and tries to hasten matters by clutching actively at the string. When its contents are shown her, she examines them gravely, and then, with a sigh of relief, settles down to repose. The slightest noise disturbs and irritates her until she discovers its cause. If she hears a footstep in the hall, she runs out to see whose it is, and, like certain troublesome little people I have known, she dearly loves to go to the front door every time the bell is rung. From my window she surveys the street with tranquil scrutiny, and, if boys are playing below, she follows their games with a steady scornful stare, very different from the wistful eagerness of a friendly dog, quivering to join in the sport. Sometimes the boys catch sight of her, and shout up rudely at her window; and I can never sufficiently admire Agrippina's conduct upon these trying occasions, the well-bred composure with which she affects neither to see nor to hear them, nor to be aware that there are such objectionable creatures as children in the world. Sometimes, too, the terrier that lives next door comes out to sun himself in the street, and, beholding my cat sitting well out of reach, he dances madly up and down the pavement, barking with all his might, and rearing himself on his short hind legs, in a futile attempt to dislodge her. Then the spirit of evil enters Agrippina's little heart. The window is open, and she creeps to the extreme edge of the stone sill, stretches herself at full length, peers down smilingly at the frenzied dog, dangles one paw enticingly in the air, and exerts herself with quiet malice to drive him to desperation. Her sense of humor is awakened by his frantic efforts, and by her own absolute security; and not until he is spent with exertion, and lies panting and exhausted on the bricks, does she arch her graceful little back, stretch her limbs lazily in the sun, and with one light bound spring from the window to my desk. Wisely has Moncrif observed that a cat is not merely diverted by everything that moves, but is convinced that all nature is occupied exclusively with catering to her diversion.

There is a charming story told by M. Champfleury, who has written so much and so admirably about cats, of a poor hermit whose piety and asceticism were so great that in a vision he was permitted to behold his place in heaven, next to that of St. Gregory, the sovereign pontiff of Christendom. The hermit, who possessed nothing upon earth but a female cat, was abashed by the thought that in the next world he was destined to rank with so powerful a prince of the Church; and perhaps—for who knows the secret springs of spiritual pride?—he fancied that his self-inflicted poverty should win for him an even higher reward. Whereupon a second revelation made known to him that his detachment from the world was by no means so complete as he imagined, for that he loved and valued his cat, the sole companion of his solitude, more than St. Gregory loved and valued all his earthly possessions. The Pope on his throne was the truer ascetic of the two.

This little tale conveys to us, in addition to its excellent moral,—never more needed than at present,—a pleasing truth concerning the lovability of cats. While they have never attained, and never deserve to attain, the widespread and somewhat commonplace popularity of dogs, their fascination is a more potent and irresistible charm. He who yields himself to the sweet seductiveness of a cat is beguiled forever from the simple, honorable friendship of the more generous and open-hearted beast. The small domestic sphinx whose inscrutable eyes never soften with affection; the fetich animal that comes down to us from the far past, adored, hated, and feared,—a god in wise and silent Egypt, a plaything in old Rome, a hunted and unholy creature, suffering one long martyrdom throughout the half-seen, dimly-fathomed Middle Ages,—even now this lovely, uncanny pet is capable of inspiring mingled sentiments of horror and devotion. Those who are under its spell rejoice in their thralldom, and, like M. Champfleury's hermit, grow strangely wedded to this mute, unsympathetic comradeship. Those who have inherited the old, half-fearful aversion render a still finer tribute to the cat's native witchery and power. I have seen middle-aged women, of dignified and tranquil aspect, draw back with unfeigned dismay at the sight of Agrippina, a little ball of gray and yellow fur, curled up in peaceful slumber on the hearth-rug. And this instinctive shrinking has nothing in common with the perfectly reasonable fear we entertain for a terrier snapping and snarling at our heels, or for a mastiff the size of a calf, which our friend assures us is as gentle as a baby, but which looks able and ready to tear us limb from limb. It may be ignominious to be afraid of dogs, but the emotion is one which will bear analysis and explanation; we know exactly what it is we fear; while the uneasiness with which many people behold a harmless and perfectly indifferent cat is a faint reflection of that superstitious terror which the nineteenth century still borrows occasionally from the ninth. We call it by a different name, and account for it on purely natural principles, in deference to progress; but the mediæval peasant who beheld his cat steal out, like a gray shadow, on St. John's Eve, to join in unholy rites, felt the same shuddering abhorrence which we witness and wonder at to-day. He simplified matters somewhat and eased his troubled mind by killing the beast; for cats that ventured forth on the feast of St. John, or on Halloween, or on the second Wednesday in Lent, did so at their peril. Fires blazed for them in every village, and even quiet stay-at-homes were too often hunted from their chimney-corners to a cruel death. There is a receipt signed in 1575 by one Lucas Pommoreux,—abhorred forever be his name!—to whom has been paid the sum of a hundred *sols parisis* "for having supplied for three years all the cats required for the fire on St. John's Day;" and be it remembered that the gracious child afterwards Louis XIII. interceded with Henry IV. for the lives of these poor animals, sacrified to wicked sport and an unreasoning terror.

Girt around with fear and mystery and subtle associations of evil, the cat comes down to us through the centuries; and from every land fresh traditions of sorcery claim it for their own. In Brittany is still whispered the dreadful tale of the cats that danced with sacrilegious glee around the crucifix until their king was killed; and in Sicily men know that if a black cat serve seven masters in turn he carries the soul of the seventh into hell. In Russia black cats become devils at the end of seven years, and in southern Europe they are merely serving their apprenticeship as witches. Norwegian folk lore is rich in ghastly stories like that of the wealthy miller whose mill has been twice burned down on Whitsun night, and for whom a traveling tailor offers to keep watch. The tailor chalks a circle on the floor, writes the Lord's prayer around it, and waits until midnight, when a troop of cats rush in and hang a great pot of pitch over the fireplace. Again and again they try to overturn this pitch, but every time the tailor frightens them away; and when their leader endeavors stealthily to draw him outside of his magic circle, he cuts off her paw with his knife. Then they all fly howling into the night, and the next morning the miller sees with joy his mill standing whole and unharmed. But the miller's wife cowers under the bedclothes, offering her left hand to the tailor, and hiding as best she can her right arm's bleeding stump.

Finer even than this tale is the well-known story which "Monk"

Lewis told to Shelley of a gentleman who, late one night, went to visit a friend living on the outskirts of a forest in east Germany. He lost his path, and, after wandering aimlessly for some time, beheld at last a light streaming from the windows of an old and ruined abbey. Looking in, he saw a procession of cats lowering into a grave a small coffin with a crown upon it. The sight filled him with horror, and, spurring his horse, he rode away as fast as he could, never stopping until he reached his destination, long after midnight. His friend was still awaiting him, and at once he recounted what had happened; whereupon a cat that lay sleeping by the fire sprang to its feet, cried out, "Then I am the king of the cats!" and disappeared like a flash up the chimney.

For my part, I consider this the best cat story in all literature, full of suggestiveness and terror, yet picturesque withal, and leaving ample room in the mind for speculation. Why was not the heir apparent bidden to the royal funeral? Was there a disputed succession, and how are such points settled in the mysterious domain of cat-land? The notion that these animals gather in ghost-haunted churches and castles for their nocturnal revels is one common to all parts of Europe. We remember how the little maiden of the Mountain Idyl confides to Heine that the innocent-looking cat in the chimney-corner is really a witch, and that at midnight, when the storm is high, she steals away to the ruined keep, where the spirits of the dead wait spellbound for the word that shall waken them. In all scenes of impish revelry cats play a prominent part, although occasionally, by virtue of their dual natures, they serve as barriers against the powers of evil. There is the old story of the witch's cat that was grateful to the good girl who gave it some ham to eat,—I may observe here, parenthetically, that I have never known a cat that would touch ham; and there is the fine bit of Italian folk lore about the servant maid who, with no other protector than a black cat, ventures to disturb a procession of ghosts on the dreadful Night of the Dead. "It is well for you that the cat lies in your arms," the angry spirit says to her; "otherwise what I am you also would be." The last pale reflex of a universal tradition I found two years ago in London, where the bad behavior of the Westminster cats—proverbially the most dissolute and profligate specimens of their race—has given rise to the pleasing legend of a country house whither these rakish animals retire for nights of gay festivity, and whence they return in the early morning, jaded, repentant, and forlorn.

Of late years there has been a rapid and promising growth of what disaffected and alliterative critics call the "cat cult," and poets and painters vie with one another in celebrating the charms of this long-neglected pet. Mr. M. H. Spielmann's beautiful volume in praise of Madame Henriette Ronner and her pictures is a treasure upon which many an ardent lover of cats will cast wandering and wistful glances. It is impossible for even the most disciplined spirit not to yearn over these little furry darlings, these gentle, mischievous, lazy, irresistible things. As for Banjo, that dear and sentimental kitten, with his head on one side like Lydia Languish, and a decorous melancholy suffusing his splendid eyes, let any obdurate scorner of the race look at his loveliness and be converted. Mrs. Graham R. Tomson's pretty anthology, Concerning Cats, is another step in the right direction; a dainty volume of selections from French and English verse, where we may find old favorites like Cowper's Retired Cat and Calverly's Sad Memories, graceful epitaphs on departed pussies, some delightful poems from Baudelaire, and three, no less delightful, from the pen of Mrs. Tomson herself, whose preface, or "foreword," is enough to win for her at once the friendship and sympathy of the elect. The book, while it contains a good deal that might well have been omitted, is necessarily a small one; for poets, English poets especially, have just begun to sing the praises of the cat, as they have for generations sung the praises of the horse and dog. Nevertheless, all English literature, and all the literatures of every land, are full of charming allusions to this friendly animal,—allusions the brevity of which only enhances their value. Those two delicious lines of Herrick's, for example,

"And the brisk mouse may feast herself with crumbs,
   Till that the green-eyed kitling comes,"

are worth the whole of Wordsworth's solemn poem The Kitten and Falling Leaves. What did Wordsworth know of the innate vanity, the affectation and coquetry, of kittenhood? He saw the little beast gamboling on the wall, and he fancied her as innocent as she looked, —as though any living creature could be as innocent as a kitten looks! With touching simplicity he believed her all unconscious of the admiration she was exciting.

> *"What would little Tabby care*
> *For the plaudits of the crowd?*
> *Over happy to be proud,*
> *Over wealthy in the treasure*
> *Of her own exceeding pleasure!"*

Ah, the arrant knavery of that kitten! The tiny imposter, showing off her best tricks, and feigning to be occupied exclusively with her own infantile diversion! We can see her now, prancing and paddling after the leaves, and all the while peeping out of "the tail o' her ee" at the serene poet and philosopher, and waving her naughty tail in glee over his confidence and condescension.

Heine's pretty lines,

> *"And close beside me the cat sits purring,*
> *Warming her paws at the cheery gleam;*
> *The flames keep flitting, and flicking, and whirring;*
> *My mind is wrapped in a realm of dream,"*

find their English echo in the letter Shelley writes to Peacock, describing, half wistfully, the shrines of the Penates, "whose hymns are the purring of kittens, the hissing of kettles, the long talks over the past and dead, the laugh of children, the warm wind of summer filling the quiet house, and the pelting storm of winter struggling in vain for entrance." How incomplete would these pictures be, how incomplete is any fireside sketch, without its purring kitten or drowsy cat!

> *"The queen I am o' that cozy place;*
> *As with ilka paw I dicht my face,*
> *I sing an' purr with mickle grace."*

This is the sphinx of the hearthstone, the little god of domesticity, whose presence turns a house into a home. Even the chilly desolation of a hotel may be rendered endurable by these affable and discriminating creatures; for one of them, as we know, once welcomed Sir Walter Scott, and softened for him the unfamiliar and unloved surroundings. "There are no dogs in the hotel where I lodge," he writes to Abbotsford from London, "but a tolerably conversable cat *who* eats a mess of cream with me in the morning." Of course it did, the wise and lynx-eyed beast! I make no doubt that, day after day and week after week, that cat had wandered superbly amid the common throng of lodgers, showing favor to no none, and growing cynical and disillusioned by constant contact with a crowd. Then, one morning, it spied the noble, rugged face which neither man nor beast could look upon without loving, and forthwith tendered its allegiance on the spot. Only "tolerably conversable" it was, this reserved and town-bred animal; less urbane because less happy than the much-respected retainer at Abbotsford, Master Hinse of Hinsefeld, whom Sir Walter called his friend. "Ah, mon grand ami, vous avez tué mon autre grand ami!" he sighed, when the huge hound Nimrod ended poor Hinse's placid career. And if Scott sometimes seems to disparage cats, as when he unkindly compares Oliver le Dain to one, in Quentin Durward, he atones for such indignity by the use of the little pronoun "who" when writing of the London puss. My own habit is to say "who" on similar occasions, and I am glad to have so excellent an authority.

It were an endless though a pleasant task to recount all that has been said, and well said, in praise of the cat by those who have rightly valued her companionship. Théophile Gautier's charming pages are too familiar for comment. Who has not read with delight of the Black and White Dynasties that for so long ruled with gentle sway over his hearth and heart; of Madame Théophile, who thought the parrot was a green chicken; of Don Pierrot de Navarre, who deeply resented his master's staying out late at night; of the graceful and fastidious Seraphita; the gluttonous Enjolras; the acute Bohemian, Gavroche; the courteous and well-mannered Éponine, who received M. Gautier's guests in the drawing-room and dined at his table, taking each course as it was served, and restraining any rude distaste for food not to her fancy. "Her place was laid without a knife and fork, indeed, but with a glass, and she went regularly through dinner, from soup to dessert, awaiting her turn to be helped, and behaving with a quiet propriety which most children might imitate with advantage. At the first stroke of the bell she would appear, and when I came into the dining-room she would be at her post, upright on her chair, her forepaws on the edge of the tablecloth; and she would present her smooth forehead to be kissed, like a well-bred little girl who was affectionately polite to relatives and old people."

I have read this pretty description several times to Agrippina, who is extremely wayward and capricious about her food, rejecting plaintively one day the viands which she had eaten with apparent enjoyment the day before. In fact, the difficulty of catering to her is so well understood by tradesmen that recently, when the house-maid carried her on an errand to the grocery,—Agrippina is very fond of these jaunts and of the admiration she excites,—the grocer, a fatherly man, with cats of his own, said briskly, "Is this the little lady who eats the biscuits?" and presented her on the spot with several choice varieties from which to choose. She is fastidious, too, about the way in which her meals are served; disliking any other dishes than her own, which are of blue and white china; requiring that her meat should be cut up fine and all the fat removed, and that her morning oatmeal should be well sugared and creamed. Milk she holds in scorn. My friends tell me sometimes that it is not the common custom of cats to receive so much attention at table, and that it is my fault Agrippina is so exacting; but such grumblers fail to take into consideration the marked individuality that is the charm of every kindly treated puss. She differs from her sisters as widely as one woman differs from another, and reveals varying characteristics of good and evil, varying powers of intelligence and adaptation. She scales splendid heights of virtue, and, unlike Sir Thomas Browne, is "singular in offenses." Even those primitive instincts which we believe all animals hold in common are lost in acquired ethics and depravity. No heroism could surpass that of the London cat that crawled back five times under the stage of the burning theatre to rescue her litter of kittens, and, having carried four of them to safety, perished devotedly with the fifth. On the other hand, I know of a cat that drowned her three kittens in a water-butt, for no reason, apparently, save to be rid of them, and that she might lie in peace on the hearth-rug,—a murder well planned, deliberate, and cruel.

> *"So Tiberius might have sat,*
> *Had Tiberius been a cat."*

Only in her grace and beauty, her love of comfort, her dignity of bearing, her courteous reserve, and her independence of character does puss remain immutable and unchanged. These are the traits which win for her the warmest corner by the fire, and the unshaken regard of those who value her friendship and aspire to her affection. These are the traits so subtly suggested by Mrs. Tomson in a sonnet which every true lover of cats feels in his heart *must* have been addressed to his own particular pet:—

> "Half gentle kindliness, and half disdain,
>   Thou comest to my call, serenely suave,
>   With humming speech and gracious gestures grave,
>   In salutation courtly and urbane;
>   Yet must I humble me thy grace to gain,
>   For wiles may win thee, but no arts enslave;
>   And nowhere gladly thou abidest, save
>   Where naught disturbs the concord of thy reign.
>
> "Sphinx of my quiet hearth! who deignst to dwell
>   Friend of my toil, companion of mine ease,
>   Thine is the lore of Ra and Rameses;
>   That men forget dost thou remember well,
>   Beholden still in blinking reveries,
>   With sombre sea-green gaze inscrutable."

HODGE, THE CAT

BY *Susan Coolidge*

Burly and big, his books among,
　Good Samuel Johnson sat,
With frowning brows and wig askew,
His snuff-strewn waistcoat far from new;
So stern and menacing his air,
　That neither Black Sam, nor the maid
To knock or interrupt him dare;
　Yet close beside him, unafraid,
　　Sat Hodge, the cat.

"This participle," the Doctor wrote,
　"The modern scholar cavils at,
But,"—even as he penned the word,
A soft, protesting note was heard;
The Doctor fumbled with his pen,
　The dawning thought took wings and flew,
The sound repeated, came again,
　It was a faint, reminding "Mew!"
　　From Hodge, the cat.

"Poor Pussy!" said the learned man,
　Giving the glossy fur a pat,
"It is your dinner time, I know,
And,—well, perhaps I ought to go;
For if Sam every day were sent
　Off from his work your fish to buy,
Why, men are men, he might resent,
　And starve or kick you on the sly;
　　Eh! Hodge, my cat?"

The Dictionary was laid down,
  The Doctor tied his vast cravat,
And down the buzzing street he strode,
Taking an often-trodden road,
And halted at a well-known stall:
  "Fishmonger," spoke the Doctor gruff,
"Give me six oysters, that is all;
  Hodge knows when he has had enough,
    Hodge is my cat."

Then home; Puss dined, and while in sleep
  He chased a visionary rat,
His master sat him down again,
Rewrote his page, renibbed his pen;
Each "i" was dotted, each "t" was crossed,
  He labored on for all to read,
Nor deemed that time was waste or lost
  Spent in supplying the small need
    Of Hodge, the cat.

The dear old Doctor! fierce of mien,
  Untidy, arbitrary, fat,
What gentle thoughts his name enfold!
So generous of his scanty gold.
So quick to love, so hot to scorn,
  Kind to all sufferers under heaven,
A tend'rer despot ne'er was born;
  His big heart held a corner, even
    For Hodge, the cat.

JAMES GOES SERENADING

BY *Jennie Laird*

*"The Devil hath not, in all his quiver's choice.
An arrow for the heart like a sweet voice."*
BYRON

LATE THAT NIGHT Muffet sat on the top of her bicycle shed, looking out over the neighboring gardens. All around her the white world was at peace. Asleep in their beds, the flowers were folded tight, wet-headed with dew, while in their nests the smaller birds lay silent; though the hunting owl that lived in Muffet's own elm tree was awake and hooting. Huddled in their houses, the human beings breathed heavily, some too heavily, in preparation for another day's toil in the service of those who own the earth and stalk it fearlessly at night.

Only the Armstrongs' rough-haired buffoon seemed disconsolate, as he sat outside his kennel and mourned. Perhaps, poor fool, he longed for the pale-gold moon that hung in the clear night sky. Or regretted, perhaps, the bareness of the bone that lay before him, gnawed and polished into ivory.

As Muffet sat ghostly white on her bicycle shed, she became aware of stealthy agitation in the gardens all around her. Dark shapes were moving, dark shadows were gathering, and where a few moments ago all had been pale and still, the earth was opening and giving forth multiple living forms that slid soundlessly along the paths, walls and fences. Expressionlessly she stared down at the shifting scene, noting with little surprise that out of the many furtive shapes the majority were headed in the direction of the Andersons' dustbin. . . . Black, tawny and striped, old, middling and young, one-eyed, battle-scarred or sound of limb, a spectral army thronged to answer the summons of the young spring night.

On other roof tops, shed tops, fences and back porches lesser and plainer Helens sat waiting for the tournament to begin. The yellow-and-green jewels of their eyes were dotted in an irregular string through the dark-blue air. Mothers of families many of them, as well as inexperienced girls and their elderly chaperones—all were young at heart, all inwardly illumined by the white-hot flame of anticipation, and they took their breath deliberately to steady the speed of their heartbeats.

But among them Muffet was queen. She shone in the palm of the moon's hand, softer than snow dust, whiter than nougat. . . . Her wide eyes gave forth a sea-blue incandescence. As the heroes silently assembled, she noted with satisfaction that those whose ears, eyes and limbs appeared the most intact were moving toward the Andersons' dustbin, and presently she stood up, arched her back, and began to make her way thither.

> *"How shall I woo thee, O beautiful she-cat*
> *Piercing my soul with the spears of thy glances?*
> *How can I tell thee the tale of my love?*
> *Queen Cleopatra looks under thine eyelids,*
> *Venus anew in thy person advances,*
> *Come to me, come, my Medusa, my dove."*

James was rehearsing his serenade as he trotted along the road toward the Anderson establishment. His heart was full of love and expectation, and as he padded along the shining road, inhaling the fragrance of the Garden City spring, he ignored the scurrying snacks that bolted across the road in front of him. Small mice, adolescent rabbits—various little rodents suffered unnecessary palpitations as he passed, singlehearted, murmuring to himself, "Come to me, come, my Medusa."

It was the custom for a suitor to compose a song for his ladylove. He would rough it out beforehand, and relying on the inspiration of the moment, half remember, half improvise when the time came for him to sing it. The merit of the song was as important a factor in courtship as the power of one's personality or the beauty of one's physique. Some overromantic shes could be won by a male of quite miserable appearance, as long as he possessed a full, rich voice and the gift of fluency. Ah, yes, with the willful blindness of her sex, many a she would ignore the merits of some fine, steady cat who unfortunately could not sing a note, and cast herself upon the bosom of a tuneful seducer who desired no more than a moment's pleasure.

James himself sang very well, and up to now would have frankly placed himself in the second category. But as he thought of the charms of Muffet, he felt more than ordinarily moved; indeed, he could almost imagine her forever lovely and himself forever faithful —he quickened his pace, for here was Westward Ho.

He entered the front garden through a gap in the hedge and followed the crazy paving around to the back of the house. Where was she, where, the adorable, the white one? Clearing his throat in readiness, he sang a few notes to get the pitch; and even as he did so the song died in his throat. At a glance, he knew that he was betrayed.

There she sat, the Queen of Perfidy, enthroned on the dustbin; not for him alone, but holding court. She was surrounded by a semicircle of silent, motionless figures, and other figures were spaced at intervals over the garden. The air was charged with tension. Every ear was pricked up to its most acute, every brain alert, and every furred chest contained a strongly determined heart. This was no love tryst, as he had expected, but a tournament, a public contest for a she, a ceremony ranking in importance second only to the Council. James took the scene in at a glance; and even as he watched, the tournament began.

A low, throaty cry two gardens away gave the signal, and one of Muffet's company—a sturdy ginger with white whiskers, diabolically slanting eyes and a crescent-shaped scar on his nose—lifted up his slightly nasal tenor in the first round of the competition. He was followed by a heavy black basso profundo, whose rich cadences began to swell forth with such fruity ardor that feminine hearts gave a bound, and a young she-tabby whispered on a roof top, "Who is that handsome black male with the beautiful voice?"

"Oh, he lives at Singapore," replied her neighbor. "Not a bad type, but rather pompous. I knew him rather well last year," she added nonchalantly. "What was that?" They listened attentively. James had suddenly come to his senses. He flung back his head, and even as the third competitor was opening his mouth to begin, James's full baritone forestalled him. Hot with anger and determination, he stood where he was and sang out to the stars with all the passion in his nature. As the wild notes pealed forth, all heads swung in his direction, and Muffet laid back her ears to listen. In the garden of Aburi, the Armstrongs' buffoon moaned and rattled his chains.

Two competitors rose and walked away, overcome by James's technique. But a bold and brindled suitor was not afraid to open his mouth, and after him two more—one of whom, being tone-deaf, was immediately counted out by a low, disapproving chorus of moans and hisses from all sides. Muffet stood up, stretched, turned sideways to the assembly to show her profile, and the second round began.

Rising to his feet and moving a few paces forward, the ginger cat again opened his mouth and let inspiration carry him away. So far did it carry him that before long a window was flung open, a head protruded, and the raucous voice of Mr. Anderson cried, "Aaaaaaaahh! Get away!" Unhesitatingly, the ginger cat swallowed his uprising notes and side-stepped, avoiding the splash of cold water which his instinct told him would follow. As he expected, it fell on his neighbor, the basso profundo, who gave a high-pitched scream and shot behind a lavender bush. The assembly froze into position. Silence reigned, save for an occasional ejaculation·from behind the lavender bush, where a frantic toilet was being performed.

"Geeeeeeertcha!" repeated the domestic threateningly, and hearing no more, shut the window and went back to bed.

The vulgar interruption was no surprise to the competitors, familiar as they were with human nature. Persecution of the sublime by the ridiculous was to them an everyday occurrence, and after the usual ninety-six seconds' pause the contest was fearlessly resumed. It was not long before James's turn came around again. He took a deep breath, closed his eyes, and once more summoned Apollo to his aid.

He sang in a tender, throaty voice that made the sleeping flowers unconsciously unfold their leaves, and Muffet's chilly little heart begin to grow warm. . . . Tears welled up in the spectators' eyes. . . . But the slant-eyed ginger tenor sat, with offensive indifference, washing his feet. This did not escape James, who when he had finished, stalked to the foot of the dustbin, seated himself and glared a challenge at the reduced semicircle. A fortunate move, for at that

SERENADING. Peggy Bacon. *From "Jennie and Macarthur"*

very moment half a dozen windows were flung up, and half a dozen voices bellowed in fury, and half a dozen arms hurled assorted missiles at the place where he had been standing. An article of footwear narrowly missed Muffet, bouncing off the dustbin with a clang. She looked at it scornfully and did not budge. As the bombardment continued, the cavaliers leaped to their feet, but not in flight. Skillfully they dodged, crouched and side-stepped, avoiding the hurtling objects as narrowly as possible, for coolness and daring in the face of danger was one of their knightly virtues.

Conspicuous in the moonlight and exquisitely groomed, the basso profundo reappeared from behind the lavender bush, and strolled down the middle of the lawn toward the rockery, daring Fate. But alas! It was his unlucky night. A piece of hard fruit struck him on the side of the head, and staggering slightly, he moved to the side and sat down. Presently he quitted the scene. But he need not have despaired. Her heart brimming with love and pity, the young she-tabby slipped down from the roof and made her way softly toward him. . . .

Then James arose, advanced to the dustbin and, looking Muffet straight in the eyes, lifted up his heavenly voice. Her gaze fell before the meaning in his. Nervously dabbing at a fern, she averted her head and listened while he sang. Three more competitors threw up the sponge and walked away.

But the red knight had also advanced to the foot of the rock, and sat grimly waiting. The remaining competitors gave up hope and settled down to watch.

Hardly had James uttered the last note when it was taken up and derisively repeated in a voice that made the moon rock in the sky. The Armstrongs' buffoon bellowed more loudly than ever, many human voices joined in, the owl hooted, a young domestic cried, a gun went off, and there were sounds of breaking crockery, and of boots thudding on wooden sheds, and windows were noisily opened and closed, and competitors from other gardens all around fell silent in order to listen to the tremendous din. Higher and higher, louder and louder in admirable counterpoint strove the alternating voices of James and his rival, paying no heed to the whizzing missiles nor to the cries of despair from the servants' quarters. Pandemonium reigned, and sleep fled precipitate from the Garden City.

Now James reached the climax of his song. Quivering from head to foot, his eyes fixed on Muffet, his haunches tensed, he crouched ready to spring and claim her under the very nose of the other.

> "Now comes thine hour, O thou frozen enchantress,
> Now shalt thou yield, for thy fate is pursuing,
> Now is the union of Venus and Mars.
> Vain are thy prayers and thy loud lamentations,
> Beautiful she, thou hast met thine undoing—
> Now art thou mine in the sight of the stars!"

As the verse ended the red one sensed James's intention, and sprang even as he sprang, and turned to face him with snarl and uplifted paw. James paused to calculate his aim, and struck!

This was no hasty battle, but one of few blows, carefully timed and unexpectedly aimed. The two were expert strategists; a feint with a left paw, a dab with the right, and then a long sweep at the face with the left. Suddenly they would clinch, and clasping each other around the neck, sway as if in a dance, seeking to bite each other's throat or ear. Absorbed in the struggle, they soon forgot about the white shape crouching on the rockery and fought on for the wild pleasure alone. It was a strange, nightmarish performance, with all the controlled grace of ballet and all the menace of death. Silently, like shadows on a screen, the two dark figures bobbed and swayed, anonymous in the uncertain light, and all around them a ring of colored pinpricks blinked attentively. Save for low murmurs from the spectators' throats and an occasional stifled cry from one of the combatants as he lunged or parried, there was no sound. Mr. Anderson took the cotton wool out of his ears and sighed with relief, then felt for the rubber hot-water bottle with his feet. It was cold, and he kicked it out of bed, then settled down to sleep again, under the impression that all was over.

He was mistaken. A second later there came a wild squawk from outside, where the young she-tabby, though still full of admiration for the basso profundo, was finding his behavior a little unnerving. Mr. Anderson leaped out of bed, flung up the window, seized the hot-water bottle and hurled it from him with all his force. Alas! It landed fair and square on James, knocking him off his balance, bursting open at the seam and soaking him with water. He turned his head, dazed and unwary, and unscrupulously the red one fell on him, bit his ear, tore his face open, dealt him a couple of violent blows and leaped victoriously up onto the dustbin. James shut his eyes. His senses left him in a blind; whirling flash. . . . Thirty seconds elapsed before he could focus—to discover that Muffet, the red cat, and all the spectators had disappeared.

When he left the garden a little later, all was quiet, save for a rustling and a whispering among the bushes, which swayed a little, perhaps with the night wind. No voice spoke, and it must have been in his imagination that he heard, mockingly repeated, the last line of the last verse of his own love song—

"Now art thou mine in the sight of the stars!"

With a wail of despair, he turned and made off, dripping, down the road for home.

BIRL FORMS A FRIENDSHIP

BY *Alexander M. Frey*

BIRL HURRIED DOWN THE LADDER, stepping from one rung to the next with the elegant agility of a cat, and never missing a single one of the thin rounds. She was in haste because she wanted to be at her post. If it should happen to be George coming home she felt it her duty to hand over the estate of which she had been unofficial caretaker.

The door opened—and it was George who came in. Birl did not know him, for she had not yet been born when he departed. But she found out at once that it was he, for behind him entered the two men who had come after the old woman's death, and the one rattling the bunch of keys boomed: "Well, Mr. Trumm, we hereby faithfully hand over your house to you. It is just as your deceased mother left it."

Birl heard George reply in a low, sad voice. "Alas that my mother is dead," he said. "Through many a long and cold night in foreign parts I thought of her. I was often warmed by the thought of sitting with her again in this room."

"Sorrowing won't help," the gruff man answered. "What's gone is gone. . . . Let's open the shutters." And he pulled the shutters roughly apart, letting in the light.

Birl watched while George stood shivering in the bare and dusty room and looking around him—George, the son of the kind old woman with whom she had lived happily for so many years. Would she not also get on well with the son? He was pale and thin and there were lines of grief around his youthful mouth. But although he now seemed distant and unhappy, Birl felt instantly drawn to him.

However, she did not like these two men who had made such grand and boastful gestures and had said, "We hereby hand over your house to you, Mr. Trumm." What had they done for the

house? They had made it dark, locked it up and left it to its fate—
the sad fate of all deserted houses: gradual decay and ruin. No one
had stirred a hand to replace a rotting board here or a broken roof
slate there. The mice would long since have chewed hundreds upon
hundreds of holes in everything, perhaps would have brought down
the whole trembling structure, if she, Birl, had not been there. But
these two men who had done nothing at all for Master George's
house were now saying with hypocritical pompousness: "We have
taken good care of your property."

But if Birl did not like them, the two men had no liking for her
either. In the bright daylight that now flooded into the room they
caught sight of Birl, and they began to bellow: "There's that worth-
less beast, still here. It isn't our fault, Mr. Trumm. We took care
to chase her out before we locked the place up. Take our word for
it, we were unremitting in our care for your property. But the vile
creature must have crept in again through one of the holes in the
wall or the roof—there are lots of them. And of course, Mr. Trumm,
we couldn't do anything about that; we couldn't be expected to
make repairs."

After repeating these assurances several times, they tried to make
Birl responsible for the deplorable state of things which was now
revealed. "Look at that!" they exclaimed. "The filthy cat has dragged
all the straw out of the mattress, and she's gnawed a huge hole in
the cupboard over here. Horrible beast!"

In George's heart sorrow over this sad homecoming was mingled
with a mounting rage. The two men succeeded in their purpose;
they turned his mind from the thought that possibly it was the fault
of human beings that his house now presented such a shabby appearance. They had diverted him very cunningly, and now they
cast all the blame for neglect and damage upon Birl.

For the moment at least George believed them. "Get out!" he
too shouted, and kicked out at the cat. Birl realized that he was so
angry and depressed that he could not think clearly, and therefore
she decided that it was best to abandon the field for the present.
Without a sound, and before the heavy boots of her two enemies
started to swing toward her, she slipped out of the room. Behind
her she heard one of the men reviling her: "The ugly beast must
be always getting into fights. Her nose is all torn up and the whole
floor is stained with spots of blood."

Birl left the three men to themselves. There was no chance of reasoning with them, since two were hardhearted and bad men who did not want to be different and the third had been deceived and roused to anger by the other two. But she did not feel that George was lost to her. She hoped he would soon come to his senses and examine the house. Then he would see whether or not Birl was really a good-for-nothing.

She sat down on the plank over the stream and watched the little fish. But none of them was inclined to swim near her paw today. And so she passed the time reflecting on the ways of men. People are always accusing cats of being deceitful, she thought. And of course, any cat treated as I have just been treated would have to become deceitful. Bad treatment creates badness. That is true of men and no less true of cats. How unjust human beings tend to be. Their observation of animals is shoddy and often they don't understand at all what we really want. When our claws sometimes hook a bit of their skin while we're playing with their fingers, they ought to realize that we never meant to hurt them. Anyway, why do they have such a tender skin instead of a pelt? If they had fur our sharp claws would slip off without hiding them. It isn't our fault that they're so unformed.

It is a sad truth, Birl reflected further, that people know so little about us animals. George is really a good man at heart—I can sense that with my feline intuition. But those two nasty hypocrites have talked him into believing something utterly stupid. He *is* gullible to believe that I made that hole in the cupboard. Do those idiots really imagine we cats can gnaw holes in wooden boards? We certainly couldn't, even if we wanted to. My dear George, you might have spent dull moments in that forest of yours, meditating whether cats enjoy gnawing round holes in the doors of cupboards. If you'd thought about it, you might have realized that such things are done by quite another kind of creature. It's really insulting to have men in their ignorance lump us together with rats and other rodents.

❧

Amid such musings the afternoon passed. When dusk fell, a strong breeze sprang up over the stream, parting Birl's white fur in places so that her pink skin was exposed to the cool air. Then Birl decided to risk a visit to the house.

The two bad men had gone long ago. Birl squeezed in through the tiniest of her loop-holes. We'll see what mood he's in, she thought wisely. She waited in the farthest corner of the kitchen until she saw that George continued to sit motionless at the table, staring at the flame of a candle which was again burning tonight, after so long a time. Then, moving with graceful diffidence, Birl emerged from her corner.

The man looked very lonesome; although the room was small, he seemed to be surrounded by vast areas of solitude.

Birl saw that he had before him the letter her old mistress had been writing when she died. The paper still lay on the same spot. The overturned ink had long since dried on the page and on the table around it. The great blot of ink was already covered with a thick layer of dust.

Now George picked up the letter, brushed away the dust, and brought the paper toward the light of the candle. But his efforts to decipher the writing were in vain. All he could make out was the salutation, which read: "My dear son." Shaking his head, he finally gave up the attempt to read the remainder of the letter. He looked at the salutation once more, and in a low voice he repeated the words to the empty room: "My dear son." Then he fell silent, sat woodenly hunched in his chair, and stared into the night.

Birl saw that he was weeping silently. He sat stiffly in his chair while the tears of sorrow, glittering as if they had caught up all the feeble candlelight, rolled down his cheeks. Then Birl knew that the moment had come for her to make the bold venture.

She uttered a chirping sound, a kind of purring twitter to which she owed her name, that bespoke sympathy and an attempt to encourage him. She could, her voice promised, drive away the terrible solitude around him and replace it by the solidarity of companionship. And suiting the action to her words, she approached with a confident and confiding air and rubbed up against the man's feet.

Do not drive me away, not now; don't do that to yourself, don't shut yourself off in your loneliness, her chirping voice begged.

Every human being who can still listen to the promptings of his heart is conquered when a cat volunteers such a graceful and tender caress, and George too was moved. He stooped, lifted the happy puss, and set her before him in the middle of the table.

"Are you Birl whom my mother used to write about all the time?" he asked her. "Look here!"—he picked up the illegible letter—"here is a word, and here's another, and here and here, and all of them might be 'Birl.' Sometimes your name was all I could decipher in her letters. . . . You were named after your voice. . . . Yes, of course, you must be the one. . . . Your white fur fits her description. But you've certainly got very lean. Well, then, we suit each other pretty well. . . . Did I kick you this afternoon? Forgive me. Those two fools tried to make me believe that black is white, I mean that rats are cats and that you gnawed holes in the cupboard and door. But after you left I threw the hypocrites out. I know cats don't do that sort of thing. I was just weak and helpless and so confused by sorrow that I couldn't think clearly, and they took advantage of me."

While George murmured this apology he stroked Birl gently. And Birl felt wonderfully contented and proud—proud not so much because she was now being caressed as because George, her new master, was a good man.

Purring, she lay down close to his elbow which was propped on the table, and George pressed his cheek against her warm white coat. And so the two of them found shelter in one another and overcame the loneliness of the night.

☙

THE   PROVIDENT   CAT

THE CAT

BY *Mary E. Wilkins*

THE SNOW WAS FALLING, and the Cat's fur was stiffly pointed with it, but he was imperturbable. He sat crouched, ready for the death-spring, as he had sat for hours. It was night—but that made no difference—all times were as one to the Cat when he was in wait for prey. Then, too, he was under no constraint of human will, for he was living alone that winter. Nowhere in the world was any voice calling him; on no hearth was there a waiting dish. He was quite free except for his own desires, which tyrannized over him when unsatisfied as now. The Cat was very hungry—almost famished, in fact. For days the weather had been very bitter, and all the feebler wild things which were his prey by inheritance, the born serfs to his family, had kept, for the most part, in their burrows and nests, and the Cat's long hunt had availed him nothing. But he waited with the inconceivable patience and persistency of his race; besides, he was certain. The Cat was a creature of absolute convictions, and his faith in his deductions never wavered. The rabbit had gone in there between those low-hung pine boughs. Now her little doorway had before it a shaggy curtain of snow, but in there she was. The Cat had seen her enter, so like a swift gray shadow that even his sharp and practised eyes had glanced back for the substance following, and then she was gone. So he sat down and waited, and he waited still in the white night, listening angrily to the north wind starting in the upper heights of the mountains with distant screams, then swelling into an awful crescendo of rage, and swooping down with furious white wings of snow like a flock of fierce eagles into the valleys and ravines. The Cat was on the side of a mountain, on a wooded terrace. Above him a few feet away towered the rock ascent as steep as the wall of a cathedral. The Cat had never climbed it—trees were the ladders to his heights of life. He had often looked with wonder at the rock, and miauled bitterly and resentfully as man does in the face of a forbidding Providence. At his left was the sheer precipice. Behind him, with a short stretch of woody growth between, was the frozen perpendicular fall of a mountain stream. Before him was the way to his home. When the rabbit came out she was trapped; her little cloven feet could not scale such unbroken steeps. So the Cat waited. The place in which he was looked like a maelstrom of the wood. The tangle of trees and bushes clinging to the mountain-side with a stern clutch of roots, the prostrate trunks and branches, the vines embracing everything with strong knots and coils of growth, had a curious effect, as of things which had whirled for ages in a current of raging water, only it was not water, but wind, which had disposed everything in circling lines of yielding to its fiercest points of onset. And now over all this whirl of wood and rock and dead trunks and branches and vines descended the snow. It blew down like smoke over the rock-crest above; it stood in a gyrating column like some death-wraith of nature, on the level, than it broke over the edge of the precipice, and the Cat cowered before the fierce backward set of it. It was as if ice needles pricked his skin through his beautiful thick fur, but he never faltered and never once cried. He had nothing to gain from crying, and everything to lose; the rabbit would hear him cry and know he was waiting.

It grew darker and darker, with a strange white smother, instead of the natural blackness of night. It was a night of storm and death superadded to the night of nature. The mountains were all hidden, wrapped about, overawed, and tumultuously overborne by it, but in the midst of it waited, quite unconquered, this little, unswerving, living patience and power under a little coat of gray fur.

A fiercer blast swept over the rock, spun on one mighty foot of whirlwind athwart the level, then was over the precipice.

Then the Cat saw two eyes luminous with terror, frantic with the impulse of flight, he saw a little, quivering, dilating nose, he saw two pointing ears, and he kept still, with every one of his fine nerves and muscles strained like wires. Then the rabbit was out—there was one long line of incarnate flight and terror—and the Cat had her.

Then the Cat went home, trailing his prey through the snow.

The Cat lived in the house which his master had built, as rudely as a child's blockhouse, but stanchly enough. The snow was heavy on the low slant of its roof, but it would not settle under it. The two windows and the door were made fast, but the Cat knew a way in. Up a pine-tree behind the house he scuttled, though it was hard work with his heavy rabbit, and was in his little window under the eaves, then down through the trap to the room below, and on his master's bed with a spring and a great cry of triumph, rabbit and all. But his master was not there; he had been gone since early fall, and it was now February. He would not return until spring, for he was an old man, and the cruel cold of the mountains clutched at his vitals like a panther, and he had gone to the village to winter. The Cat had known for a long time that his master was gone, but his reasoning was always sequential and circuitous; always for him what had been would be, and the more easily for his marvellous waiting powers, so he always came home expecting to find his master.

When he saw that he was still gone, he dragged the rabbit off the rude couch which was the bed to the floor, put one little paw on the carcass to keep it steady, and began gnawing with head to one side to bring his strongest teeth to bear.

It was darker in the house than it had been in the wood, and the cold was as deadly, though not so fierce. If the Cat had not received his fur coat unquestioningly of Providence, he would have been thankful that he had it. It was a mottled gray, white on the face and breast, and thick as fur could grow.

The wind drove the snow on the windows with such force that it rattled like sleet, and the house trembled a little. Then all at once the Cat heard a noise, and stopped gnawing his rabbit and listened, his shining green eyes fixed upon a window. Then he heard a hoarse shout, a halloo of despair and entreaty; but he knew that it was not his master come home, and he waited, one paw still on the rabbit. Then the halloo came again, and then the Cat answered. He said all that was essential quite plainly to his own comprehension. There was in his cry of response inquiry, information, warning, terror, and finally, the offer of comradeship; but the man outside did not hear him, because of the howling of the storm.

Then there was a great battering pound at the door, then another, and another. The Cat dragged his rabbit under the bed. The blows came thicker and faster. It was a weak arm which gave them, but it was nerved by desperation. Finally the lock yielded, and the stranger came in. Then the Cat, peering from under the bed, blinked with a sudden light, and his green eyes narrowed. The stranger struck a match and looked about. The Cat saw a face wild and blue with hunger and cold, and a man who looked poorer and older than his poor old master, who was an outcast among men for his poverty and lowly mystery of antecedents; and he heard a muttered, unintelligible voicing of distress from the harsh, piteous mouth. There was in it both profanity and prayer, but the Cat knew nothing of that.

The stranger braced the door which he had forced, got some wood from the stock in the corner, and kindled a fire in the old stove as quickly as his half-frozen hands would allow. He shook so pitiably as he worked that the Cat under the bed felt the tremor of it. Then the man, who was small and feeble and marked with the scars of suffering which he had pulled down upon his head, sat down in one of the old chairs and crouched over the fire as if it were the one love and desire of his soul, holding out his yellow hands like yellow claws, and he groaned. The Cat came out from under the bed and leaped up on his lap with the rabbit. The man gave a great shout and start of terror, and sprang, and the Cat slid clawing to the floor, and the rabbit fell inertly, and the man leaned, gasping with fright, and ghastly, against the wall. The Cat grabbed the rabbit by the slack of its neck and dragged it to the man's feet. Then he raised his shrill, insistent cry, he arched his back high, his tail was a splendid waving plume. He rubbed against the man's feet, which were bursting out of their torn shoes.

The man pushed the Cat away, gently enough, and began searching about the little cabin. He even climbed painfully the ladder to the loft, lit a match, and peered up in the darkness with straining eyes. He feared lest there might be a man, since there was a cat. His experience with men had not been pleasant, and neither had the experience of men been pleasant with him. He was an old wandering Ishmael among his kind; he had stumbled upon the house of a brother, and the brother was not at home, and he was glad.

He returned to the Cat, and stooped stiffly and stroked his back, which the animal arched like the spring of a bow.

Then he took up the rabbit and looked at it eagerly by the firelight. His jaws worked. He could almost have devoured it raw. He fumbled—the Cat close at his heels—around some rude shelves and a table, and found, with a grunt of self-gratulation, a lamp with oil in it. That he lighted; then he found a frying-pan and a knife, and skinned the rabbit, and prepared it for cooking, the Cat always at his feet.

When the odor of the cooking flesh filled the cabin, both the man and the Cat looked wolfish. The man turned the rabbit with one hand, and stooped to pat the Cat with the other. The Cat thought him a fine man. He loved him with all his heart, though he had known him such a short time, and though the man had a face both pitiful and sharply set at variance with the best of things. It was a face with the grimy grizzle of age upon it, with fever hollows in the cheeks, and the memories of wrong in the dim eyes, but the Cat accepted the man unquestioningly and loved him. When the rabbit was half cooked, neither the man nor the Cat could wait any longer. The man took it from the fire, divided it exactly in halves, gave the Cat one, and took the other himself. Then they ate.

Then the man blew out the light, called the Cat to him, got on the bed, drew up the ragged coverings, and fell asleep with the Cat in his bosom.

The man was the Cat's guest all the rest of the winter, and the winter is long in the mountains. The rightful owner of the little hut did not return until May. All that time the Cat toiled hard, and he grew rather thin himself, for he shared everything except mice with his guest; and sometimes game was wary, and the fruit of the patience of days was very little for two. The man was ill and weak, however, and unable to eat much, which was fortunate, since he could not hunt for himself. All day long he lay on the bed, or else sat crouched over the fire. It was a good thing that firewood was ready at hand for the picking up, not a stone's throw from the door, for that he had to attend to himself.

The Cat foraged tirelessly. Sometimes he was gone for days together, and at first the man used to be terrified, thinking he would never return; then he would hear the familiar cry at the door, and stumble to his feet and let him in. Then the two would dine together, sharing equally; then the Cat would rest and purr, and finally sleep in the man's arms.

Towards spring the game grew plentiful; more wild little quarry were tempted out of their homes, in search of love as well as food. One day the Cat had luck—a rabbit, a partridge, and a mouse. He could not carry them all at once, but finally he had them together at the house door. Then he cried, but no one answered. All the mountain streams were loosened, and the air was full of the gurgle of many waters, occasionally pierced by a bird whistle. The trees rustled with a new sound to the spring wind; there was a flush of rose and gold-green on the breasting surface of a distant mountain seen through an opening in the wood. The tips of the bushes were swollen and glistening red, and now and then there was a flower; but the Cat had nothing to do with flowers. He stood beside his booty at the house door, and cried and cried with his insistent triumph and complaint and pleading, but no one came to let him in. Then the Cat left his little treasures at the door, and went around to the back of the house to the pine-tree, and was up the trunk with a wild scramble, and in through his little window, and down through the trap to the room, and the man was gone.

The Cat cried again—that cry of the animal for human companionship which is one of the sad notes of the world; he looked in all the corners; he sprang to the chair at the window and looked out; but no one came. The man was gone, and he never came again.

The Cat ate his mouse out on the turf beside the house; the rabbit and the partridge he carried painfully into the house, but the man did not come to share them. Finally, in the course of a day or two, he ate them up himself; then he slept a long time on the bed, and when he waked the man was not there.

Then the Cat went forth to his hunting-grounds again, and came home at night with a plump bird, reasoning with his tireless persistency in expectancy that the man would be there; and there was a light in the window, and when he cried his old master opened the door and let him in.

His master had strong comradeship with the Cat, but not affection. He never patted him like that gentler outcast, but he had a pride in him and an anxiety for his welfare, though he had left him alone all winter without scruple. He feared lest some misfortune might have come to the Cat, though he was so large of his kind, and a mighty hunter. Therefore, when he saw him at the door in all the glory of his winter coat, his white breast and face shining like snow in the sun, his own face lit up with welcome, and the Cat embraced his feet with his sinuous body vibrant with rejoicing purrs.

The Cat had his bird to himself, for his master had his own supper already cooking on the stove. After supper the Cat's master took his pipe, and sought a small store of tobacco which he had left in his hut over winter. He had thought often of it; that and the Cat seemed something to come home to in the spring. But the tobacco was gone; not a dust left. The man swore a little in a grim monotone, which made the profanity lose its customary effect. He had been, and was, a hard drinker; he had knocked about the world until the marks of its sharp corners were on his very soul, which was thereby calloused, until his very sensibility to loss was dulled. He was a very old man.

He searched for the tobacco with a sort of dull combativeness of persistency; then he stared with stupid wonder around the room. Suddenly many features struck him as being changed. Another stove-lid was broken; an old piece of carpet was tacked up over a window to keep out the cold; his fire-wood was gone. He looked, and there was no oil left in his can. He looked at the coverings on his bed; he took them up, and again he made that strange remonstrant noise in his throat. Then he looked again for his tobacco.

Finally he gave it up. He sat down beside the fire, for May in the mountains is cold; he held his empty pipe in his mouth, his rough forehead knitted, and he and the Cat looked at each other across that impassable barrier of silence which has been set between man and beast from the creation of the world.

❧

THE   DIVERSIFIED   CAT

HOW A CAT WAS ANNOYED
AND A POET WAS BOOTED

BY *Guy Wetmore Carryl*

A Poet had a cat.
There is nothing odd in that—
   (I *might* make a little pun about the *Mews!*)
But what is really more
Remarkable, she wore
   A pair of pointed patent-leather shoes.
     And I doubt me greatly whether
      E'er you heard the like of that:
     Pointed shoes of patent-leather
      On a cat!

His time he used to pass
Writing sonnets, on the grass—
   (I *might* say something good on *pen* and *sward!*)
While the cat sat near at hand
Trying hard to understand
   The poems he occasionally roared.
     (I myself possess a feline,
      But when poetry I roar
     He is sure to make a bee-line
      For the door.)

The poet, cent by cent,
All his patrimony spent—
    (I *might* tell how he went from *verse* to *worse!*)
Till the cat was sure she could,
By advising, do him good,
    So addressed him in a manner that was terse:
        "We are bound toward the scuppers,
            And the time has come to act,
        Or we'll both be on our uppers,
            For a fact!"

On her boot she fixed her eye,
But the boot made no reply—
    (I *might* say: "Couldn't speak to save its *sole!*")
And the foolish bard, instead
Of responding, only read
    A verse that wasn't bad upon the whole:
        And it pleased the cat so greatly,
            Though she knew not what it meant,
        That I'll quote approximately
            How it went:—

"If I should live to be
The last leaf on the tree"—
    (I *might* put in: "I think I'd just as *leaf!*")
"Let them smile, as I do now,
At the old, forsaken bough"—
    Well, he'd plagiarized it bodily, in brief!
        But that cat of simple breeding
            Couldn't read the lines between,
        So she took it to a leading
            Magazine.

She was jarred and very sore
When they showed her to the door,
    (I *might* hit off the door that was a *jar!*)
To the spot she swift returned
Where the poet sighed and yearned,
    And she told him that he'd gone a little far.

"Your performance with this rhyme has
    Made me absolutely sick,"
She remarked, "I think the time has
    Come to kick!"

I could fill up half a page
With descriptions of her rage—
    (I *might* say that she went a bit *too fur!*)
When he smiled and murmured, "Shoo!"
"There is one thing I can do!"
    She answered with a wrathful kind of purr.
      "You may shoo me, and it suit you
        But I feel my conscience bid
      Me as tit for tat, to boot you!"
        (Which she did.)

The *Moral* of the plot
    (Though I say it, as should not!)
    Is: An editor is difficult to suit.
But again, there 're other times
When the man who fashions rhymes
    Is a rascal, and a bully one to boot!

THE VEGETARIAN CAT

THE LONG-CAT

BY *Colette*

A SHORT-HAIRED BLACK CAT always looks longer than any other cat. But this particular one, Babou, nicknamed the Long-cat, really did measure, stretched right out flat, well over a yard and a quarter. If you did not arrange him properly, he was not much more than a yard. I used to measure him sometimes.

"He's stopped growing longer," I said one day to my mother. "Isn't it a pity?"

"Why a pity? He's too long as it is. I can't understand why you want everything to grow bigger. It's bad to grow too much, very bad indeed!"

It's true that it always worried her when she thought that children were growing too fast, and she had good cause to be anxious about my elder half-brother, who went on growing until he was twenty-four.

"But I'd love to grow a bit taller."

"D'you mean you'd like to be like that Brisedoux girl, five-foot-seven tall at twelve years old? A midget can always make herself liked. But what can you do with a gigantic beauty? Who would want to marry her?"

"Couldn't Babou get married, then?"

"Oh, a cat's a cat. Babou's only too long when he really wants to be. Are we even sure he's black? He's probably white in snowy weather, dark blue at night, and red when he goes to steal strawberries. He's very light when he lies on your knees, and very heavy when I carry him into the kitchen in the evenings to prevent him from sleeping on my bed. I think he's too much of a vegetarian to be a real cat."

For the Long-cat really did steal strawberries, picking out the ripest of the variety called Docteur-Morère which are so sweet, and of the white Hautboys which taste faintly of ants. According to the season he would also go for the tender tips of the asparagus, and when it came to melons his choice was not so much for cantaloups as for the kind called Noir-des-Carmes whose rind, marbled light and dark like the skin of a salamander, he knew how to rip open. In all this he was not at all exceptional. I once had a she-cat who used to crunch rings of raw onion, provided they were the sweet onions of the South. There are cats who set great store by oysters, snails, and clams.

When the Long-cat went off to poach strawberries from our next-door neighbour, Monsieur Pomié, he went by way of the wall, which was covered with such dense ivy that the cats could walk along under cover, their presence revealed only by the quivering of the leaves, the mist of yellow pollen and the golden cloud of bees.

He loved this leafy tunnel but, do what he would, he had to

come out of it at the end since Madame Pomié kept the top of the wall bare where it overlooked her garden. Once out in the open, he adopted a very off-hand manner, especially if he met Madame de Saint-Aubin's beautiful cat, who was black, with a white face and belly. I found this wall a good place to study tomcats, not so much their habits as their ceremonial procedure, governed by a kind of choreography. Unlike the females, they are more noisy than war-like and they try to gain time by palavers. Hence all the snarling preambles. Not that they do not know how to fight cruelly once they come to grips; but as a rule they are far removed from the silent and furious grapplings of the females. The she-cat we had at the same time as the Long-cat literally flew into battle if a female ventured into her haunts. Barely touching the ground, she would pounce on the enemy, even if it were her own offspring. She fought as a bird does, going for her adversary's head. I never saw her chastise a male, except for a few cuffs, for as soon as the males saw her they fled, while she followed them with a look of inexpressible contempt. When July and January came, she settled her amorous encounters in forty-eight hours. On the morning of the third day, when the chosen partner, in fine fettle and with renewed appetite, approached her with a self-confident, prancing gait and a deep-throated song, she would root him to the spot with a mere look.

"I've come," he would begin, "I . . . I came to resume our agree-able conversation of yesterday . . ."

"Excuse me," the she-cat interrupted, "you were saying? I didn't quite catch. What agreeable conversation?"

"Why . . . the one we had at ten o'clock in the morning . . . and the one at five in the afternoon . . . and especially our conversation at ten in the evening, near the well."

The she-cat, perched on top of the pergola, raised herself a little on her delicately-boned paws.

"Near the well, a conversation, you, with ME? Who do you suppose is going to believe that? You don't expect ME to! Take yourself off! It'll be the worse for you if you don't, I can tell you. Take yourself off!"

"But . . . but I love you. And I'm ready to prove it to you again."

Standing upright there the she-cat towered over the tom as Satan, jutting out from Notre Dame, broods over Paris. The look she cast on him from her tawny-gold eyes was such as he could not long

endure; and the outcast would make off with the shambling gait of
someone who has been driven away.

As I was saying then, the Long-cat, impelled by a vegetarian
craving which those who have not experienced it can never understand, would go after the strawberries, the melons and the asparagus. On his return, a little green or rosy pulp remained, as evidence
of his pillagings, in the grooves between his curved claws, and this
he licked casually during his siesta.

"Show your hands!" my mother used to say to him, and thereupon
he surrendered to her a long front paw, adept at every kind of
mischief, with pads as hard as a road parched with drought.

"Have you been opening a melon?"

I dare say he understood. His gentle yellow eyes met Sido's
penetrating look, but since his innocence was only assumed, he
could not help squinting a little.

"Yes, you *have* opened a melon. And I expect it was the pretty
little one I had my eye on, the one that looked like a globe with
yellow continents and green seas." She released the long paw which
fell back limp and expressionless.

"That deserves a good slap," said I.

"I know. But just think that instead of a melon he might have
slit open a bird, or a little rabbit, or have eaten a chick."

She scratched the flat skull which he stretched up against her
hand, and the half-bald temples which showed bluish between the
sparse black hairs. A tremendous purring rose from his thick neck
with its white patch under the chin. The Long-cat loved no one but
my mother, followed no one but her and looked to her for everything. If I took him in my arms he would imperceptibly glide out
of them as though he were melting away. Except for the ritual
battles and during the brief seasons of love-making, the Long-cat
was nothing but silence, sleep and nonchalant night-prowlings.

I naturally preferred our she-cats to him. The females of the
feline tribe are so unlike the males that they seem to regard the tom
as a stranger and often as an enemy. The only exceptions are the
cats of Siam who live in couples like the wild beasts. Perhaps it is
because the cats in our countries are such a hybrid collection of
every coat and colour that they develop a taste for change and fickle-
ness. In my home we were never without two or three she-cats who
graced the lawns, crowned the pump and slept in the wistaria,

THE BIG CAT. *Cornelius Visscher. Courtesy Cooper Union Museum*

which they had hollowed into a hammock. They confined their charming sociability to my mother and myself. As soon as January and July, the compulsory seasons of love, were over, they regarded the male once again as a suspect, a lout, and a wicked devourer of newly-born kittens, and their conversations with the Long-cat consisted chiefly of crisp insults, whenever he assumed the bland, gentle manner and the innocent smile of the cat who has never harboured any evil intentions, or even thoughts. Sometimes they seemed about to play, but this never came to anything. The females took fright at the strength of the male, and at that furious excitement which, in an uncastrated cat, turns playfulness into a murderous combat.

By virtue of his serpent-like build, the Long-cat excelled at strange leaps in which he nearly twisted himself into a figure of eight. In full sunlight his winter coat, which was longer and more satiny than in summer, revealed the waterings and markings of his far-off tabby ancestor. A tom will remain playful until he is quite old; but even in play his face never loses the gravity that is stamped on it. The Long-cat's expression softened only when he looked at my mother. Then his white whiskers would bristle powerfully, while into his eyes crept the smile of an innocent little boy. He used to follow her when she went to pick violets along the wall that

separated M. de Fourolles' garden from ours. The close-set border
provided every day a big bunch which my mother let fade, either
pinned to her bodice or in an empty glass, because violets in water
lose all their scent. Step by step the Long-cat followed his stooping
mistress, sometimes imitating with his paw the gesture of her hand
groping among the leaves, and imitating her discoveries also. "Ha,
ha!" he would cry, "me too!" and thereupon show his prize: a bom-
bardier beetle, a pink worm or a shrivelled cockchafer.

"My goodness, how silly you are," Sido would say to him, affectionately. "Never mind, what you've found is very pretty."

When we rejoined my elder brother in the Loiret, we took with
us our favourite she-cat and the Long-cat. Both of them seemed to
mind much less than I did exchanging a lovely house for a small
cottage, and the vast grounds of our family property for a narrow
garden. I have referred elsewhere to the stream which danced at
the end of this garden. Left to itself, it was sufficiently clear and
sparkling, and had enough soap-wort and wild radishes clinging to
the walls which hemmed it in, to beautify any village, if the village
had respected it. But those who lived on its banks polluted it.

At the end of our new garden there was a little wash-house
which protected the straw palliasse on which the washerwomen
knelt, the sloping board, white as a scraped bone, where they
pressed the frothing linen, the washerwomen's battledores, the
brushes made of couch-grass and the sprinklers. Soon after our arrival the she-cat laid claim to the palliasse, gave birth to her litter
on it, and brought up there the one little tabby which we left her.
Whenever the sun shone I joined her there and sat on the soaping-
board. The tabby kitten, soft and heavy with milk, watched the re-
flections of the little river forming broken rings, gold serpents and
wavelets on the tiled roof of the penthouse. At six weeks he was
already trotting, and following the flight of the flies with eyes that
were still blue, while his mother, with a coat as finely marked as
his, saw herself mirrored in the beauty of her son.

Excluded though he was from this family happiness, the Long-
cat for all that adopted an air of serenity that was vaguely patri-
archal, the detached bearing of those fathers who are content to
leave the care of their offspring to their worthy spouse. He confined
himself to the parsley bed which the she-cat let him have, and there
he would sprawl, warming his long belly, with its withered teats,

in the sun. Or else he would drape himself over the heap of fire-wood, as if the spiky faggots were wool and down. For a cat's idea of what is comfortable and what is not is incomprehensible to a human.

Spring drenched our retreat with precocious warmth, and in the light air of May the scents of lilac, young tarragon and red-brown wallflower intermingled. I was at that time a prey to homesickness for my native village, and this I nursed in silence in the new village, amidst the bitterness of spring and its first flowers. There I sat, an anæmic young girl, leaning my cheeks and my little waxen ears against a wall already warm, the end of one of my over-long plaits always trailing far from me over the fine, sieved leaf-mould of a seed-bed.

One day when we were all dozing, the she-cat on her palliasse, the tom on his couch of spiky firewood-bundles, and I at the foot of the wall where the sun lingered longest, the little cat, who was wide awake and busy chasing flies on the edge of the river, fell into the water. True to the code of his tribe, he uttered no cry and began to swim by instinct as soon as he came to the surface. I happened to see him tumble in, and just as I was setting off for the house to seize the butterfly net, run down the road, and rejoin the river at the first little bridge, where I could have fished out the swimming kitten, the Long-cat threw himself into the water. He swam like an otter, ears flat and only his nostrils out of the water.

It is not every day that one sees a cat swim, swim of his own free will, I mean. He can glide unerringly through water like a serpent, but he never makes use of this gift except to save his life if he is in danger of drowning. Helped by the current, the Long-cat forged ahead strongly in pursuit of the kitten, the swift, transparent waters of the pent-up river on its bed of pebbles and broken shards making his long body look like a leech. I lost half a minute through stopping to watch him.

He seized the little cat by the scruff of its neck, turned right round and set off upstream, not without effort, for the current was strong and the kitten, inert like all little cats when you hold them by the scruff of their necks, weighed his full weight. The sight of the Long-cat struggling nearly made me jump into the water too. But the rescuer clambered up on to the washing-board and laid his dripping burden on the bank, after which he shook himself and looked in stupefaction at the drenched kitten. That was the moment when the rescued one, silent hitherto, elected to cough and sneeze and set up a terrific shrill lamentation which awoke the mother cat.

"Horrors!" she cried. "What do I see? You baby-snatcher! You wrecker, you devourer of infants, you stinking beast, what have you done to my son?"

Even as she jerked out these insults at the top of her voice, she was already encircling the little cat with her own body and sniffing him, finding time too to turn him all over and lick the river water off his coat.

"But," ventured the Long-cat, "but . . . but on the contrary, I jumped into the water to get him. Now I come to think of it, I don't know what made me do it!"

"Out of my sight! Or in another moment I'll bite your nose off and crush the breath out of you! I'll blind you, I'll slit your throat, I'll. . ."

She made ready to suit the action to the word, and I admired the furious beauty which animates a female when she pits herself against danger or an adversary bigger than herself.

The Long-cat took to his heels and, still dripping, gained the ladder leading to the cosy hay-loft warm under its tiled roof. The she-cat, changing her tone, led her son to the palliasse where he found once again the warm maternal belly with its milk, healing care and restoring sleep.

But the she-cat never forgave the Long-cat. Whenever she met him she never forgot to call him "baby-snatcher, drowner of little cats, assassin," accompanying this with snarls and yells, while the Long-cat strove each time to clear himself: "Now look here! I tell you that, on the contrary, it was I who, obeying only my own heart, overcame my loathing for cold water . . ."

I genuinely pitied him and used to call him "poor, misunderstood Long-cat."

"Misunderstood," said my mother, "that remains to be seen."

She could see deep into souls; and she was not one to be taken in by the equivocal meekness, the flickering yellow gleam in the eye of a tom-cat, whenever it lights on tender, defenseless flesh.

TUT AS A MUSIC CRITIC

BY *John Hosford Hickey* AND *Priscilla Beach*

THE LIST OF SUBJECTS in King Tut's college curriculum was never disclosed to us. In some of the liberal arts, however, Tut felt himself qualified to instruct human, as well as feline, pupils.

We have heard of cats who were considered critics of considerable worth. George Moore's cat, "the great black tom cat of Ebury Street," was the first audience to Moore's work *Avowals*. The cat sat sedately in an armchair blinking his green eyes while his master made his famous plea in defense of censored literature.

Tut would have done excellently in such a capacity, as we observed time after time through different radio lecturers to whom Tut listened. When someone on the radio would speak intelligently, in mellow tones with proper inflections, Tut would listen respectfully, often going close to the radio, where he would sit lion fashion to catch every word. But if the speaker spoke in rasping tones or ranted, Tut would meow back at him. As the speaker's voice would rise, Tut's would rise in an effort to drown him out. If he didn't subside, Tut would look up at us with a most distressed expression and meow pleadingly with us, "Please shut this fellow off—he is really getting in my fur!"

His laws of musical criticism were no less stringent. He had his favorite radio programs, taking great pleasure in the philharmonic orchestras, and was bored with swing. With singers he was pretty severe; few pleased him. At the sound of a badly performed passage he would mew disgustedly and frown, sitting up with a shiver, as if in great discomfort. He generally got up and walked away from the radio. But when female crooners wailed their blues, Tut opened up on them in a full and loud soprano, showing them how it really should be done.

265

Gautier's cat, Madame Théophile, also was known to be highly critical of singers.

> Sitting on a pile of scores she listened attentively and with visible signs of pleasure to singers. But piercing notes made her nervous and at the high A she never failed to close the mouth of the singer with her soft paw. This was an experiment which it amused many to make and which never failed. It was impossible to deceive this cat dilettante on the note in question. . . .

Jenny Lind, when a young girl, used to sing all her songs to her cat. Her eldest son writes: "Her favorite seat with her cat was in the window . . . which looked out on the lively street leading up to the church of St. Jacob's, and here she sat and sang to it; and the people passing in the street used to hear, and wonder."

Many cats, no doubt, have held such an honored place. Mademoiselle Dupuy, for instance, a great harpist of the seventeenth century, attributed her success to her cat, whose signs of displeasure or delight she noticed as she played. The composer Sacchini declared he could compose only when surrounded by his cats. According to Charles Larcom Graves's *Diversions of a Music Lover,* no less an artist than Paderewski received graciously the praise and encouragement of a cat when he made his London debut at St. James's. There were only a hundred persons in the hall. Nervously the young pianist turned to the St. James's cat, sitting by his chair, and whispered, "Wish me luck!" Pussy, never loath to recognize genius, promptly jumped on his lap and purred. After giving a brilliant performance Paderewski paid homage to his feline patron by playing in her honor Scarlatti's *"Cat's Fugue"** in the Artists' Room.

Tut was passionately fond of the piano. Whenever I played he was at my side.

One day, as I had just played the last chords of Debussy's "Clair de Lune," Florence stuck her head in the door. "Tut does love that piece, Miss Beach," she said, "whatever it is. As soon as you start to play it, no matter what I'm doing for him, he rushes to get in to you—he won't stay another minute."

---

* The theme of this composition is supposed to have been suggested to the composer by his musical cat taking a stroll up the keyboard.

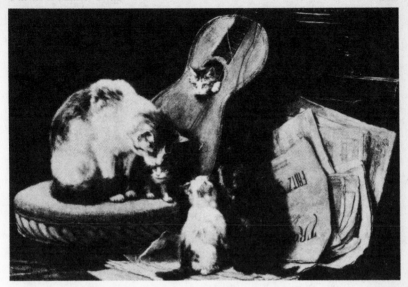

THE MUSIC ROOM. Henriette Ronner

Florence had a peculiar expression on her face, as if I might not believe that Tut were capable of a musical preference. "Yes, I know he likes this, Florence," I said. "That's why I play it so often."

When I wanted to find Tut and couldn't see him anywhere, all I had to do was to start "Clair de Lune." Almost immediately Tut would mysteriously appear from nowhere and walk quietly over to the side of the piano, where he would stretch out in his leonine pose, with his front paws straight out. How he would listen!—not with sleepy satisfaction but with an air of rapt attention. The whole body was relaxed, except that his head swayed as rhythmically as a conductor's baton. If I wanted to dismiss my audience, I had only to start Bach's "Chromatic Fantasy and Fugue in D Minor." Tut would go like a shot out of a gun.

"What is that you play that makes Tut so mad, Miss Beach?" asked Florence on another occasion. "Please forgive me, I don't like to mention it, but every time you play that thing Tut comes into the kitchen in a rage, and argues with me about it. If I don't watch out, he bites my ankles. He says, 'Meow-ow ow-ow-ow!' in such a distressed way! It seems to me just as if he is saying. 'She's at it again—please go over and stop her, won't you, Florence? Please, I can't stand it, that's all.'

"When he looks up at you with those appealing eyes of his," she went on, "they seem to run right through you. You can't refuse him anything, can you?"

As a result of Tut's definite reactions to music, I had the strange experience that when Tut was listening, I became more acutely aware of the quality of the music I was playing, and also of the effectiveness of my own execution. A broken phrase or a carelessly interpreted rubato, would make Tut's eyes open critically, and a faulty touch on a sforzando, or a wrong note, would send an electric shuddering down his spine. It was as if I had a conductor constantly beating time and measuring the accuracy of every bar of the score.

As the music changed in its mood, so did Tut change in his visible reaction. He listened to a concert of Mendelssohn, Brahms, Johann Strauss, Verdi, Wagner, and some of my own compositions as if soothed and carried away. The romantic melodies and chromatic progressions in Chopin and the subtle impressionism of Debussy were above everything else deeply moving to Tut. It was as if these two composers had penetrated the ideal harmony of the cat soul. If he had gone out for an intermission during my playing of Bach, at the strains of "Arabesques" or *Pelléas et Mélisande* or a Chopin *étude*, he would quietly saunter back again in a softly triumphant manner and resume his post of attentive absorption.

"That's beautiful," he would seem to say, as he looked up into my face with a smile. "E-e-ew! meow! That's what I call music."

The development sections of certain sonatas and symphonies, which I had studied since childhood until I had absorbed every detail, suddenly appeared to me to be labored, and I wondered if they bored Tut. I looked around at him during one of these passages and saw him just finishing a yawn. It might have been a coincidence, of course. Likewise, I felt somewhat embarrassed when certain themes recurred again and again and again. I may have imagined that Tut sighed and meowed impatiently, "W-h-a-at? Tha-at again? I heard you the first time."

He gave me a peculiar look when I played Schönberg. I could not help thinking he looked amused, but since he did not walk out I assumed he was somewhat pleased with the dissonant harmonies and irregular rhythms. I did not fully understand his reactions, however, until the evening I went with the noted pianist Norma Boleslavski, a prodigy pupil of Ethel Leginska and wife of the late Richard Boleslavski, famous producer of Hollywood, to hear the first performance of Schönberg's *Creation*. There was an awed silence before the *première*, while the audience prepared to be carried back to that first dawn when the command came: "Let there be light!" Then the music started. I saw several people convulsively hold their breath as the first bars squeaked and squirmed. While the squeaks labored into agitated groans, people smiled and tittered. A hundred mice being held by their tails could not have given a less awe-inspiring performance than the orchestra. I began to see the similarity between Tut's reactions and that audience's at listening to Schönberg's works. Tut, although not a college graduate, surprised me by his depth of musical perception. He had exposed these monstrosities I had been educated into admiring. Why was it, I wondered, that Tut should have perceived the emptiness of these pieces, when I, with all my musical training, had not fathomed it? Tut, it seemed, understood music better than I did. I should take lessons from him if I did not want to risk sounding like Sontag in Heinrich Heine's poem "The Young Cats' Club for Poetry and Music":

> And loudest of all was heard a voice
>   Which sounded languid and shrieking
> As Sontag's voice became at last
>   When utterly broken and squeaking.

I decided to pay more attention to Tut's attitudes, which apparently were a reflection of the way an audience would respond. Whenever I saw that supercilious smile come over Tut's face while I was playing, I forced myself to throw out all I had learned about music and listen without bias, as a child does—or a cat.

On one of these days when I was playing and Tut was sitting by the piano, in bounced Puccini, the little silver Persian cat. Tut looked embarrassed as she walked in and took her place beside him. I continued playing, including many of Tut's favorite pieces. Puccini did not move but seemed to absorb and enjoy the whole thing, looking up at me pensively with her great big blue eyes. The two cats seemed as if lost to the world. I felt that I couldn't stop. I had to play. This tableau continued for some time—how long I don't know. When I stopped, Tut jumped on the bench beside me, put his paws on my shoulder, and kissed my face. Puccini, not to be outdone, jumped up on the other side and followed Tut's example. I petted them both, while they gave little soft meows, as if to say, "Thank you, thank you, I've had a wonderful time!"

This was the first time Puccini had been in our house. She had broken the master's rule. He wouldn't introduce her, so she introduced herself. After that, when she heard the piano she came hurrying in, the same as Tut. We found she lived not far from us and had been christened Puccini because of her extreme fondness for music.

Puccini's grace and charm brought additional refinement to the class of gentleman cats. We noticed after the arrival of her ladyship the other cats became more fastidious in their manners and paid especial attention to their grooming. Pepper, in particular, hung his hat up for Puccini.

THE WELL-BEHAVED CAT

GRISETTE DINES

BY *Antoinette Deshoulières*

Always well behaved am I,
Never scratch and never cry;
Only touch the diner's hand,
So that he can understand
That I want a modest share
Of the good things that are there.
If he pay but scanty heed
To my little stomach's need,
I beg him with a mew polite
To give me just a single bite.
Greedy though that diner be,
He will share his meal with me.

CAT CATCHING A MOUSE. Gottfried Mind

THE IMMORTAL CAT

BY *Karel Capek*

THIS STORY ABOUT A CAT (with the inconsequence which is the very characteristic of reality) is at the beginning about a tomcat, in fact, about a tomcat which was presented to me. Every gift has about it something supernatural; each comes, so to speak, from another world, it drops from heaven, is sent upon us, invades our lives independently of its own and with some kind of exuberance, especially if it happens to be a particular tomcat with a blue ribbon round his neck. And he was called Philip, Percy, Scamp, and Rogue, in accordance with his various moral qualities; he was

271

an Angora kitten, but dishevelled and carrotty like any other Christian scamp. One day on a tour of exploration he fell from the balcony onto the head of some female person; on the one hand she was scratched by it, on the other deeply offended, and she brought out a charge against my cat as a dangerous animal which springs from balconies onto people's heads. As a matter of fact I established the innocence of this Seraphic little beast; but three days later the little animal breathed his last, poisoned with arsenic and human malice. Just as through a strange mist I saw how with his last tremor his hips had sunken in, there was a mew on my doorstep; a stray brindled kitten was trembling there, as scraggy as a ridge-tile, and as frightened as a wandering child. Well, come here, Pussy; perhaps it is the finger of God, the will of Fate, a mysterious sign or whatever it is called; most probably the departed has sent you in his place; unfathomable is the continuity of life.

Such then was the first arrival of a cat which for her modesty was given the name of Pudlenka; as you see, she came from the Unknown, but I bear witness that she in no way puffed herself up on account of her mysterious and perhaps even supernatural origin. On the contrary, she behaved like every normal cat: she drank milk and stole the meat, she slept in one's lap and roamed in the night; and when her time had come, she gave birth to five kittens of which one was red, one black, one mixed, one brindled, and one Angora. And I began to accost all the people I knew. "Listen," I began magnanimously, "I've got a marvellous kitten for you." Some of them (out of extreme modesty, very likely) managed to extricate themselves, saying that they would love to, but that unfortunately they couldn't, and so on; but others were so taken by surprise that before they could utter a word I had pressed their hand, and declared that it was settled then, they needn't worry, I was going to send them that kitten in due course; and already I was off after the next. Nothing is more charming than such a cat's maternal happiness; you ought to have a cat for yourself, if for nothing else but for those kittens. After six weeks Pudlenka let the kittens be kittens, and went to listen at first hand to the heroic baritone of the tomcat from the adjoining street. In fifty-three days she delivered six young ones. In a year and a day they added up to seventeen. Most probably that miraculous fertility was a legacy and post-mortem mission of the deceased bachelor little cat.

Cats on a Trouser Leg.
Karel Capek. From *"The
Immortal Cat"*

I always used to be of the opinion, may the deuce take them, that I had heaps of acquaintances, but from the time that Pudlenka threw herself into producing kittens, I found that in this life of ours I was terribly alone; for instance, I had no one to present with the twenty-sixth kitten. When I had to make myself known to someone I mumbled my name, and said: "Don't you want a kitten?" "What kitten?" they enquired dubiously. "I don't know yet," was my general answer; "but I think that I shall be having some kittens again." Soon I began to have the feeling that people were avoiding me; perhaps it was out of envy because I had such luck with kittens. According to Brehm cats bear young twice a year; Pudlenka had them three to four times a year without any regard to the seasons; she was a supernatural cat—apparently she had a higher mission, to revenge and replace a hundredfold the life of that tomcat which was done to death.

After three years of fertile vigour Pudlenka suddenly perished; some caretaker broke her back on the undignified pretext that according to him she had eaten a goose in his larder. The very same day that Pudlenka disappeared, her youngest daughter came back to us, a cat which I had pressed onto the people next door; and she lived with us under the name of Pudlenka II as a direct continuation of her deceased mother. She continued her to perfection; she was still a girlish adolescent when she began to swell, and then brought into the world four kittens. One was black, and had a noble, carrotty colour of the Vršovice race, one the elongated nose

of the Strašnice cats, while the fourth was spotty like a bean, as the
cats of Malâ Strana are. Pudlenka II produced kittens three times
a year with the regularity of a law of Nature; in two and a quarter
years she enriched the world with one and twenty kittens, of all
colours and breeds, except that of the cats of the Isle of Man which
are born without tails. For the twenty-first kitten I really had no
market. I was just making up my mind that I ought to join the
Free Thought or the Rosary Brotherhood, to gain a new circle of
acquaintances when our neighbour's Rolf bit to death Pudlenka II.
We carried her home and laid her on the bed; her chin still was
trembling. Then the chin stopped shaking and from her dense coat
fleas rapidly crawled away; this is the unmistakable sign of death
with a cat. So then her surviving kitten for whom there was no
market remained with us as Pudlenka III. In four months' time
Pudlenka III gave birth to five kittens; from that time on she has
conscientiously fulfilled her task of this life at regular intervals of
fifteen weeks; only during those great frosts of this year did she miss
one term.

You might not perhaps say of her that she had such a big and
immortal mission; to look at, she seems an ordinary, many-coloured
democratic puss, who spends the whole day long dozing on the
family patriarch's lap, or on the bed. She has a highly-developed
sense for her personal comfort, maintains a healthy distrust of men
and animals, and when it comes to it she can defend her interests
dente unguibusque. But when her fifteen weeks are over she begins
to be excited and restless, and she sits nervously by the door giving
one to understand: "Man, let me out quickly, I have got the tummy
ache." After this, she dashes out like an arrow into the evening
darkness, and doesn't return till morning, with a drawn face and
rings round her eyes. At such times a huge black tomcat comes from
the North, where the Olšany Cemeteries are; from the South,
where Vršovice is, appears a carrotty and one-eyed fighter; from the
West, the seat of civilization, arrives an Angora cat, with a bush of
ostrich feathers; from the East, where there is nothing, a mysterious
white animal appears with a curved-up tail. In their midst sits the
simple many-coloured Pudlenka III, and with burning fascinated
eyes she listens to their howling, stifled exclamations, screams as of
murdered children, roar of drunken mariners, saxophones, roll of
drums and other instruments in the Cats' Symphony. To put it

clearly, not only are strength and courage necessary for a tomcat, but also perseverance; sometimes for a week at a time these four tomcats of the Apocalypse besiege Pudlenka's home, blockade the gate, make their way through the windows into the house, and leave behind them merely a hellish stench. At last the night arrives when Pudlenka III no longer has any desire to go out. "Let me sleep," she says. "Let me sleep, sleep for ever. Sleep, dream. . . . Ah, I'm so unhappy!" After this, at the proper time, she delivers five kittens. On this question I have already had a certain amount of experience: there will be five of them. I already see them, those dear, sweet little lumps, stumping, and padding about over the house, pulling over electric lamps, making little puddles in slippers, crawling up my legs, onto my lap (my legs are scratched by them, like Lazarus's), I see myself finding a kitten in the sleeve when I'm putting on my coat, and my tie under the bed when I want to put it on—Children are worrying, everybody will tell you that. It isn't enough just to bring them up; you have to ensure their future.

In the editorial office everybody now has got a kitten from me; very well, I shall have to get taken on at another place. I am ready to put my name down for any society, or organization, if they will assure me of the disposal of at least twenty-one kittens. While I shall be struggling along in a hostile world to find room for more generations, Pudlenka III, or Pudlenka IV, will be purring, her paws folded up beneath her, and spinning the immortal thread of cat life. She will dream of the cats' world, of the hosts of cats, of cats, when there will be enough of them, seizing power to rule over the universe. For it is a Great Task which was imposed upon her by the little Angora tomcat, innocently done to death.

Seriously, now, wouldn't you like a kitten?

THIS MUFF OF FUR

BY *Mildred R. Howland*

The Devil's soul
Is not more black
Than Smudge my cat
Who has more yen
For mice than men.

Narrowed to slits
His topaz eyes
Fixed on a hole
As there he sits
With fierce control
For hours
And glowers—
Claws curved, intent,
On murder bent.

The glossy brute
Fears not one hoot
My lame pursuit,
And every night
Sneaks out to fight,
Seduce, and prowl;
Long after three,
I hear him yowl
To waken me;
Dizzy with sin,
He staggers in.

Damn his black skin.

No angel's smile
Has half the wile
Of his smug purr
In a feigned nap—
This muff of fur
Curled on my lap.

In my castle
He is the king
And I his vassal.
Bound to appease,
Beseeching paws
With indrawn claws
Pad my old knees;
He knows how weak
I am—the sneak,
Softer than silk
Close by my side,
Milder than milk.

Bless his black hide.

THE PERFECT CAT

CALVIN

BY *Charles Dudley Warner*

CALVIN IS DEAD. His life, long to him, but short for the rest of us, was not marked by startling adventures, but his character was so uncommon and his qualities were so worthy of imitation, that I have been asked by those who personally knew him to set down my recollections of his career.

His origin and ancestry were shrouded in mystery; even his age was a matter of pure conjecture. Although he was of the Maltese race, I have reason to suppose that he was American by birth as he certainly was in sympathy. Calvin was given to me eight years ago by Mrs. Stowe, but she knew nothing of his age or origin. He walked into her house one day out of the great unknown and became at once at home, as·if he had been always a friend of the family. He appeared to have artistic and literary tastes, and it was as if he had inquired at the door if that was the residence of the author of *Uncle Tom's Cabin,* and, upon being assured that it was, had decided to dwell there. This is, of course, fanciful, for his antecedents were wholly unknown, but in his time he could hardly have been in any household where he would not have heard *Uncle Tom's Cabin* talked about. When he came to Mrs. Stowe, he was as large as he ever was, and apparently as old as he ever became. Yet there was in him no appearance of age; he was in the happy maturity of all his powers, and you would rather have said in that maturity he had found the secret of perpetual youth. And it was as difficult to believe that he would ever be aged as it was to imagine that he had ever been in immature youth. There was in him a mysterious perpetuity.

After some years, when Mrs. Stowe made her winter home in Florida, Calvin came to live with us. From the first moment, he fell into the ways of the house and assumed a recognized position in the family—I say recognized, because after he became known he was always inquired for by visitors, and in the letters to the other members of the family he always received a message. Although the least obtrusive of beings, his individuality always made itself felt.

His personal appearance had much to do with this, for he was of royal mould, and had an air of high breeding. He was large, but he had nothing of the fat grossness of the celebrated Angora family; though powerful, he was exquisitely proportioned, and as graceful in every movement as a young leopard. When he stood up to open a door—he opened all the doors with old-fashioned latches—he was portentously tall, and when stretched on the rug before the fire he seemed too long for this world—as indeed he was. His coat was the finest and softest I have ever seen, a shade of quiet Maltese; and from his throat downward, underneath, to the white tips of his feet, he wore the whitest and most delicate ermine; and no person was ever more fastidiously neat. In his finely formed head you saw something of his aristocratic character; the ears were small and

He Gambolled Like a Dog.
Peggy Bacon

cleanly cut, there was a tinge of pink in the nostrils, his face was handsome, and the expression of his countenance exceedingly intelligent—I should call it even a sweet expression if the term were not inconsistent with his look of alertness and sagacity.

It is difficult to convey a just idea of his gaiety in connection with his dignity and gravity, which his name expressed. As we know nothing of his family, of course it will be understood that Calvin was his Christian name. He had times of relaxation into utter playfulness, delighting in a ball of yarn, catching sportively at stray ribbons when his mistress was at her toilet, and pursuing his own tail, with hilarity, for lack of anything better. He could amuse himself by the hour, and he did not care for children; perhaps something in his past was present to his memory. He had absolutely no bad habits, and his disposition was perfect. I never saw him exactly angry, though I have seen his tail grow to an enormous size when a strange cat appeared upon his lawn. He disliked cats, evidently regarding them as feline and treacherous, and he had no association with them. Occasionally there would be heard a night concert in the shrubbery. Calvin would ask to have the door opened, and then you would hear a rush and a "pestzt," and the concert would explode, and Calvin would quietly come in and resume his seat on the hearth. There was no trace of anger in his manner, but he wouldn't have any of that about the house. He had the rare virtue of magnanimity. Although he had fixed notions about his own rights, and extraordinary persistency in getting them, he never showed temper at a repulse; he simply and firmly persisted till he had what he wanted. His diet was one point; his idea was that of the scholars about dictionaries,—to "get the best." He knew as well as anyone what was in the house, and would refuse beef if turkey was to be had; and if there were oysters, he would wait over the turkey to see if the oysters would not be forthcoming. And yet he was not a gross gourmand; he would eat bread if he saw me eating it, and thought he was not being imposed on. His habits of feeding, also, were refined; he never used a knife, and he would put up his hand and draw the fork down to his mouth as gracefully as a grown person. Unless necessity compelled, he would not eat in the kitchen, but insisted upon his meals in the dining-room, and would wait patiently, unless a stranger were present; and then he was sure to importune the visitor, hoping that the latter was ignorant of the rule of the house, and would give him something. They used to say that he preferred as his table-cloth on the floor a certain well-known church journal; but this was said by an Episcopalian. So far as I know, he had no religious prejudices, except that he did not like the association with Romanists. He tolerated the servants, because they belonged to the house, and would sometimes linger by the kitchen stove; but the moment visitors came in he arose, opened the door, and marched into the drawing-room. Yet he enjoyed the company of his equals, and never withdrew, no matter how many callers—whom he recognized as of his society—might come into the drawing-room. Calvin was fond of company, but he wanted to choose it; and I have no doubt that his was an aristocratic fastidiousness rather than one of faith. It is so with most people.

The intelligence of Calvin was something phenomenal, in his rank of life. He established a method of communicating his wants, and even some of his sentiments; and he could help himself in many things. There was a furnace register in a retired room, where he used to go when he wished to be alone, that he always opened when he desired more heat; but never shut it, any more than he shut the door after himself. He could do almost everything but speak; and you would declare sometimes that you could see a pathetic longing to do that in his intelligent face. I have no desire to overdraw his qualities, but if there was one thing in him more noticeable than another, it was his fondness for nature. He could content himself for hours at a low window, looking into the ravine and at the great trees, noting the smallest stir there; he delighted, above all things, to accompany me walking about the garden, hearing the birds, getting the smell of the fresh earth, and rejoicing in the sunshine. He followed me and gambolled like a dog, rolling over on the turf and exhibiting his delight in a hundred ways. If I worked, he sat and watched me, or looked off over the bank, and kept his ear open to the twitter in the cherry-trees. When it stormed, he was sure to sit at the window, keenly watching the rain or the snow, glancing up and down at its falling; and a winter tempest always delighted him. I think he was genuinely fond of birds, but, so far as I know, he usually confined himself to one a day; he never killed, as some sportsmen do, for the sake of killing, but only as civilized people do,—from necessity. He was intimate with the flying-squirrels who dwelt in the chestnut-trees,—too intimate, for almost every day in the summer he would bring in one, until he nearly discouraged them. He was, indeed, a superb hunter, and would have been a devastating one, if his bump of destructiveness had not been offset by a bump of moderation. There was very little of the brutality of the lower animals about him; I don't think he enjoyed rats for themselves, but he knew his business, and for the first few months of his residence with us he waged an awful campaign against the horde, and after that his simple presence was sufficient to deter them from coming on the premises. Mice amused him, but he usually considered them too small game to be taken seriously; I have seen him play for an hour with a mouse, and then let him go with a royal condescension. In this whole matter of "getting a living," Calvin was a great contrast to the rapacity of the age in which he lived.

I hesitate to speak of his capacity for friendship and the affectionateness of his nature, for I know from his own reserve that he would not care to have it much talked about. We understood each other perfectly, but we never made any fuss about it; when I spoke his name and snapped my fingers, he came to me; when I returned home at night, he was pretty sure to be waiting for me near the gate, and would rise and saunter along the walk, as if his being there were purely accidental,—so shy was he commonly of showing feeling; and when I opened the door he never rushed in, like a cat, but loitered, and lounged, as if he had had no intention of going in, but would condescend to. And yet, the fact was, he knew dinner was ready, and he was bound to be there. He kept the run of dinnertime. It happened sometimes, during our absence in the summer, that dinner would be early, and Calvin walking about the grounds, missed it and came in late. But he never made a mistake the second day. There was one thing he never did,—he never rushed through an open doorway. He never forgot his dignity. If he had asked to have the door open, and was eager to go out, he always went deliberately; I can see him now, standing on the sill, looking about at the sky as if he was thinking whether it were worthwhile to take an umbrella, until he was near having his tail shut in.

His friendship was rather constant than demonstrative. When we returned from an absence of nearly two years, Calvin welcomed us with evident pleasure, but showed his satisfaction rather by tranquil happiness than by fuming about. He had the faculty of making us glad to get home. It was his constancy that was so attractive. He liked companionship, but he wouldn't be petted, or fussed over, or sit in any one's lap a moment; he always extricated himself from such familiarity with dignity and with no show of temper. If there was any petting to be done, however, he chose to do it. Often he would sit looking at me, and then, moved by a delicate affection, come and pull at my coat and sleeve until he could touch my face with his nose, and then go away contented. He had a habit of coming to my study in the morning, sitting quietly by my side or on the table for hours, watching the pen run over the paper, occasionally swinging his tail round for a blotter, and then going to sleep among the papers by the inkstand. Or, more rarely, he would watch the writing from a perch on my shoulder. Writing always interested him, and, until he understood it, he wanted to hold the pen.

He always held himself in a kind of reserve with his friend, as if he had said, "Let us respect our personality, and not make a 'mess' of friendship." He saw, with Emerson, the risk of degrading it to trivial conveniency. "Why insist on rash personal relations with your friends? Leave this touching and clawing." Yet I would not give an unfair notion of his aloofness, his fine sense of the sacredness of the me and the not-me. And, at the risk of not being believed,

I will relate an incident, which was often repeated. Calvin had the practice of passing a portion of the night in the contemplation of its beauties, and would come into our chamber over the roof of the conservatory through the open window, summer and winter, and go to sleep at the foot of my bed. He would do this always exactly in this way; he never was content to stay in the chamber if we compelled him to go upstairs and through the door. He had the obstinacy of General Grant. But this is by the way. In the morning, he performed his toilet and went down to breakfast with the rest of the family. Now, when the mistress was absent from home, and at no other time, Calvin would come in the morning, when the bell rang, to the head of the bed, put up his feet and look into my face, follow me about when I rose, "assist" at the dressing, and in many purring ways show his fondness, as if he had plainly said, "I know that she has gone away, but I am here." Such was Calvin in rare moments.

He had his limitations. Whatever passion he had for nature, he had no conception of art. There was sent to him once a fine and very expressive cat's head in bronze, by Frémiet. I placed it on the floor. He regarded it intently, approached it cautiously and crouchingly, touched it with his nose, perceived the fraud, turned away abruptly, and never would notice it afterward. On the whole, his life was not only a successful one, but a happy one. He never had but one fear, so far as I know: he had a mortal and a reasonable terror of plumbers. He would never stay in the house when they were here. No coaxing could quiet him. Of course he didn't share our fear about their charges, but he must have had some dreadful experience with them in that portion of his life which is unknown to us. A plumber was to him the devil, and I have no doubt that, in his scheme, plumbers were foreordained to do him mischief.

In speaking of his worth, it has never occurred to me to estimate Calvin by the worldly standard. I know that it is customary now, when anyone dies, to ask how much he was worth, and that no obituary in the newspapers is considered complete without such an estimate. The plumbers in our house were one day overheard to say that, "They say that *she* says that *he* says that he wouldn't take a hundred dollars for him." It is unnecessary to say that I never made such a remark, and that, so far as Calvin was concerned, there was no purchase in money.

As I look back upon it, Calvin's life seems to me a fortunate one, for it was natural and unforced. He ate when he was hungry, slept when he was sleepy, and enjoyed existence to the very tips of his toes and the end of his expressive and slow-moving tail. He delighted to roam about the garden, and stroll among the trees, and to lie on the green grass and luxuriate in all the sweet influences of summer. You could never accuse him of idleness, and yet he knew the secret of repose. The poet who wrote so prettily of him that his little life was rounded with a sleep, understated his felicity; it was rounded with a good many. His conscience never seemed to interfere with his slumbers. In fact, he had good habits and a contented mind. I can see him now walk in at the study door, sit down by my chair, bring his tail artistically about his feet, and look up at me with unspeakable happiness in his handsome face. I often thought that he felt the dumb limitation which denied him the power of language. But since he was denied speech, he scorned the inarticulate mouthings of the lower animals. The vulgar mewing and yowling of the cat species was beneath him; he sometimes uttered a sort of articulate and well-bred ejaculation, when he wished to call attention to something that he considered remarkable, or to some want of his, but he never went whining about. He would sit for hours at a closed window, when he desired to enter, without a murmur, and when it was opened he never admitted that he had been impatient by "bolting" in. Though speech he had not, and the unpleasant kind of utterance given to his race he would not use, he had a mighty power of purr to express his measureless content with congenial society. There was in him a musical organ with stops of varied power and expression, upon which I have no doubt he could have performed Scarlatti's celebrated cat's-fugue.

Whether Calvin died of old age, or was carried off by one of the diseases incident to youth, it is impossible to say; for his departure was as quiet as his advent was mysterious. I only know that he appeared to us in this world in his perfect stature and beauty, and that after a time, like Lohengrin, he withdrew. In his illness there was nothing more to be regretted than in all his blameless life. I suppose there never was an illness that had more of dignity and sweetness and resignation in it. It came on gradually, in a kind of listlessness and want of appetite. An alarming symptom was his preference for the warmth of a furnace-register to the lively sparkle of the open wood-fire. Whatever pain he suffered, he bore it in silence, and seemed only anxious not to obtrude his malady. We tempted him with the delicacies of the season, but it soon became impossible for him to eat, and for two weeks he ate or drank scarcely anything. Sometimes he made an effort to take something, but it was evident that he made the effort to please us. The neighbors— and I am convinced that the advice of neighbors is never good for anything—suggested catnip. He wouldn't even smell it. We had the attendance of an amateur practitioner of medicine, whose real office was the cure of souls, but nothing touched his case. He took what was offered, but it was with the air of one to whom the time for pellets was passed. He sat or lay day after day almost motionless, never once making a display of those vulgar convulsions or contortions of pain which are so disagreeable to society. His favorite place was on the brightest spot of a Smyrna rug by the conservatory, where the sunlight fell and he could hear the fountain play. If we went to him and exhibited our interest in his condition, he always purred in recognition of our sympathy. And when I spoke his name, he looked up with an expression that said, "I understand it, old fellow, but it's no use." He was to all who came to visit him a model of calmness and patience in affliction.

I was absent from home at the last, but heard by daily postal-card of his failing condition; and never again saw him alive. One sunny morning, he rose from his rug, went into the conservatory (he was very thin then), walked around it deliberately, looking at all the plants he knew, and then went to the bay-window in the dining-room, and stood a long time looking out upon the little field, now brown and sere, and toward the garden, where perhaps the happiest hours of his life had been spent. It was a last look. He turned and walked away, laid himself down upon the bright spot in the rug, and quietly died.

It is not too much to say that a little shock went through the neighborhood when it was known that Calvin was dead, so marked was his individuality; and his friends, one after another, came in to see him. There was no sentimental nonsense about his obsequies; it was felt that any parade would have been distasteful to him. John, who acted as undertaker, prepared a candle-box for him, and I believe assumed a professional decorum; but there may have been the usual levity underneath, for I heard that he remarked in the kitchen that it was the "dryest wake he ever attended." Everybody, however, felt a fondness for Calvin, and regarded him with a certain respect. Between him and Bertha there existed a great friendship, and she apprehended his nature; she used to say that sometimes she was afraid of him, he looked at her so intelligently; she was never certain that he was what he appeared to be.

When I returned, they had laid Calvin on a table in an upper chamber by an open window. It was February. He reposed in a candle-box, lined about the edge with evergreen, and at his head stood a little wine-glass with flowers. He lay with his head tucked down in his arms,—a favorite position of his before the fire,—as if asleep in the comfort of his soft and exquisite fur. It was the involuntary exclamation of those who saw him, "How natural he looks!" As for myself, I said nothing. John buried him under the twin hawthorn-trees,—one white and the other pink,—in a spot where Calvin was fond of lying and listening to the hum of summer insects and the twitter of birds.

Perhaps I have failed to make appear the individuality of character that was so evident to those who knew him. At any rate, I have set down nothing concerning him but the literal truth. He was always a mystery. I did not know whence he came; I do not know whither he has gone. I would not weave one spray of falsehood in the wreath I lay upon his grave.

THE PARADISE OF CATS

BY *Emile Zola*

A<small>N AUNT BEQUEATHED ME</small> an Angora cat, which is certainly
the most stupid animal I know of. This is what my cat related
to me, one winter night, before the warm embers.

i

I was then two years old, and I was certainly the fattest and most
simple cat any one could have seen. Even at that tender age I displayed all the presumption of an animal that scorns the attractions
of the fireside. And yet what gratitude I owed to Providence for
having placed me with your aunt! The worthy woman idolised me.
I had a regular bedroom at the bottom of a cupboard, with a feather
pillow and a triple-folded rug. The food was as good as the bed; no
bread or soup, nothing but meat, good underdone meat.

Well! amidst all these comforts, I had but one wish, but one
dream, to slip out by the half-open window, and run away on to
the tiles. Caresses appeared to me insipid, the softness of my bed
disgusted me, I was so fat that I felt sick, and from morn till eve I
experienced the weariness of being happy.

I must tell you that by straining my neck I had perceived the
opposite roof from the window. That day four cats were fighting
there. With bristling coats and tails in the air, they were rolling on
the blue slates, in the full sun, amidst oaths of joy. I had never wit-
nessed such an extraordinary sight. From that moment my convictions were settled. Real happiness was upon that roof, in front of
that window which the people of the house so carefully closed. I
found the proof of this in the way in which they shut the doors of
the cupboards where the meat was hidden.

I made up my mind to fly. I felt sure there were other things in
life than underdone meat. There was the unknown, the ideal. One

287

day they forgot to close the kitchen window. I sprang on to a small roof beneath it.

ii

How beautiful the roofs were! They were bordered by broad gutters exhaling delicious odours. I followed those gutters in raptures of delight, my feet sinking into fine mud, which was deliciously warm and soft. I fancied I was walking on velvet. And the generous heat of the sun melted my fat.

I will not conceal from you the fact that I was trembling in every limb. My delight was mingled with terror. I remember, particularly, experiencing a terrible shock that almost made me tumble down into the street. Three cats came rolling over from the top of a house towards me, mewing most frightfully, and as I was on the point of fainting away, they called me a silly thing, and said they were mewing for fun. I began mewing with them. It was charming. The jolly fellows had none of my stupid fat. When I slipped on the sheets of zinc heated by the burning sun, they laughed at me. An old tom, who was one of the band, showed me particular friendship. He offered to teach me a thing or two, and I gratefully accepted. Ah! your aunt's cat's meat was far from my thoughts! I drank in the gutters, and never had sugared milk seemed so sweet to me. Everything appeared nice and beautiful. A she-cat passed by, a charming she-cat, the sight of her gave me a feeling I had never experienced before. Hitherto, I had only seen these exquisite creatures, with such delightfully supple backbones, in my dreams. I and my three companions rushed forward to meet the newcomer. I was in front of the others, and was about to pay my respects to the bewitching thing, when one of my comrades cruelly bit my neck. I cried out with pain.

"Bah!" said the old tom, leading me away; "you will meet with stranger adventures than that."

iii

After an hour's walk I felt as hungry as a wolf.

"What do you eat on the roofs?" I inquired of my friend the tom.

"What you can find," he answered shrewdly.

This reply caused me some embarrassment, for though I carefully searched I found nothing. At last I perceived a young work-girl in a garret preparing her lunch. A beautiful chop of a tasty red colour was lying on a table under the window.

"There's the very thing I want," I thought, in all simplicity.

And I sprang on to the table and took the chop. But the work-girl, having seen me, struck me a fearful blow with a broom on the spine, and I fled, uttering a dreadful oath.

"You are fresh from your village then?" said the tom. "Meat that is on tables is there for the purpose of being longed for at a distance. You must search in the gutters."

I could never understand that kitchen meat did not belong to cats. My stomach was beginning to get seriously angry. The tom put me completely to despair by telling me it would be necessary to wait until night. Then we would go down into the street and turn over the heaps of muck. Wait until night! He said it quietly, like a hardened philosopher. I felt myself fainting at the mere thought of this prolonged fast.

iv

Night came slowly, a foggy night that chilled me to the bones. It soon began to rain, a fine, penetrating rain, driven by sudden gusts of wind. We went down along the glazed roof of a staircase. How ugly the street appeared to me! It was no longer that nice heat, that beautiful sun, those roofs white with light where one rolled about so deliciously. My paws slipped on the greasy stones. I sorrowfully recalled to memory my triple blanket and feather pillow.

We were hardly in the street when my friend the tom began to tremble. He made himself small, very small, and ran stealthily along beside the houses, telling me to follow as rapidly as possible. He rushed in at the first street door he came to, and purred with satisfaction as he sought refuge there. When I questioned him as to the motive of his flight, he answered:

"Did you see that man with a basket on his back and a stick with an iron hook at the end?"

"Yes."

"Well! if he had seen us he would have knocked us on the heads and roasted us!"

"Roasted us!" I exclaimed. "Then the street is not ours? One can't eat, but one's eaten!"

v

However, the boxes of kitchen refuse had been emptied before the street doors. I rummaged in the heaps in despair. I came across two or three bare bones that had been lying among the cinders, and I then understood what a succulent dish fresh cat's meat made. My friend the tom scratched artistically among the muck. He made me run about until morning, inspecting each heap, and without showing the least hurry. I was out in the rain for more than ten hours, shivering in every limb. Cursed street, cursed liberty, and how I regretted my prison!

At dawn the tom, seeing I was staggering said to me with a strange air:

"Have you had enough of it?"

"Oh yes," I answered.

"Do you want to go home?"

"I do, indeed; but how shall I find the house?"

"Come along. This morning, when I saw you come out, I understood that a fat cat like you was not made for the lively delights of liberty. I know your place of abode and will take you to the door."

The worthy tom said this very quietly. When we had arrived, he bid me "Good-bye," without betraying the least emotion.

"No," I exclaimed, "we will not leave each other so. You must accompany me. We will share the same bed and the same food. My mistress is a good woman——"

He would not allow me to finish my sentence.

"Hold your tongue," he said sharply, "you are a simpleton. Your effeminate existence would kill me. Your life of plenty is good for bastard cats. Free cats would never purchase your cat's meat and feather pillow at the price of a prison. Good-bye."

And he returned up on to the roofs, where I saw his long outline quiver with joy in the rays of the rising sun.

When I got in, your aunt took the whip and gave me a thrashing which I received with profound delight. I tasted in full measure the pleasure of being beaten and being warm. Whilst she was striking me, I thought with rapture of the meat she would give me afterwards.

vi

You see—concluded my cat, stretching itself out in front of the embers—real happiness, paradise, my dear master, consists in being shut up and beaten in a room where there is meat.

I am speaking from the point of view of cats.

❧

THE ABSENT CAT

THE CATS

BY *Adriaan Morriën*

WHEN THE WAR WAS OVER we all discovered, as if intuitively, that there were no cats left in our ill-treated town. What had become of them? They had vanished from the scene just as, in more peaceful times, they used to slip out of a living room: noiselessly—that is, if the door was open. Now, too, a door must have been open, for nobody had heard them meow. Had people eaten them? Had they starved to death or failed to reproduce themselves? Nobody knew. But everybody longed for them, once it was summer and there was no lack of milk. They were part of the furniture; they added the finishing touch to a cozy home; they were a solace to old folk, an example to young married couples awaiting the arrival of their first child. The milk saucers in the kitchens of many families stood conspicuously empty. The rats and mice grew bolder and bolder so that one almost felt impelled to offer these voracious creatures a seat at the table, which was once again well laden, or to apologize for the appetite of one's family. A balance had been upset—in the lower regions of domestic economy, it is true—but none the less it was intolerable. For even the gutter and the sewer have their rights.

Articles on the cat problem appeared in the newspapers. Conversations would begin with the statement that someone had seen a cat. In the afternoons, when the men were still at work in offices

or factories, the women had nothing to pet or to talk to. But most
to be pitied were the old people, who with a black or spotted
tomcat in their lap found it easier to face the end. Never had it been
so clearly appreciated that heads being rubbed, paws sticking out,
and tails curled high were part of the indispensable décor of our
lives. If only there had been a rationing of cats! Many a person
would willingly have sacrificed his candy coupons.

Gradually details about the disappearance of the cats became
known, though for the time being statistics on feline mortality during the last winter of the war were lacking. With tears in their eyes
and remorse in their hearts, many people had eaten their pets—
melancholy meals by the light of a candle or an oil lamp, with
everyone imagining he heard a meow. Other cats had died of
hunger. Misled by their fur, their friends had often not noticed till
after their death how badly off the poor animals had been, for it is
deceptive to go around in a fur coat when one is down and out.

Cats had fled in bewilderment from the houses where they were
born and bred—where they had become mother, grandmother, great-
grandmother, and great-great-grandmother—in search of the food
that no one could give them; they were lost in the snow that then
lay on the streets; hunted perhaps; frozen to death, and amazed at
what was happening to them. At the time, nobody took any notice
of them except for some sentimental girl or short-sighted old gentleman. Now, they were lamented by everyone. The burgomaster
turned his attention to them. A new political party, cutting across
the traditional party lines, came close to being formed. But after a
short period of vacillation which we referred to as "mature consideration," politics reverted to its usual concerns.

Not all the cats had died out, however. Here and there one still
lived, unconscious of the general pity its species had aroused. When
they, too, had taken the edge off their hunger—at first with bread
and diluted milk, but presently with chitterlings and heads of fish—
they emerged from their anonymity and became individuals. They
rediscovered the world one radiant summer morning in the sunshine
near a window, or some evening on the eaves where the last damp-
ness had been evaporating, while people were once more going for
walks and children were playing in the streets. A solitary cat's head
would suddenly be filled with cherished memories. Peace had actually come, and spring and summer had been selected for the pur-

pose. A cat does not have much difficulty in recognizing that life is touching and beautiful. Furthermore, it has more opportunities for changing its point of view. A cat looks at the world from between trouser legs and women's stockings, then it looks down from a roof at the tree-tops, with the street lights burning between them, and the water of the canal glistening far below. A cat outlives all noise in the still of the night, when it is alone with its fellow cats and the fine game of chimneys and fences begins. More than once, coming home late, I have caught the suprised look of a tomcat interrupting his nightly task to watch me putting my key in the lock; and I would compare my sleepiness with his robust, pungent lust for life.

ii

The tomcats were pretty busy that summer. Females being scarce, they often had to go far afield, crossing a street, a square, or a bridge to pay their visits. They developed an intimate knowledge of a part of the town's layout. People would sometimes come across their tomcat in some distant street, apparently ashamed of its presence there; occasionally the animal would forget all its intentions in joyful recognition of its master and would go home feigning hunger or a need for companionship. It would lie in a chair throughout the evening, full of magnanimous indolence, but become restless as soon as the family began to get ready for bed.

Anyone with a tabby-cat might at any moment of the day find a band of tomcats sitting in front of his house—a strange mixed company, evidently not related by ties of blood; moody, jealous, but at the same time trustful or full of misplaced faith; melancholy and resigned. Tomcats are not at their best in company. At night the house would seem surrounded by cats, with a cordon of tomcats across the street as though some strange sort of maneuver were being held. Traffic was heavy along the eaves. A lot of worldly wisdom was wasted unseen or, at best, glimpsed by a sleepless lodger from an attic window. Was there a special shortage of females, or were the males so faithless?

The news of the cat shortage in our country had traveled abroad, even across the ocean; and with the first parcels of food and clothing there also arrived small shipments of cats. They were unloaded at one of the ports in the south of the country, and were welcomed by a committee headed by the burgomaster, hat in hand. The cats were housed in oblong baskets partitioned off into little pens. If you lifted the lid, you could see them sitting under a wicker latticework —cats of all shades standing on their hind legs to rub their heads against the warmly responsive fingers of the committee members. One old lady went around with a bag of smoked sprats. There was passionate meowing beneath the blue sky. The same angelic smile played about everyone's mouth; and even the stevedores, strong matter-of-fact characters, interrupted their work to gaze affectionately at the animals and the people welcoming them. In the tepid air of morning there floated over the wharf the pungent smell of cat's urine, which, to the people sniffing it, was a reminder that their freedom had been regained and a promise of renewed domesticity.

That same day the cats lapped their first taste of our country's milk from white and flowered saucers, while parents and children observed this solemn performance through which a corner of the kitchen was consecrated. Slowly, gingerly, sniffing all over the place, pussy would make its way to the living room followed by the family, which had to adapt its movements to the animal's fancy. Once more there was the sound of purring in the room, a sound that is talking, laughing, and singing all in one. Cats lay in cherished places, curled up like a horn, rustling in their sleep.

As soon as the foreign cats had got settled, they went reconnoitering the neighborhood. Even while they were still shut up, nocturnal meowing from neighboring roofs had already given them warning that for them the world held no frontiers. One day they would come out and trot shivering over the damp stones of the street. There was always one of their kind who had been waiting for this moment and would open its eyes wide, petrified in an expectation which we take for enmity. Unhampered by language barriers, considerations of decency, or all-too-human shyness, they would recognize one another as street urchins do, but with the patience of their species that makes summer afternoons endless. The consequences were soon noticeable. Even before summer was over, kittens were born: a new generation which had not known the war or the distant country its parents came from, and which appropriated the world as its inalienable domain.

DON MANUEL OSARIO DE ZUNIGA (detail). Francisco de Goya. *Courtesy The Metropolitan Museum of Art, The Jules S. Bache Collection*

Meanwhile the unknown donors overseas had been requested not to send any more cats. The shortage threatened to turn into over-population; instinct does not need encouragement. The cat committee suspended its activities reluctantly, for an organization had been created, and it is hard to abandon a task even when it has become pointless.

Presently an old lady, perhaps the dispenser of the sprats, hit upon a charming idea. A monument should be erected in our town in honor of the cats who, albeit unintentionally, had given their lives in the liberation of our country. At first it was considered an idiotic, irreverent suggestion. But when one wants something, one has only to think about it, to want it more and more passionately. There were many who wanted the monument, and were still capable of surrendering to these crazy impulses that can make our lives so much more beautiful.

The committee resumed its work, somewhat hesitant at first because its purpose had been altered, but a fluent fountain pen can rid us of all our hesitations. Circulars were drawn up and money was collected—banknotes from rich eccentrics, but also unsightly prewar coins conscientiously hoarded in old-fashioned purses. Even the children donated their pennies. A small but moving justification had been added to the machinery of our lives.

The town council approved the erection of the monument in the largest park in town. This decision was preceded by a stormy council meeting, at which even the basic problems of life entered into the discussion.

The following summer, on a Saturday afternoon, the monument was unveiled. The ceremony came a year too late; for in almost every family, kittens were once more being drowned in kitchen pails or simply thrown into the canal. Even rationing was coming to an end. You could drink as much milk as you wanted.

It was raining, and the rain on the jasmine bushes in bloom and the well-kept lawns somehow reminded us, by the very contrast, of the war years. Somebody made a speech, standing under an umbrella—a speech ridiculous to anyone who could not switch off his intellect. It was a remarkable gathering of people who could not otherwise have been brought together outdoors so easily—inveterate stay-at-homes who think about a fire even in summer; meditative pipe-smokers and dreamers; old women as full of worries as though there would never be an end to their lives; lame children; bachelors with water on the brain; cripples too poor to buy an artificial leg; and an occasional blind person with a smile on his face as though his eyesight had been restored. But also a beautiful young woman with luxurious clothes, jewelry, and shoes of fine, expensive leather, shaking her damp curls.

A pious mischief was in the air; a feeling that for a moment one had left the earth, just as at meetings of spiritualists, vegetarians, novices in politics, and magazine editors. This impression was confirmed by the clothing—cloth caps and leather jackets, a nineteenth-century shawl, a peasant brooch on an urban bosom. There were beards, mustaches, powder and lipstick on withered faces, unwashed hands, and a vague smell of cats that hovered over the scent of the jasmine. The monument was simple—a pedestal with a bronze cat reclining on it.

Whenever I go walking in the park with my children, I never fail to go past it. The monument is already beginning to lose its color to the weather and turn gray. My children look at it with cheerful innocence and wonder, not having learned yet to count back to the war years when the snow refused to melt and when getting from the warm bed to the frozen kitchen was like traveling across the world.

It is good to live in a town where a statue has been erected to the cats. May the rats and mice forgive us.

THE SOCIETY CAT

PARK AVENUE CAT

BY *Frances Frost*

This was a thing the saints never knew:
By the Church of Saint Bartholomew,
Lean and lanky, there he sat—
A dusky, gold-eyed gentleman cat.
Proud, aloof, and pondering evil,
Consort of witches and the devil,
On Saturday at half-past two,
He sat and stared at Park Avenue.

Cat of a pent-house, son of the city,
He was rich in scorn and poor in pity.
He had paraded up and down
This peacock street of a soaring town,
All day he had listened while doormen muttered
Tales of brokers egged-and-buttered,
All day he had heard how the glittering ladies
Raised publicly their private hades.

Doormen's legs are splendid and braided:
He rubbed them well as he paraded.
Scanning the motors where pretty creatures
Embarked with furs and lifted features,
He applauded his own unerring taste
For feminine cats with slender waists,
For cats with small, swift feet that flew
At midnight down Park Avenue.

Now his whiskers twitched, his eyes were bright
With the memories of Friday night;
But the end of the week yields a better day
For sin, when there's only the devil to pay.
Near R. K. A.'s unhallowed steeple,
From Bartholomew's steps, he watched the people.
Toward the Waldorf cliffs he suddenly turned,
And his black tail lashed and his gold eyes burned.

In the fenced-in yard at the right of the church,
Somebody left a tree in the lurch,
And it grows there, slanted and scrawny and small,
Crouched 'neath the Waldorf mountain-wall.
And the gentleman cat, his fur awry,
Went up like a shot and yowled at the sky,
And shook the tree and grinned with mirth
And sniffed at the folk on the common earth.

Decorous and meek and mild,
Innocent as a month-old child,
Freed of his humor's violent taint,
Angelic as a new-made-saint,
The gentleman cat, his black fur flat,
On the steps of Saint Bartholomew's sat,
And pious and prim, if a little rude,
Stared at the passing multitude.

The afternoon wore on toward three,
And still he sat there delicately,
His whiskers calm on his rakish face,
In keeping with the hour and place.

His tail was wound round his lanky feet,
His golden eyes were great and sweet
As he gazed toward the spot where the sky begins,
Thought of Saturday night and his coming sins.

❦

THE PRODIGAL CAT

NELLIE AND TOM

BY *Marvin R. Clark*

I WAS A BOY of eighteen years of age when my mother brought home with her, all the way from the State of Maine, a Maltese Pussy, of full breed. We called her "Nellie." After mother had buttered Nellie's feet, a process which she said would always keep a cat from running away from home, the aristocratic Nellie became an important member of our household, and never deserted us.

One day I brought home to Nellie a companion who had been presented to me by a friend. "Tom," as we called the boy, was a pure Maltese, and a giant of his kind, a cheerful, clever and peaceable fellow and an ornament and pet, for he was admired by everybody who saw him. His feet were also buttered, and after a little spat with Nellie, who, at first, could see no just reason why Tom should encroach upon her domain, the two became fast friends, and finally married and raised several litters of pure Maltese kittens, all of whom we gave to longing friends save one, which we kept for Nellie's sake.

Tom remained true to his marriage vows for a long time, but one day, about six months after his advent in the household, he was missing, and the neighborhood was searched for Tom. He remained away until the following afternoon, when he returned, looking sheepish, while his appearance bore unmistakable evidence of his having been indulging in a debauch. Tom was very crestfallen and expressed his sorrow to his spouse Nellie, who would have nothing to do with him for several days. Poor Tom was disconsolate, and applied to me for sympathy. Of course every member of the family reproved Tom for his waywardness, but the story of the "Prodigal Son" and his return, in tatters, was not forgotten, although the fatted calf was omitted, and I was the first to forgive and console Tom. I used my influence so successfully with Nellie, who was very fond of me, that once more Tom was taken into Nellie's favor and everything went on as usual, excepting that Nellie gave every evidence of keeping a close eye upon her erring liege-lord, who was not fully restored to her confidence.

Some five weeks after, while Nellie was nursing a new brood of kittens, Tom turned up missing again. We did not go to any trouble that time to search for him, nor did we feel any anxiety concerning the wandering minstrel, knowing from our former experience that he was big enough and old enough to take care of himself. Three weary weeks for Nellie went by while she was worrying for her Romeo, although she tried to conceal her anxiety behind an appearance of unconcern, while lavishing her affections upon her infants. At the end of the third week Tom leisurely strolled into the house and sought Nellie's presence. He bore an air of bravado which seemed to say that he was lord and master of his own family, that he had a right to go whither, and stay there as long as he pleased. But he was battered and torn, almost beyond recognition. One eye was completely closed, much of his fur was gone, he limped when he walked, one ear was entirely bitten through and a portion of it missing, and his head was covered with bloody wounds, while his general appearance was emaciated, tattered and forlorn. Nellie's tail was a sight to behold when she spied Tom, and she raised herself to a sitting posture and threw upon the debauchee a withering look of contempt which sent his tail between his legs in less time than it takes to tell it, while he completely lost his braggadocio air and slunk off to a corner of the room and Nellie returned to her babies.

After the tramp had received a scolding from each one of the family, and been thoroughly cleansed and his wounds dressed, he sat down a few feet from his lawful wife and moaned and cried for an hour or more, without once attracting a look of pity from her. After that he approached Nellie and attempted to ask her forgiveness for his absence upon some fictitous ground, but that faithful one raised herself upon her hind legs, spat upon the battered tramp and then deliberately beat him with her paws and scratched him

The Beast Has Had the
Time of His Life. Rube
Goldberg

with her claws until he slunk out of the room, a well reproved if
not a better Cat. For more than a week, every time Tom made overtures looking toward a reconciliation, Nellie repeated her chastise-
ment, and I fully believe if any other Maltese Tom had presented
himself during that time, she would have taught Tom a lesson
which he would have remembered to the end of his life, by adopting him in Tom's place, and, with his assistance, driven out upon
the charity of a cold world, her wayward and presumably unfaithful
consort. But, although we refused to intercede for him with Nellie,
in the course of time Tom was partly forgiven and was again kept
under the watchful eye of Nellie.

Three months later the vagabond again forgot his marriage vows
and disappeared. This time we gave him up for lost, as he did not
return for a month. Considering him a thing of the beautiful past,
I bought another Tom and brought him home to Nellie. Singularly
enough, the two did not fraternize, although it was not the fault
of the new Tom, and Nellie remained, as she supposed, a widow,
with her kittens as her constant care. Upon them she lavished all
of her affections, spitting at and boxing the new Tom whenever he
approached them.

One fine day, to our utter astonishment, the scoundrel, Tom
strolled in upon the scene as nonchalantly as if he had not been
off on a long protracted cruise. But this time he was covered with
sores, and had, in addition, the mange. He was a sorry-looking Tom,
and an animal to avoid. Even in that condition, I am sure, Nellie
would have nursed him and doctored him until he recovered, had
he been faithful to her. But there was no hope of it now. She had

evidently been thinking deeply about the newcomer, and was making comparisons.

At first he showed contrition, but when he discovered the new Tom, who he supposed had assumed his duties in the household, he did not become an Enoch Arden, but, with fire in his evil eye and without making proper inquiries concerning Nellie's unexceptionable conduct, with a great bologna sausage of a fuzzy tail and a fearful shriek for vengeance, he made for Tom Number Two with the speed of lightning, in the stereotyped manner of an outraged husband whose lapses of fealty and so on are forgotten in the greater sin of an interloper.

What might have become of the innocent new fellow was illustrated in the story of the Kilkenny cats, with this difference, that one of the two would have been left on the earth, and it wouldn't have been the new fellow, for Tom was the maddest Cat you ever saw. When the tocsin of war was sounded by the mangy deserter, Nellie sprang for him and there ensued a battle royal. There was war to the knife, from the point to the hilt. The screams of the combatants were terrific, and the dining-room floor was covered with a constantly accumulating mass of Maltese fur. In both the new Tom and Nellie, who, alone, was a host in herself, the mangy Tom found more than his match, and he was beaten, torn, wounded at every point, and a total wreck when he scurried out of the house and took his sorrowful way down the street, toward the dock at the foot of Hubert street. Whether or not he did the best thing he could have done under the circumstances, and went and drowned himself, is unknown, but Nellie never knew him more, for the new fellow thereafter succeeded to his lares and penates and Nellie and he lived happily together until Tom number two was shot by some cruel person. After that Nellie mourned his loss and refused to be comforted with another, although, of course, there were many Toms who would have lain down and died for her. She lived but a short time after the death of her second husband, and died regretted by all of us.

FELISSA — A KITTEN OF SENTIMENT

Anonymous

I DID NOT PERFECTLY COMPREHEND the nature of this conversation, but I saw my mistress look pleased, and so I hoped that we were going to lose this troublesome woman and her tasks. For my own part, I hated her; for I had overheard her say, "If that kitten were but out of the house, one might stand some chance for a few minutes' attention the course of the day:"—but Lady Dashley declared she had never heard such a cruel proposition in her life, and said positively that the dear creature should not be deprived of her pretty playfellow. With all this kind encouragement, we both set Miss Allworth at defiance, and did just what we pleased.

But the day before she was to quit the family, my young mistress took a whim of having a christening, as she called it, and I was to perform the part of the baby. She had somehow contrived to get at the beautiful laced robe and cap in which she herself had been christened; and while putting it upon me, she so rolled and tumbled me about upon her knee, that I (having been nearly as much spoiled as herself) grew peevish and impatient with her; and when she was pinning the back of my robe, she was heedless enough to run the pin half way through my back;—I could then bear it no longer, but leaped up, and not being able to appeal to her pity in her own language, and utter my sufferings in a comprehensible manner, I made them known by sticking my little claws, with all my force, in her pretty face.—It was torn in the most merciless manner; her shrieks and screams brought the whole family to her assistance, and, the apartment which we were in being next to her mother's, brought her also. They were all horror-struck at my mistress's appearance—her face streaming with blood, and scored all over as if with a knife. She accused me in the bitterest manner, and vowed never to play with me again.

303

I was aware, from observation, that Lady Dashley set a far higher value upon her daughter's face than she did upon the improvement and virtues of her mind, and that this crime would never be forgiven, though all my other sins had been so mildly treated. All now I knew was over with me, and therefore endeavoured to extricate myself from my finery, and make my escape. I was hid behind a screen, and in disentangling myself from my rich drapery, which was composed of the most costly muslin and lace, tore them all to atoms. Here I was at last discovered by Mrs. Tricksey, who seized me by the neck, carried me out of the room, and, by way of expedition and revenge, inhumanly threw me over the banisters of the stairs into the hall. Luckily for our race, we have a faculty of generally lighting upon our feet, which I did upon mine, and being very small and light, I felt little more than a violent shock and a temporary giddiness.

I was picked up by the porter, who was very busy looking over his visiting list, to give to his lady, when I descended. He knew not of my crime, and thought my fall accidental, till Mrs. Tricksey came down stairs, in a great flurry, to desire "that abominable, wicked, ungrateful kitten," might be drowned immediately. I sickened with terror and indignation—for I knew myself to be neither wicked nor ungrateful. I had been severely hurt, and had borne it as long as I could, and, at length, had recourse to the only means of defense with which nature had supplied me, and was quite unconscious of the extent of the mischief that had ensued;—besides, I had been spoiled and petted, and, like *all other* spoiled and petted kittens, was inclined to become peevish, discontented, and selfish.

The old porter, however, who knew much of life and the ways of our family, pitied me, and only said, "Well, well, we must get rid on it somehow, to be sure."—"Yes, and it must be drowned or hanged, my lady says, as all such ungrateful beastesses ought to be," screamed Mrs. Tricksey. The porter made no reply, but took me down stairs, and gave me to Lady Arabella Markwell's gamekeeper, who had just brought up some game, and was returning immediately to Markwell Park. He admired my beauty, and said that the Rector of their parish had asked him for a kitten a few days ago, and he would present me to him.

I had but a disagreeable journey, being shut up in a bag and thrown into the cart, where I could hardly breathe, and the rum-

LITTLE MISS HONE. Samuel F. B. Morse. *Courtesy Boston Museum of Fine Arts*

bling and jumbling of the cart over the stones, added to the agitation of my mind, kept me from sleeping; but I tried to console myself with the thoughts of having escaped hanging or drowning, and hoped for better times. I was taken, the same night that we arrived at the Park, to the Rector's.

The game-keeper carried me himself into the parlour, where the good old gentleman sat; and he was so much pleased with my appearance, that he gave John Grouse a nice new half-crown. For a week I lived in perfect peace and quiet, well fed, and I might have been well taught, for my master used to read both instructive and entertaining things to his sister every evening, while she worked; but soon this happiness was interrupted by the arrival of two of my master's nephews, fine boys from the age of fifteen to seventeen. The eldest was a midshipman in His Majesty's service, and was come to pass a few weeks with his uncle, while his ship was undergoing some repairs. The other had not finished his education, and was invited for the remainder of his holidays to the Rectory.

These boys had not been in the room ten minutes, before Guildford, the youngest, caught me up by the tail, and swung me round in the air; which put me into the greatest terror, and brought back all my nervous symptoms. I was then held up by my ears, which, he said, wanted cropping, and were not "knowing ears;" likewise my tail did not suit his taste, being, I found, infinitely too long for a kitten of fashion. In fact, the whole turn of his conversation, though chiefly to himself (while his brother was talking with my master at a distant part of the room), filled me with inconceivable alarm; and not without reason, for in a few days I was shod with walnut-shells, harnessed into a cart, and underwent a variety of other cruel experiments which nothing but a cowardly, mischievous, idle school-boy knows how to invent, or an unhappy, defenseless animal can with patience endure. This little contemptible tyrant, however, always took the opportunity of tormenting me when his brother Marcus was absent: the brave, he knew, were always compassionate, and would never ill-treat *any thing,* but particularly not that which was weak, helpless, and in their power. Indeed, through every vicissitude of my eventful life, I have observed this to mark the difference between mean and generous spirits: in the former, I have always found thoughtlessness, wantonness, and cruelty; in the latter, attention, kindness, and protection.

One unlucky day for me, my master and his eldest nephew went out to call upon some friends in the neighbourhood, and I was left at the sole mercy of my tyrant, who thought that he would take this opportunity of cropping my ears, and clipping off a part of my tail. I was sitting on a green, sunny bank in the garden, when I saw him coming along with a large pair of garden-shears. Recollecting what I had heard him say, and knowing that he never came near me but to torment me, I flew for refuge to a very high tree, which I ascended with the utmost rapidity, followed by my pursuer. Irritated at my escape, he vowed the most dreadful vengeance, when he should reach me; but his haste and passion rendering him incautious, and being also encumbered with the shears in his hand, he stepped upon a high branch, unequal to his weight, which gave way immediately, and he fell headlong to the very bottom; where he lay roaring and screaming, with the utmost violence of mingled pain and passion, till the gardener came to his assistance.

Cruel as this boy was, I felt a little shocked and grieved when the man cried out that his young master's leg was broken; but all compassion for my persecutor soon ceased, when I heard him using the most outrageous expressions, wickedly swearing, and exclaiming, with a shocking oath, that it was "all owing to that diabolical Cat:" —words which no boy should ever use, because they are vulgar and disgusting to the ears of man, and highly offensive to God. His threats, however, reminded me that the best thing I could do was, to make my escape; so, while the gardener, with the assistance of the other servants, was carrying him upon a plank to the house, I ran down from my tree, bounded over the garden wall, and fled, I knew not whither,—regardless of the future, in my anxiety to escape the present danger; for I heard the gardener receive express orders to catch and destroy me, for which he was to be liberally rewarded by cruel Guildford.

THE GRINNING CAT

ALICE AND THE CHESHIRE CAT

BY *Lewis Carroll*

ALICE WAS JUST BEGINNING to think to herself, "Now, what am I to do with this creature when I get it home?" when it grunted again, so violently, that she looked down into its face in some alarm. This time there could be *no* mistake about it: it was neither more nor less than a pig, and she felt that it would be quite absurd for her to carry it any further.

So she set the little creature down, and felt quite relieved to see it trot away quietly into the wood. "If it had grown up," she said to herself, "it would have been a dreadfully ugly child: but it makes rather a handsome pig, I think." And she began thinking over other children she knew, who might do very well as pigs, and was just saying to herself, "if one only knew the right way to change them—" when she was a little startled by seeing the Cheshire Cat sitting on a bough of a tree a few yards off.

The Cat only grinned when it saw Alice. It looked good-natured, she thought: still it had *very* long claws and a great many teeth, so she felt it ought to be treated with respect.

"Cheshire Puss," she began, rather timidly, as she did not at all know whether it would like the name: however, it only grinned a little wider. "Come, it's pleased so far," thought Alice, and she went on, "Would you tell me, please, which way I ought to walk from here?"

"That depends a good deal on where you want to get to," said the Cat.

"I don't much care where—" said Alice.

"Then it doesn't matter which way you walk," said the Cat.

"—so long as I get *somewhere*," Alice added as an explanation.

"Oh, you're sure to do that," said the Cat, "if you only walk long enough."

Alice felt that this could not be denied, so she tried another question. "What sort of people live about here?"

"In *that* direction," the Cat said, waving its right paw round, "lives a Hatter: and in *that* direction," waving the other paw, "lives a March Hare. Visit either you like: they're both mad."

"But I don't want to go among mad people," Alice remarked.

"Oh, you can't help that," said the Cat: "we're all mad here. I'm mad. You're mad."

"How do you know I'm mad?" said Alice.

"You must be," said the Cat, "or you wouldn't have come here."

Alice didn't think that proved it at all; however, she went on: "and how do you know that you're mad?"

"To begin with," said the Cat, "a dog's not mad. You grant that?"

"I suppose so," said Alice.

"Well then," the Cat went on, "you see a dog growls when it's angry, and wags its tail when it's pleased. Now I growl when I'm pleased, and wag my tail when I'm angry. Therefore I'm mad."

THE CHESHIRE CAT. John Tenniel. *From "Alice in Wonderland"*

"I call it purring, not growling," said Alice.

"Call it what you like," said the Cat. "Do you play croquet with the Queen to-day?"

"I should like it very much," said Alice, "but I haven't been invited yet."

"You'll see me there," said the Cat, and vanished.

Alice was not much surprised at this, she was getting so well used to queer things happening. While she was still looking at the place where it had been, it suddenly appeared again.

"By-the-bye, what became of the baby?" said the Cat. "I'd nearly forgotten to ask."

"It turned into a pig," Alice answered very quietly, just as if the Cat had come back in a natural way.

"I thought it would," said the Cat, and vanished again.

Alice waited a little, half expecting to see it again, but it did not appear, and after a minute or two she walked on in the direction in which the March Hare was said to live. "I've seen hatters before," she said to herself: "the March Hare will be much the most interesting, and perhaps as this is May it won't be raving mad—at least not so mad as it was in March." As she said this, she looked up, and there was the Cat again, sitting on a branch of a tree.

"Did you say pig, or fig?" said the Cat.

"I said pig," replied Alice; "and I wish you wouldn't keep appearing and vanishing so suddenly: you make one quite giddy."

"All right," said the Cat; and this time it vanished quite slowly, beginning with the end of the tail, and ending with the grin, which remained some time after the rest of it had gone.

"Well! I've often seen a cat without a grin," thought Alice; "but a grin without a cat! It's the most curious thing I ever saw in all my life!"

❖

The players all played at once without waiting for turns, quarrelling all the while, and fighting for the hedgehogs; and in a very short time the Queen was in a furious passion, and went stamping about, and shouting, "Off with his head!" about once in a minute.

Alice began to feel uneasy: to be sure, she had not as yet had any dispute with the Queen, but she knew that it might happen any minute, "and then," thought she, "what would become of me? They're dreadfully fond of beheading people here: the great wonder is, that there's any one left alive!"

She was looking about for some way of escape, and wondering whether she could get away without being seen, when she noticed a curious appearance in the air: it puzzled her very much at first, but after watching it a minute or two she made it out to be a grin, and she said to herself, "It's the Cheshire Cat: now I shall have somebody to talk to."

"How are you getting on?" said the Cat, as soon as there was mouth enough for it to speak with.

Alice waited till the eyes appeared, and then nodded. "It's no use speaking to it," she thought, "till its ears have come, or at least one of them." In another minute the whole head appeared, and then Alice put down her flamingo, and began an account of the game, feeling very glad she had some one to listen to her. The Cat seemed to think that there was enough of it now in sight, and no more of it appeared.

"I don't think they play at all fairly," Alice began, in rather a complaining tone, "and they all quarrel so dreadfully one can't hear one's-self speak—and they don't seem to have any rules in particular; at least, if there are, nobody attends to them—and you've no idea how confusing it is all the things being alive; for instance, there's the arch I've got to go through next walking about at the other end of the ground—and I should have croqueted the Queen's hedgehog just now, only it ran away when it saw mine coming!"

"How do you like the Queen?" said the Cat in a low voice.

"Not at all," said Alice: "she's so extremely—" Just then she noticed that the Queen was close behind her, listening: so she went on "—likely to win, that it's hardly worth while finishing the game."

The Queen smiled and passed on.

"Who *are* you talking to?" said the King, coming up to Alice, and looking at the Cat's head with great curiosity.

"It's a friend of mine—a Cheshire Cat," said Alice: "allow me to introduce it."

"I don't like the look of it at all," said the King: "however, it may kiss my hand if it likes."

"I'd rather not," the Cat remarked.

"Don't be impertinent," said the King, "and don't look at me like that!" He got behind Alice as he spoke.

"A cat may look at a king," said Alice. "I've read that in some book, but I don't remember where."

"Well, it must be removed," said the King very decidedly, and he called to the Queen, who was passing at the moment, "My dear! I wish you would have this cat removed!"

The Queen had only one way of settling all difficulties, great or small. "Off with his head!" she said without even looking round.

"I'll fetch the executioner myself," said the King eagerly, and he hurried off.

Alice thought she might as well go back and see how the game was going on, as she heard the Queen's voice in the distance, screaming with passion. She had already heard her sentence three of the players to be executed for having missed their turns, and she did not like the look of things at all, as the game was in such confusion that she never knew whether it was her turn or not. So she went off in search of her hedgehog.

The hedgehog was engaged in a fight with another hedgehog, which seemed to Alice an excellent opportunity for croqueting one of them with the other: the only difficulty was, that her flamingo was gone across to the other side of the garden, where Alice could see it trying in a helpless sort of way to fly up into a tree.

By the time she had caught the flamingo and brought it back, the fight was over, and both the hedgehogs were out of sight: "but it doesn't matter much," thought Alice, "as all the arches are gone from this side of the ground." So she tucked it away under her arm, that it might not escape again, and went back to have a little more conversation with her friend.

When she got back to the Cheshire Cat, she was surprised to find quite a large crowd collected round it: there was a dispute going on between the executioner, the King, and the Queen, who were all talking at once, while all the rest were quite silent, and looked very uncomfortable.

The moment Alice appeared, she was appealed.to by all three to settle the question, and they repeated their arguments to her, though, as they all spoke at once, she found it very hard to make out exactly what they said.

The executioner's argument was, that you couldn't cut off a head unless there was a body to cut it off from: that he had never had to do such a thing before, and he wasn't going to begin at his time of life.

The King's argument was, that anything that had a head could be beheaded, and that you weren't to talk nonsense.

The Queen's argument was, that if something wasn't done about it in less than no time, she'd have everybody executed, all round. (It was this last remark that had made the whole party look so grave and anxious.)

Alice could think of nothing else to say but "It belongs to the Duchess: you'd better ask *her* about it."

"She's in prison," the Queen said to the executioner: "fetch her here." And the executioner went off like an arrow.

The Cat's head began fading away the moment he was gone, and, by the time he had come back with the Duchess, it had entirely disappeared: so the King and the executioner ran wildly up and down looking for it, while the rest of the party went back to the game.

PUSS IN BOOTS

BY *Charles Perrault*

ONCE UPON A TIME there was a miller who left no more riches to the three sons he had than his mill, his ass, and his cat. The division was soon made. Neither the lawyer nor the attorney was sent for. They would soon have eaten up all the poor property. The eldest had the mill, the second the ass, and the youngest nothing but the cat.

The youngest, as we can understand, was quite unhappy at having so poor a share.

"My brothers," said he, "may get their living handsomely enough by joining their stocks together; but, for my part, when I have eaten up my cat, and made me a muff of his skin, I must die of hunger."

The Cat, who heard all this, without appearing to take any notice, said to him with a grave and serious air:—

"Do not thus afflict yourself, my master; you have nothing else to do but to give me a bag, and get a pair of boots made for me, that I may scamper through the brambles, and you shall see that you have not so poor a portion in me as you think."

Though the Cat's master did not think much of what he said, he had seen him play such cunning tricks to catch rats and mice— hanging himself by the heels, or hiding himself in the meal, to make believe he was dead—that he did not altogether despair of his helping him in his misery. When the Cat had what he asked for, he booted himself very gallantly, and putting his bag about his neck, he held the strings of it in his two forepaws, and went into a warren where was a great number of rabbits. He put bran and sow-thistle into his bag, and, stretching out at length, as if he were dead, he waited for some young rabbits, not yet acquainted with the deceits of the world, to come and rummage his bag for what he had put into it.

Scarcely was he settled but he had what he wanted. A rash and foolish young rabbit jumped into his bag, and Monsieur Puss, immediately drawing close the strings, took him and killed him at once. Proud of his prey, he went with it to the palace, and asked to speak with the King. He was shown upstairs into his Majesty's apartment, and, making a low bow to the King, he said:—

"I have brought you, sire, a rabbit which my noble Lord, the Master of Carabas" (for that was the title which Puss was pleased to give his master) "has commanded me to present to your Majesty from him."

"Tell thy master," said the King, "that I thank him, and that I am pleased with his gift."

Another time he went and hid himself among some standing corn, still holding his bag open; and when a brace of partridges ran into it, he drew the strings, and so caught them both. He then went and made a present of these to the King, as he had done before of the rabbit which he took in the warren. The King, in like manner, received the partridges with great pleasure, and ordered his servants to reward him.

The Cat continued for two or three months thus to carry his Majesty, from time to time, some of his master's game. One day when he knew that the King was to take the air along the riverside, with his daughter, the most beautiful princess in the world, he said to his master:—

"If you will follow my advice, your fortune is made. You have nothing else to do but go and bathe in the river, just at the spot I shall show you, and leave the rest to me."

The Marquis of Carabas did what the Cat advised him to, without knowing what could be the use of doing it. While he was bathing, the King passed by, and the Cat cried out with all his might:—

"Help, help! My Lord the Marquis of Carabas is drowning!"

At this noise the King put his head out of the coach window, and seeing the Cat who had so often brought him game, he commanded his guards to run immediately to the assistance of his Lordship the Marquis of Carabas.

While they were drawing the poor Marquis out of the river, the Cat came up to the coach and told the King that, while his master was bathing, there came by some rogues, who ran off with his

Puss in Boots.
Gustave Doré.
*From "Mother
Goose Tales"*

clothes, though he had cried out, "Thieves! thieves!" several times,
as loud as he could. The cunning Cat had hidden the clothes under
a great stone. The King immediately commanded the officers of his
wardrobe to run and fetch one of his best suits for the Lord Marquis
of Carabas.

The King was extremely polite to him, and as the fine clothes he
had given him set off his good looks (for he was well made and
handsome), the King's daughter found him very much to her liking,
and the Marquis of Carabas had no sooner cast two or three respect-
ful and somewhat tender glances than she fell in love with him to
distraction. The King would have him come into the coach and take
part in the airing. The Cat, overjoyed to see his plan begin to
succeed, marched on before, and, meeting with some countrymen,
who were mowing a meadow, he said to them:—

"Good people, you who are mowing, if you do not tell the King
that the meadow you mow belongs to my Lord Marquis of Carabas,
you shall be chopped as small as herbs for the pot."

The King did not fail to ask the mowers to whom the meadow they were mowing belonged.

"To my Lord Marquis of Carabas," answered they all together, for the Cat's threat had made them afraid.

"You have a good property there," said the King to the Marquis of Carabas.

"You see, sire," said the Marquis, "this is a meadow which never fails to yield a plentiful harvest every year."

The Master Cat, who went still on before, met with some reapers, and said to them:—

"Good people, you who are reaping, if you do not say that all this corn belongs to the Marquis of Carabas, you shall be chopped as small as herbs for the pot."

The King, who passed by a moment after, wished to know to whom belonged all that corn, which he then saw.

"To my Lord Marquis of Carabas," replied the reapers, and the King was very well pleased with it, as well as the Marquis, whom he congratulated thereupon. The Master Cat, who went always before, said the same thing to all he met, and the King was astonished at the vast estates of my Lord Marquis of Carabas.

Monsieur Puss came at last to a stately castle, the master of which was an Ogre, the richest ever known; for all the lands which the King had then passed through belonged to this castle. The Cat, who had taken care to inform himself who this Ogre was and what he could do, asked to speak with him, saying he could not pass so near his castle without having the honor of paying his respects to him.

The Ogre received him as civilly as an Ogre could do, and made him sit down.

"I have been assured," said the Cat, "that you have the gift of being able to change yourself into all sorts of creatures you have a mind to; that you can, for example, transform yourself into a lion, or elephant, and the like."

"That is true," answered the Ogre, roughly; "and to convince you, you shall see me now become a lion."

Puss was so terrified at the sight of a lion so near him that he immediately climbed into the gutter, not without much trouble and danger, because of his boots, which were of no use at all to him for walking upon the tiles. A little while after, when Puss saw that the Ogre had resumed his natural form, he came down, and owned he had been very much frightened.

"I have, moreover, been informed," said the Cat, "but I know not how to believe it, that you have also the power to take on you the shape of the smallest animals; for example, to change yourself into a rat or a mouse, but I must own to you I take this to be impossible."

"Impossible!" cried the Ogre; "you shall see." And at the same time he changed himself into a mouse, and began to run about the floor. Puss no sooner perceived this than he fell upon him and ate him up.

Meanwhile, the King, who saw, as he passed, this fine castle of the Ogre's, had a mind to go into it. Puss, who heard the noise of his Majesty's coach coming over the drawbridge, ran out, and said to the King, "Your Majesty is welcome to this castle of my Lord Marquis of Carabas."

"What! my Lord Marquis," cried the King, "and does this castle also belong to you? There can be nothing finer than this courtyard and all the stately buildings which surround it; let us see the interior, if you please."

The Marquis gave his hand to the young Princess, and followed the King, who went first. They passed into the great hall, where they found a magnificent collation, which the Ogre had prepared for his friends, who were that very day to visit him, but dared not to enter, knowing the King was there. His Majesty, charmed with the good qualities of my Lord of Carabas, as was also his daughter, who had fallen violently in love with him, and seeing the vast estate he possessed, said to him:—

"It will be owing to yourself only, my Lord Marquis, if you are not my son-in-law."

The Marquis, with low bows, accepted the honor which his Majesty conferred upon him, and forthwith that very same day married the Princess.

Puss became a great lord, and never ran after mice any more except for his diversion.

HURRLI, BOLD, PROUD, AND AMIABLE
MASTER OF THE ELK HOUSE

BY *Paul Eipper*

HURRLI LIVED AT THE REFUGE for not quite two years. Then the spreading colossus of the city reached out inexorably for our little world, no longer peaceful as it had once been; the trees around us were felled more and more ruthlessly week by week, and so we built a new house deep in the Grunewald, at a point where, on a ramble one spring, I had once seen, with happy surprise, a tall, double-stemmed birch tree standing alone between fen and conifers.

We left the Happy Refuge in the autumn. Our son Herbert drove the family out of town to the Elk House; between my wife and me stood a covered basket on the floor of the car, and in it sat the tom cat, growling.

"Patience, my conquering hero! The lid will be off in another twenty minutes' time. You have no idea of all the wonderful things waiting for you. In your place I'd be ashamed to make that noise," said my wife. "Aren't we together, after all?" Herbert echoed her words by sounding the horn in a way that Hurrli knew full well— three blows, short-long-short—and the tom was entirely reassured. He had not lived with us three weeks before he discovered that this was how all the members of the family announced their return from a trip to town, and he would always come, tail waving joyfully in the air, to welcome us at the front door, even before it was opened to us. Another thing that never failed to amaze me as an achievement of animal intelligence was the way in which Hurrli was able not only to express his wishes to us but also to show exactly how we might help him. For instance, he would appear in the garden making his special cooing noise, prod me several times with his head, and trip off in the direction of the veranda door; then come back again, a second and a third time, until I followed him. He would go straight to the umbrella-stand in the hall and rub his head against my walking stick, which I would take, anxious to execute his wish but still uncomprehending. Then Hurrli would run to the dining-room and crouch down by the glass china-cupboard, staring intently into the empty space between the cupboard and the floor. After a time, the dull creature that I am realized what was wanted, and poked my stick under the cupboard. Hurrli's ping-pong ball would emerge; it had rolled all the way to the wall, and could not be extracted by the cat's paw, even when extended to full length. Hurrli would seize the celluloid ball between his teeth and walk away in silent satisfaction. Another time we would hear the clatter of dishes in the kitchen. My wife, fearing mischief, would run to see what was happening. Hurrli had rolled his enamelled drinking bowl into the middle of the floor, and was sitting with an expectant eye cocked at the kitchen tap. "Perfectly clear," says the understanding cat-expert, "our poor boy is thirsty."

The companionship of this perfectly ordinary, common-or-garden stray added a great deal to the range of our knowledge. I believe that unprejudiced observation of an untrained animal brings you closer to understanding the mystery of the animal soul than elaborate experiments and logical reasoning. Generally speaking, we humans ought not to try to be too clever about animals; if we do, we erect artificial barriers between them and ourselves and create a rigid system of classification which remains intact only so long as we believe in it. People say, for instance, that dogs live by their noses, while cats rely almost entirely on their visual sense. Also that cats are far less attached to people than to their accustomed surroundings, furniture, kitchen and living-room. And then an ordinary tomcat like Hurrli comes along and quietly proves the exact opposite.

Let me now return to the beginning: we had travelled with Hurrli about fifteen kilometres from the Refuge to the Elk House. On the morning of our move I, in my wisdom, had given orders that special care should be taken of the cat. "The best thing would be to keep him locked on the first floor of the new house for the first five days, to give him a chance to get used to the new surroundings. If he runs out into the garden (which was then not yet fenced in) and into the wood, that will be the last we shall ever see of him; he will never find his way back to the strange house."

Well, it is easy enough for the head of the family to issue orders of this kind; but who can keep a constant eye on a freedom-loving cat that has never been locked up before, in the midst of unpacking endless trunks and boxes, especially when there is a constant flow of strangers through every room of the house? Briefly, in the afternoon of the third day Hurrli had vanished.

"Well, that's that. We shall never see him again," said I. "Most likely he will get shot by a gamekeeper for poaching." Great agitation, and much conscience-searching all round. In spite of all the piled-up work, my wife found time every so often to go out and sadly call her darling cat; but all in vain. Evening came, and not a trace of Hurrli. . . .

We went to bed late, partly on account of the unpacking, partly in the hope that we might still hear the familiar mew at the front door.

Towards five o'clock in the morning I suddenly awoke. The new day was beginning to dawn faintly through the wide open window, and outside there was a scratching on the level of the window-sill. "Impossible," said my reason, "this is the first floor, fifteen feet above the ground."

"And yet there's something scratching," said my hearing, "and now it has moved higher still."

As I sat up, I heard my wife whisper: "Can you hear it, too?" And in the same instant there was a despairing yowl from outside, and a dark body shot like a torpedo, twisting round to the left, through the open window and landed with a bounce on my blankets: Hurrli, our tom, not in the least contrite at having startled us so. For a few moments he twisted and turned, trying to find the most comfortable position, then fell cosily asleep at once.

Only the next morning, taking stock of the situation outside the house, was I able to understand exactly what had happened and what must have gone on in our pussy's mind.

Of course, I am only human, and I may be wrong: but this is what I *think* occurred.

Hurrli, accustomed to the peace and quiet of our old house, had been thoroughly upset by the noise of the removal men and his imprisonment in the new unfamiliar-smelling rooms. The fact that one or another of his human friends looked in to see him every now and then was no comfort. His instinct told him to get away, as quickly and as far as possible: the fundamental urge of his cave-dwelling, solitary, wild forbears.

CAT DRAWINGS. Jean Jacques Rousseau

And so, when at some point one of us had carelessly **neglected** to shut the door properly, the tabby slipped quickly and noiselessly down the stairs and out into the open. There, between the garden and the wood, many novelties awaited him: flying birds and rustling leaves, hiding-places in the grass, perhaps a mouse's track. The hours passed quickly; evening came, and all was quiet. 'This is the time to be sitting in the living-room, with the mistress: that is where I want to be.' And so Hurrli sets out to find his way back. His own tracks on the ground have long since disappeared; but the general direction must have remained in his memory, and he soon found himself back among the houses. But that is where the trouble began. Where is the home of his choice, where is his human family, his beloved mistress? There are three houses within an area of a hundred yards in the clearing, and all three are entirely strange to Hurrli.

There will have been a long period of indecision, of running this way and that, until at last, in the middle of the night, Hurrli found the house to which he had been brought three days earlier in his closed basket. I could see later from the round footmarks in the sand that Hurrli had approached the house from many different directions, circling it again and again. Everywhere he tried to find a way in, but in vain: the big front door and all the windows on the ground floor were shut.

Perhaps the poor little creature in its homesickness will have looked longingly up the four walls of the house, and its sharp night-eyes will have noticed the windows on the upper floor were open. But I think it is much more likely that the sense of smell played the decisive part on that occasion; for in the end Hurrli stopped below the window from which a familiar human scent was wafted by the still night air. 'Up there are my friends,' he will have said to himself, and he was right, for he was standing directly beneath our bedroom window. (He could not have known it; he had never been inside that room, which in addition, faced towards the east, i.e., almost 180 degrees from the north-west room in which Hurrli had been locked up for three days.)

The cat's next actions were extraordinarily courageous and intelligent. He overcame all difficulties by his brain, and found his way home without help from anyone.

Two yards away from the front wall of my house stands the old, straight birch tree; the trunk is divided, so that one-half rises vertically about a yard and a half from the bedroom window. That is where Hurrli climbed in the early dawn; that is how he came closer and closer to the scent of 'his' humans; but he climbed on, past the window, until at last he made up his mind to hurl himself downwards and sideways through the dark shaft of the window. It must have been terribly hard, suddenly to disengage all four clawed feet from the birch bark, to push off for the jump, and to take threefold, unerringly accurate aim: downwards, to the left, and forwards from the window-sill into the room. Hence the long, scratching hesitation and, at last, the despairing cry. Hurrli had staked everything on a single chance.

And I believe that only one motive force could have been strong enough in the little animal's soul: love of us, his human friends.

That was in the late summer. Winter came, and at last another spring. Hurrli had long ago settled down in his new home; he knew every corner inside and outside the house, as far as the boundary of our property, and he demanded strict observance of that boundary from all strange animals. "Really, we don't need a watchdog," my wife would often say; "just look how our proud squire is patrolling his land. All that's missing is the bark."

Hurrli was very fond of the garden, my highly unprofessional mixed forest plantation with the dense network of paths trodden by our feet. Whenever, as a change from travelling, I was able to stay and work at my desk, and if my thinking suddenly came to a halt, I would walk quietly up and down between the young leafy trees, the bushes, flowers and herbs.

Only a few minutes of solitude: then, as if conjured up from the earth, there stands my pussy by my side. At home, Hurrli is always communicative; but now he does not make a sound and expects no words from me. With his tail high in the air he follows me wherever I go (the paths are not wide enough for two abreast) and I feel very strongly that he is happy now, although I never bend down to stroke him. And Hurrli goes for such companionable walks with other members of my household, too, particularly with my wife, who is the first favourite of his manly heart.

He loves her so much that he will even tolerate the grave faults which—so he thinks—mar her character. For the truth is that she loves all animals and has a kind word for all, even the strangers; she actually goes so far as to feed the white hens and the coloured rooster belonging to some distant neighbours.

Oh, how fiercely, with what a dangerous passion does Hurrli hate these impudent fowls that go scratching and clucking all day in search of nourishment in the wood! When he goes hunting in his turn, he stalks stiffly and with averted eyes (I might almost say contemptuously) through the midst of this noisy company: disapproval personified!

Once, and only once, did the rooster dare to assault him. The tom-cat hissed, briefly, but so angrily that the bird learnt his lesson once and for all. Since then he has been wise enough to walk behind a solid advance guard of hens whenever he sees Hurrli coming.

Yes, a cat has plenty of trouble with his humans. If Hurrli

could speak in our fashion, he would surely utter many reproachful words; for, to his visible annoyance, the mistress throws vegetable scraps over the fence, day after day. That is why all the fowls in the neighbourhood come waddling and squawking through the wood whenever my wife appears on the terrace. Sometimes they even wait for her to come out, clucking and calling, spread out in a long line. 'A disgusting spectacle,' thinks Hurrli no doubt, profoundly indignant, as he emerges from the house with his mistress; but he refrains from any action, for the other day he had to listen to a long severe scolding and was not allowed into the dining-room for a whole evening. And all he had done was to pull out a miserable couple of feathers out of the cheekiest hen's tail, as a warning, no more!

But there is one point on which Hurrli will not yield even to my wife. That is the matter of distance, of physical distance between the fowls and our house. Not even at feeding times are they allowed within more than a couple of human paces from the fence. If ever a young cockerel crosses the invisible boundary in his uncontrollable greed, Hurrli jumps up—with a single, infinitely graceful movement—on top of a pointed five-foot fence pole, keeping balance precariously on all four paws between the rows of barbed wire, and looks down so threateningly that the cockerel withdraws at once, followed by all the hens.

Then Hurrli turns his head to look at his beloved mistress, coos softly, and disappears among the trees, deeply satisfied. 'There must be a boundary between the neighbours and ourselves; I hope you will not deny it, woman.'

This grey tabby possessed a nature of extraordinary variety, proud yet affectionate, brimful with tenderness, absolutely motionless in the dreamy hours, then again bursting with life.

Once Hurrli bitterly fought and completely demolished a large squirrel who also had failed to observe the boundary of our garden: and, after he had devoured the vanquished adversary, bushy tail and all, he went on at once to play gracefully with a faded leaf. His life with us seemed to be the fulfillment of every imaginable wish; Hurrli remained splendidly natural and free, even as a domestic pet; all his surroundings, near and far, remained open to him at every hour.

Until one day a speeding motor-cycle in the woodland lane ran him down, pressing the little ribs into his lungs and heart. Now only a memory remains to us of all Hurrli's sweetness.

He lies buried in the garden, under a young birch tree; many bright wild flowers grow from the soil that covers Hurrli's body. Whenever we passed the spot during the remainder of our time at the Elk House, we would repeat his special sound in melancholy greeting: "Urr-urrh!" Yet at the same time we were glad that his short life had been so rich in happiness, and that he had been spared the infirmities, the powerlessness of old age. With every breath he drew, our house cat Hurrli had enjoyed the full freedom of his wild nature and, equally, the love of human beings.

'Do you remember still, proud companion and prince, how once you came to our door, a wretched, skinny foundling, and begged your first bowl of milk from us? How long ago it is . . .'

THE ARROGANT CAT

MY LORD'S MOTORING

BY *Vincent Starrett*

He was an arrogant cat, *My Lord,*
Or ever he heard of Henry Ford.
He sat in the windows, east and west,
Amber eyes and a snow-white vest,
Watching the silly children run,
Staring haughtily at the sun:
Nothing disturbed him in the least,
Nor touched the pride of that stately beast.

Then, on a day, we went to ride
I in the wheel-seat, he beside.
Never a move that advertised
He was the slightest bit surprised;

He sat up straight as a millionaire,
A snob of snobs in a parlor chair—
But once, when I missed a boy at play,
I thought he winked in a knowing way.

☙

THE   SELF-SUPPORTING   CAT

THE MYSTERIOUS RA

BY *Margaret Benson*

R A HAD THREE PERIODS OF DEVELOPMENT. In the first, he showed himself cowardly and colorless; in the second, he sowed his wild oats with a mild and sparing paw; and in the third period it was borne in on us that whatever qualities of heart and head he displayed were but superficial manifestations, while the inner being of Ra, the why and wherefore of his actions, must forever remain shrouded in mystery.

We might have guessed this, had we been wise enough, from his appearance. His very color was uncertain. His mistress could see that he was blue—a very dark, handsome, blue Persian. Those who knew less than she did about cats called him black. One, as rash as she was ignorant, said he was brown; but as there are no brown cats Ra could not have been brown. Finally, a so-called friend named him "The Incredible Blue."

When the Incredible Blue sat at a little distance two large green eyes were all that could be discerned of his features. The blue hair was so extremely dark that it could be hardly distinguished from his black nose and mouth. This gave him an inexpressibly serious appearance.

The solemnity of his aspect was well borne out by the stolidity of his behavior. There is little to record during his youth except an unrequited attachment to a fox-terrier. In earlier days Ra's grandmother had been devoted to the same dog—a devotion as little desired and as entirely unreciprocated.

RA. *From "The Mysterious Ra"*

But it was necessary that Ra should leave the object of his devotion and come with us to live in a town; and now it became apparent that his affections had been somehow nipped in the bud. Whether it was the loss of the fox-terrier, the new fear of Taffy's boisterous pursuits, or the severity of his grandmother's treatment,—for the first time he came into close contact with that formidable lady,—whatever the reason may have been, it was plain that Ra's heart was a guarded fortress. He set himself with steady appetite to rid the house of mice, but he neither gave nor wanted affection.

He would accept a momentary caress delicately offered; but if one stroked him an instant too long, sharp, needle-like teeth took a firm hold of the hand. We apologized once to a cat-lover for the sharpness of Ra's teeth. "I think the claws are worse," was all he said.

Ra was an arrant coward. If a wild scuffle of feet was heard overhead we were certain that it was the small, agile grandmother in pursuit of Ra. If Taffy were seen careering over the lawn and leaping into the first fork of the mulberry-tree, it was because Ra had not faced him out for a moment, but was peering with dusky face and wide emerald eyes between the leaves.

Once or twice there was an atmosphere of tension in the house, no movement of cat or dog, and it was found that the three were fixed on the staircase unable to move—Taffy looking up from below with gleaming eyes, Granny malevolently scowling from above, and Ra in sight like Bagheera, in heart like a frightened mouse protected by the very fact that he was between the devil and the deep sea. Taffy did not dare to chase Ra for fear of the claws of the cat above; Granny did not care to begin a scrimmage downstairs, which would land them both under the dog's nose. So they sat, free but enthralled, till human hands carried them simultaneously away.

But the general tension of feeling grew too great. Ra's life was a burden through fear, Granny's through jealousy, Taffy's through scolding. Ra was sent off to a little house in London, and here his second stage of development began.

He had always been pompous, now he grew grand. It took ten minutes to get him through the door, so measured were his steps, so ceremonious the waving of his tail. He sat in the drawing-room in the largest armchair. Then it irked him that there was no garden, so he searched the street until he discovered a house with a garden, and he went to stay there for days together. A house opposite was being rebuilt, and Ra surveyed the premises and overlooked the workmen, sliding through empty window-frames and prowling along scaffolding with a weight of disapproval in his expression.

Thus Ra, who had hitherto caused no anxiety to his family, now became a growing responsibility; visions of cat stealers, of skin-dealers, of cat's-meat men, of policemen, and lethal chambers began to flit through the imagination whenever Ra was missing—which was almost always. So to save the nerves and sanity of his friends Ra left London.

We had now removed to the country, and greatly to our regret, though little to that of Ra, his ancient foe had passed from the scene; and although he felt it better to decline the challenges of the sandy kitten, yet he no longer believed his safety and his life to be in the balance; it was plain that he had realized his freedom, and would assume for himself a certain position in the household.

The house was a very old one; but Ra had been not long employed before the scurrying of feet over the ceiling was perceptibly lessened, and behind the mouldering wainscot the mouse no longer shrieked. That, indeed, is a lame, conventional way of describing the previous doings of the mice. Rather let us say that the mice no longer danced in the washing basins at night, nor ran races over the beds, nor bit the unsheltered finger of the sleeper, nor left the row of jam-pots clean and empty.

If Ra had confined himself to this small game all would have been well, but he proceeded to clear the garden of rabbits. Day by day he went out and fetched a rabbit, plump and tender, and ate it for his dinner. It must at least be recorded that at this time he was practically self-supporting.

Three he brought to me. The first was dead, and I let him eat it; the second showed the brightness of a patient brown eye, and while I held Ra an instant from his prey, the little thing had cleared the lawn like a duck-and-drake shot from a skillful hand, and disappeared in the hedgerow.

The third was dead. I took it and shut up Ra. We "devilled" the rabbit hot and strong; we positively filled it with mustard, and returned it. Ra ate half with the utmost enjoyment, and the sandy kitten finished the rest.

Then came Ra's final aspiration. Unwitting of strings of cats' tails, dead stoats, and the gay feathers of the jay with which the woodland was adorned, he took to the preserves. We have no reason to think he hunted anything but the innocent field mouse or a plump rabbit for us to season; but with a deadly confidence he crossed the fields evening by evening in sight of the keeper's cottage.

If we had all been ancient Egyptians we should have developed his talent. The keeper would have trained him to retrieve, and he would gayly have accompanied the shooting parties. If I had even been the Marchioness of Carabbas I should have turned the talent to account, and Ra, clad in a neat pair of Wellingtons, would have left my compliments and a pair of rabbits at all the principal houses in the neighborhood.

Prejudice was too strong for us. I won a truce for Ra until we could find a new home for him, and he departed in safety. I heard, to my relief, that he seemed quite happy and settled, and had bitten and scratched a large number of Eton boys.

Now up to his departure we had at once admired and despised Ra, but no one understood him. His appearance was so dignified, his spirit seemed so mean. He lent a silky head to be caressed, and while you still stroked him, without a sign of warning except the heavy thud of the last joint of his tail, he turned and bit. He addressed one in a small, delicate voice of complaint, yet wanted nothing. He followed me up and down in the garden with a sedate step; there were no foolish games in bushes, pretence of escape, hope of chase and capture. Happy or fearful, sociable or solitary, Ra was utterly self-contained.

Now hear the last act.

Ra began paying calls from his new home, and was established on a footing of intimacy at a neighboring house. As he sat in the drawing-room window there one morning, he watched the gardener planting bulbs. The gardener planted a hundred crocus bulbs and went home to dinner. No sooner was he gone than Ra descended, went to the bed, and dug up the bulbs from first to last. Then he returned to the drawing-room window.

The gardener came back, and lo! his hundred bulbs lay exposed. Nothing moved; no creature was to be seen but a cat with solemn face and green, disapproving eyes, who glared at him from the window.

The gardener replanted half his bulbs and went to fetch some tool; when he returned he seemed to himself to be toiling in a weird dream, for the bulbs he had replanted lay again exposed and the cat still sat like an image in the window.

Again he toiled at his replanting, and finally left the garden.

In a moment Ra descended upon it; with hasty paws he disinterred the crocuses, and laid the hundred on the earth. Then, shrouded still in impenetrable mystery, Ra returned home.

History does not relate whether or no the gardener consulted a brain specialist the following day.

THE TRAVELING CAT

CAT'S CRUISE

BY *Mazo de la Roche*

CAT WAS AS BLACK AS A CROW. This very blackness made her presence desired by sailors, who were sure it brought them good luck. She was not pretty, but she had charm which she had spent her life in exercising, to get what she wanted. She was eight years old, and she had woven into that eight years more travel and more adventure than most humans achieve in eighty. She had also brought forty-five kittens into the world.

She had been born on board a coaling vessel, the *Sultara*, in the midst of a terrible storm when the crew thought that every moment would be their last. Her mother was ginger-colored; and she had, while the vessel floundered in distress, produced three ginger-colored kittens besides this last one, black as the coal which formed the cargo. The stoker, looking gloomily at their squirming bodies, had growled:

"There'll be no need for us to drown *them*. The bloomin' sea'll do it!"

He picked up the black midget and held it in his hand. He felt an instant's compassion for it. It had come out of darkness and was so soon to return; yet there it lay, curved in his palm, bullet-headed, its intricate mechanism of tiny organs and delicate bones padded with good flesh, the flesh covered by thick silky fur, the whole animated by a spirit so vigorous that already ten little claws made themselves felt on his palm.

"If I could find a bottle the right size," he said, "I'd put you into it and chuck you into the sea. I'll bet you'd get to land!"

But there was no need to try the experiment. Miraculously, it seemed, the storm began to abate. The waves subsided; the vessel was got under control. One and all declared that they had been saved by the timely birth of the black kitten. It became the mascot, the idol of the ship.

They could not agree on a name for it. Some wanted a simple one, easy to say and descriptive of its color, such as Smut, Darkie, Jet or Nigger. Others insisted on some name which would suggest the rescue of their lives by the kitten's timely birth. One offered Nick-o'-Time, with Nick for short. But they could not agree. Then someone called her simply "Cat," and the others, in spite of themselves, acquiesced, as is often the case with names. From then on she was proudly, affectionately, known as "Cat" wherever she went.

She had a very round head, with small ears and narrow, clear green eyes. She had exceptionally long, glossy whiskers above a large mouth that displayed needle-sharp teeth in a three-cornered smile or a ferocious grin when her emotions were stirred. Her tail was sleek and sinuous and almost never still. Happy was the sailor round whose neck she wound it. Her attentions were known to bring good luck.

As she grew up she reigned supreme on the vessel. Nothing was too good for her. If what she wanted was not given her at once, she climbed on to the neck of the man who withheld it and put both arms (you could not call them forelegs, because she used them exactly like arms) round his neck and peered into his eyes out of the narrow green slits of her own. If he did not at once surrender, she pressed her stubby nose on first one side of his face, then on the other, while with her claws she massaged the weather-beaten back of his neck. If he were still obdurate, or perhaps mischievous enough still to deny her, she reversed her position and put her claws into his thigh. Gladly he gave her then whatever she desired.

She had a loud vibrant purr, and when she moved gracefully along whatever deck she was favoring with her presence, purring and swaying her long tail, a feeling of reassurance and tranquility came to all on board . . . It was a bitter thing to the crew of the coaling vessel on which she had been born when, at the time of her first litter, she deserted them for a Norwegian schooner. The captain could scarcely persuade the crew to sail. The docks at Liverpool were combed for her without success. The voyage was one of rough weather and general dissatisfaction.

At that time the Norwegians had not heard of her. They had their own cat, and did not want another. But she soon won them over, and they had the most successful voyage they had ever known. When they next called at Liverpool, the mate boasted of Cat in the hearing of one of the crew of the *Sultara*. He boasted of her intelligence, of her blackness, of the luck she brought.

On board the *Sultara* there was joy when they learned that she was safe, rage when they heard that she was living with the Norwegians. They visited the foreigners and saw for themselves the cat was "Cat." They found that she had a litter of ginger-colored kittens. But the Norwegians would not give her up. They would give up one or all of her ginger-colored litter, but they would not give up "Katts."

The crew of the *Sultara* hung about the docks with scraps of kipper in their pockets, because Cat had a weakness for kippers; but the Norwegians guarded Katt with terrible efficiency. When, however, she chose to go ashore, nothing could stop her. A morsel of kipper was proffered her at the right moment. She mounted the shoulder of the giver, and was borne in triumph to her birthplace. She gave evidence of the greatest pleasure in her reunion with the crew, who were ready to weep with joy at recovering her.

Cat remained with them for two voyages. Then again she disappeared, this time in favor of an oil tanker bound for the East ... And so it went on, this life of change and adventure. She chose her ships. She remained on them till her love of variety prompted her to seek another lodging. But wherever she sailed, she brought good luck, and at regular intervals, she returned to the *Sultara*. On all the Seven Seas she produced litters of ginger or gray kittens, but never one of her own glittering black. She held herself unique. She was Cat.

Now, on a morning in late February, she glided down the gangway of the *Greyhound,* which had just limped into port after an Antarctic relief expedition. The voyage had lasted for six months, and had been one of the mistakes of Cat's life, so far as her own pleasure was concerned.

The captain and crew of the *Greyhound* had been delighted when she sauntered aboard. The seal of success, they felt, had been set on the expedition. And they were right. The lost explorers had been discovered, living, though in desperate plight. Cat's reputation was still more enhanced.

But she herself was disgruntled, through and through. She had never, in all her years of travel, experienced such a voyage. She felt disillusioned; she felt ill. She felt like scratching the first hand that was stretched out to pat her.

"Hullo, Cat!" exclaimed a burly dock-hand. "So you're back from the Pole? And what captain are you going to sign up with next?" He bent to scratch her neck, but she eluded him and glided off with waving tail.

"Cat don't look very bright," observed another dock-hand.

"She's fed up, I expect, with the length of the last voyage," said the first speaker, staring after her. "She don't generally go for such long one. *And* the weather! *And* the grub! She could have done much better for herself, and she knows it."

He turned to one of a crew which was about to sail for Norway.

"Hi, Bob! Here's Cat! Just back from the South Pole. P'raps you can make up to her."

Bob approached, grinning. He planted himself in Cat's way, and held two thick tarry hands down to her.

"Puss, puss!" he wheedled. "Coom along wi' us. Tha can have whativer tha wants. Tha knaws me, Cat."

She knew Bob well, and liked him. She suffered herself to be laid across his breast and she gave him a long look out of her narrow green eyes. He felt her ribs with his blunt fingers.

"She's naught but fur and bone," he declared.

"Her's been frettin' fer home," said the first.

"The sea is her home," said Bob. "But she's a dainty feeder. S'll I carry thee off, Cat?"

She began softly to purr. She relaxed in every fiber. The tip of her tongue showed between her lips. She closed her eyes.

"She'll go with you," said the dock-hand, and Bob began to pick his way among the crates and bales, carrying Cat hopefully in his arms.

She heard the varied sounds of the docks, the shouts, the hoarse whistles of ships, the rattle of chains, smelled the familiar smells. It was music and sweetness to her after her long absence. She surrendered herself to the rhythmic movement of Bob's big chest.

In triumph he deposited her on his own deck. The rest of the crew stopped in their work for a moment to welcome her. The cook brought her a brace of sardines.

For politeness' sake she ate one; but left the other on the deck. She arched herself against the legs of the first mate and gave her three-cornered smile. A ray of feeble sunlight struggled through the wintry fog and fell across her. She began to think she might sail with this crew.

"Keep an eye on her," said the mate to a cabin-boy. "Don't let her out of your sight till we're away."

All about was hurry and noise. Cat sat on the deck washing the oil of the sardine from her whiskers. The pale sunshine surrounded her, but deep within her, there was dissatisfaction growing. This was not what she wanted, and soon it would be too late to return to the docks. She would be in for another long, cold voyage.

Her little round black head looked very innocent. Her eyes were tight shut. Methodically she moved her curved paw over her face.

Someone called the boy, and forgetting the earlier order, he ran off. Cat was galvanized into life and movement. She flew along the deck. In another instant she would be on the docks. But Bob saw her, and caught her in his huge hands. She liked him; still she did not weaken. She thrust her claws into his hands, and with a yell of triumph and every hair erect, escaped.

It was some time before she regained her calm. She slunk among legs, among trucks, through scattered straw and trampled mud. The fog thickened again, settling clammily on her fur. It was bitterly cold. What she wanted was solitude. She was sick of the sight and sound of men and their doings.

She entered a warehouse and passed between tiers of wooden boxes and bales, stopping to sniff now and again when some smell attracted her. The cold in this building was very penetrating. Was she never to know warmth again?

In a dim shed she found stalls, all empty except one in which a prize ram was awaiting shipment to America, where he was to be used for breeding. She clambered up the partition of the stall and perched there, gazing down at him. She did not remember having seen anything like him before. His yellow gaze was as inscrutable as hers.

With paws tucked under her breast she sat enjoying the sight of him. She stared at his massive wooly shoulders, his curly horns, his restless pawing hoofs. He lowered his head and butted the manger in front of him with his hard skull. Cat felt that she could watch him forever.

The gruff whistles of the ships shook the hoary air. The faint sunlight coming in at the cobwebbed window was shut off by a curtain of gray dusk. Cat and the ram were wrapped about by a strange intimacy. The chill increased. The docks became almost silent. The ram gave a bereft *baa* and sank to his knees.

Now he was only a pale mound in the dusk, but Cat still stared at him. He was conscious of her too; and like some earth-bound spirit, he raised his yellow gaze to the glimmering stars of her eyes.

Toward midnight the cold became unbearable to her. On the Antarctic expedition she had slept in the bunk with a well-fleshed sailor. Now a thin rime was stiffening every hair of her coat. She rose stiffly and stretched. Her tail hung powerless. Some message, some understanding, passed between her and the ram.

She leaped from the partition and landed between his shoulders. She sank into the deep oily warmth of his wool. He remained motionless, silent as the hill where he had pastured.

She stretched herself out on him with a purr of delight. She sought to feel his flesh with the fine points of her claws through the depth of his wool. A smell new to her rose from his body, and the beginning of a *baa* stirred in his throat. Their two bodies united in the quiet breathing of sleep. Her sleep was light, of a pale luminous quality, always just on the edge of waking; but his was dark and heavy, as though he were surrounded by shaggy furze and thick heather.

A dense fog rose from the sea at dawn and pressed thickly into the stall. With it crept a long gray cat with a white blaze on his face, and his ears torn by fighting. He scrambled up the partition of the stall and peered down at the two below. He dropped to the manger, and from there to the straw. He touched Cat tentatively.

She had been conscious of his approach. It had brought into her dreams a vague vision of a tawny striped cat she had met in Rio de Janeiro, where the relief ship had called. But the touch of the paw galvanized her. She gave a shriek and driving her hind paws into the ram's back, she reared herself and struck at the intruder's face as though she would put her mark on it forever.

But he was not easily frightened off. He sprang to the ram's back also, and through the fog Cat saw his white face grinning at her. He set his teeth in the back of her neck. They both shrieked.

The ram's deep, dark, warm slumber was shattered into fright. He bounded up, with a clatter of hoofs, overthrowing the cats. His white eyelashes flickered. He glared in primeval rage and lowered his head to charge.

The cats scrambled agilely over the partition and dropped to the stone floor outside, their tails enormous. They sped in opposite directions into dim corners of the shed. The battering of the ram's head against the door of the stall echoed through the fog.

As Cat reached her corner, a mouse flickered out of the gloom, squeaking in an agony of fear, and shot past her. With a graceful flourish of her limber body she turned completely round and captured the mouse with that one effective movement. She picked it up delicately in her teeth and crouched in the corner.

After a time the door opened and two men came in. They turned on a light, and the interior of the shed was revealed in foggy pallor. The men entered the stall where the ram was. There came strange bumping sounds. The men cursed. Then they appeared leading the ram, roped by the horns. He was led out helpless, his little hoofs pattering on the stone floor. He uttered a plaintive, lamblike *baa*. The men left the door open behind them.

Cat discovered the body of the mouse. It now meant nothing to her. She glided out onto the docks, wondering what ship she would sail in. She passed among them as they were dimly revealed, cargoes being loaded or unloaded, men working like ants. She felt a dim wonder at their activity, a faint disdain for their heaving bodies.

Toward noon, when a shabby blurred disk showed where the sun was, she came upon a passenger-ship just departing on a West India cruise. She had never sailed on a passenger-ship. They were an untrustworthy and strange world, and she hated the sight of women.

As she stood pessimistically surveying it, a kitchen worker tossed a slice of chicken-breast through a porthole to her. She crouched on the pier devouring it, while shivers of delight made her separate hairs quiver. She had not known that such food existed. After it was gone, she sat beaming toward the porthole, but nothing more was thrown out.

Luggage was being loaded onto the ship, and a throng of people of a sort she had never before seen, hastened up the gangway. One of them, a man, bent and gently massaged the muscles in the back of her neck, before he passed on. She beamed after him. She had not known such hands existed, so smooth, so tender. They were like the breast of chicken she had just devoured.

She rose, chilled by the clammy cold, and glided up the gangway onto the ship.

She knew that she was a stranger here, and some instinct told her that quite possibly she might not be welcome. She slunk along the innumerable white passages, making herself as nearly invisible as possible. She glanced in at the doors of staterooms, as she passed. Generally there were women inside, and sometimes the rather disgusting smell of flowers was in the air.

Cat heard the thunder of the whistle. She felt a quiver go through the ship. She had a mind to get off it while there was yet time, but she felt powerless to turn herself away from the delicious warmth that was radiated from every corner of the liner. It made her feel yielding, soft. She wanted something cozy to lie down on.

She paused at the door of a cabin that was empty except for the promise of a man's coat and hat thrown on the berth. She went in and walked round it, purring. She held her tail stiffly erect, all but the tip, which moved constantly as though it were, in some subtle way, gauging the spiritual atmosphere of the cabin.

Gregg, the swimming-instructor, found her there, curled up on his coat. They had left the docks, so she could not be put ashore. He recognized her as the cat he had caressed and supposed that she belonged on the liner. He tucked her under his arm and carried her to the kitchen quarters. The boy who had thrown her the morsel of chicken recognized her. He had once been galley-boy on an oil tanker she had favored with her presence.

"It's Cat," he explained. " 'Aven't yer never 'eard tell of Cat? W'y, we're in luck, mister! And yer ought to be proud to share your berth wiv 'er!"

But Gregg did not want to share his berth with Cat, even after he had heard her history and virtues. He dumped her down and rather glumly retraced his steps. He felt a shrinking from the long cruise that stretched ahead of him. To be sociable was a part of his job, and he hated the thought of sociability.

He had, in fact, seen too much of people. He had had more experience of society than was good for him. He was not yet thirty, but he had lost a fair-sized fortune, the woman he loved, and worst of all, his hope and his fortitude. He had been at his wits' end to find a job, when a friend had got him this post as swimming-instructor. He was in a state bordering on despair, but here he was bound to seem cheerful and gay, to take a passionate interest in the flounderings of fat passengers in the pool.

No one on board was so out of sympathy with the cruise as was he. Indeed, everyone on board was in sympathy with the cruise but Gregg and Cat, who did not at all understand cruising for pleasure.

She was there in his berth waiting for him when he returned to his cabin that night, having found her way through all the intricacy of glittering passages. He was a little drunk, for he was very attractive, and people insisted on treating him. The sight of Cat lying there on his bed angered him. He was about to put her out roughly, when she rolled over on her back, turned up her black velvet belly and round little face with the glittering eyes narrowed and the three-cornered smile showing her pink tongue. He bent over her, pleased in spite of himself.

"You're a rogue," he said. "But you can't get around me like that."

For answer she clasped her forepaws round his neck and with her hind paws clawed gently on his shirt front. She pressed her face on his, and purred loudly in his ear.

"Cheek to cheek, eh?" said Gregg, and gave himself up to her hypnotic overtures.

Morning found them snuggled close together. He sent the steward for a dish of milk for her. He appeared at the swimming-pool with her on his shoulder. She basked in the heavenly warmth of the place.

From that time, she spent her days by the pool. Tolerantly, almost benignly, she watched the skill or awkwardness of the swimmers. When the pool was deserted, she crouched by its brink gazing at her reflection, dreaming of lovely fish that might have graced it. At night she slept with Gregg. She thrived immensely.

When they were in sparkling southern waters, Cat disappeared early one evening. She met Gregg at the door of his cabin with a tremulously excited air. She advanced toward him, purring, then turned her back and flaunted her sinuous black tail. She looked back at him over her shoulder. Her head and tail met. She caught the tip of it in her mouth and lay down on her back, rolling coyly from side to side. She looked strangely slender.

"So you've been and gone and done it," said Gregg. "Not on the bed, I hope!"

No, not on the bed. In the wardrobe, where Gregg's soft dressing-gown had somehow fallen from the peg. There were three of them, all plump, all tawny, like the gentleman in Rio de Janeiro.

Next day Gregg got a nice box with a cushion and put the kittens in it. He carried them to the balmy warmth of the air that surrounded the swimming-pool, and all the bathers gathered to admire and stroke them. They were the pets of the ship. But Cat cared only for Gregg. She fussed over him far more than she did over her kittens. She refused to stay with them by the pool at night, so the box had to be carried to his cabin. There she would sit waiting for him, her glowing eyes fixed on the door, every nerve tuned for his coming.

But on one night, he did not come. She waited and waited, but he did not come. At last she sprang up from suckling her kittens, and they fell back like three tawny balls. The door was fixed ajar. She glided through the opening and began her search for him.

The smoke-room was closed; the lounge was empty, the decks deserted except for a pacing figure in uniform. At last Cat saw Gregg standing, still as a statue, in a secluded corner where a lifeboat hung. Silent as the shadows cast by moonlight, she drew near to him. But she did not rub herself against his leg as usual. She climbed into the lifeboat, and over its edge, peered down into his face.

That night Gregg felt alone—lost. In spite of the moonlight, the myriad glittering waves, the world was black to him. The life on this luxurious liner, among these spoiled shallow people, was suffocating him; he could not breathe. He looked back on his own life as a waste, on his future with despair. He had made up his mind to end it all.

Cat watched him intently as he leaned against the rail. If he had been her prey, she could not have observed him with more meticulous concentration as he mounted it. Just before he would have leaped over the side, she sprang onto his shoulders with a shriek that curdled the blood of those whose staterooms gave on that deck. She not only shrieked, but she drove every claw into Gregg. She turned herself into a black fury whose every hair stood on end, whose eyes glared with hate and fear at that gulf below . . .

"I don't know what the devil is the matter with her," Gregg said to the officer who hastened up. "She's as temperamental as a prima donna." His hand shook as he stroked her.

But she had saved him from his black mood, saved him from his despairing self. When he was undressed, he looked with wonder at the little bloody spots on his shoulders . . . Cat slept on his chest.

He made up his mind that he would never part with her. He owed her a debt which could only be repaid by the certainty of affection and gentle living for the rest of her days. He would find lodgings where she would be welcome.

But Gregg reckoned without Cat. By the time they reached port, she was sick to death of the luxury liner. There was not a smell on board that pleased her. She liked Gregg, but she could do without him. She liked her three plump kittens, but the quality of real mother love did not exist in her. She loved the sea and the men.

who spent their days in strenuous work on the sea. She disliked women and scent and all daintiness. She was Cat; she could not change herself.

In the confusion of landing, no one saw her slip ashore. She vanished like a puff of black smoke. It was as lovely a morning as any they had seen on the cruise. The air was balmy, the sky above the docks blue as a periwinkle. When Cat reached the places she was accustomed to, she purred loudly and rubbed herself against tarry trouser-legs, arched her neck to horny hands. But she was coy. She would not commit herself. For a fortnight she lived on the dock, absorbing the satisfying smells of fresh timber, straw, tar, salt fish, hemp, beer, oil and sweat. She even renewed acquaintance, this time more amiably though with loud screams, with the gray-furred gentleman who had called on her in the ram's stall.

At last she sailed on a cattle-ship, and all her past was as nothing to her!